Portraits of the Seventeenth Century

HENRI, DUC DE ROHAN
From a steel engraving

PORTRAITS
OF THE
SEVENTEENTH CENTURY

Historic and Literary

VOLUME I

by

C. A. SAINTE-BEUVE

With an Introduction by Ruth Mulhauser

ILLUSTRATED

FREDERICK UNGAR PUBLISHING CO.
NEW YORK

Translated by Katharine P. Wormeley

INTRODUCTION

Sainte-Beuve's biography defies most attempts to set it down. Not that he was a secretive man; on the contrary, he kept a meticulous record of his own doings, but despite his rigorous schedule of one published article each week for close to twenty years created by three days of reading, one of writing and revising and then reading and correcting proofs, which often took two whole days, Sainte-Beuve still managed to know most of the intellectuals in Paris during his life-time, took his Academy duties seriously and certainly did not neglect his personal friends. His general correspondence, in the exemplary edition by Jean Bonnerot, will reach twenty volumes. In short, he lived a dynamic life in many spheres, any account of which quickly tends to become a chronicle of his time.

Charles-Augustin Sainte-Beuve was born in Boulogne-sur-mer on December 23, 1804. He was the only and posthumous son of Charles-François Sainte-Beuve who, rather late in life, had married Augustine Coillot in March 1804, but died of quinsey two months before his son's birth. Sainte-Beuve, for even his mother called him that, seems to have been a grave child carefully brought up by his mother and his aunt, Madame Carmier, a widowed sister of Charles-François Sainte-

v

Beuve. Charles-Augustin was a good student and at the age of sixteen he persuaded his mother to send him to Paris to study. In his later novel, *Volupté*, the hero, Amaury, says that he wanted desperately to go to Paris to learn Greek, and Sainte-Beuve himself did, indeed, study Greek immediately upon his arrival, but after completing his baccalaureate studies, he began the study of medicine in the Hôpital Saint Louis in Paris.

One day in 1824, however, his former teacher Pierre-François Dubois, who had been dismissed from the teaching corps for his liberal political views, visited the young medical student, found him dissatisfied, at loose ends, and offered him a modest post on the staff of his budding newspaper, *Le Globe*. At first, Sainte-Beuve wrote in his spare time, but shortly he abandoned his medical career for journalism. The *Globe* was officially nonpolitical, but the atmosphere was liberal and ardently philhellenic during the Greek War for Independence. In its offices Sainte-Beuve met some of the outstanding minds of the time. Through his own short review of *Odes et Ballades* in January 1827, he became acquainted with a rising young poet who for several years was to be his closest friend until their all too much discussed rupture. The poet was, of course, Victor Hugo.

In 1827, Daunou, another Boulonnais, interested in the young man, suggested that he compete for a literary prize to be given by the French Academy for an essay on sixteenth-century French lyrical poetry. Sainte-Beuve soon saw he would not finish his work in time for the competition, but produced instead his first work, the two volume *Tableau historique et critique de la poésie et du théâtre français au XVIe siècle* (July, 1828) which played its role in revivifying mod-

ern interest in the Pléiade as well as not too indirectly
in giving status to the young Romantics by providing
them with French literary ancestors. The next year
(April, 1829) brought the first volume of his own
poetry, *Vie, poésies et pensées de Joseph Delorme,*
which is more outstanding for its cerebral innovations
than for the singing quality of its verse. Sainte-Beuve
also played his part in the "Battle of Hernani" and the
triumph of Romanticism.

The Revolution of 1830 left him disillusioned and he
turned for a time to the Christian socialism of Lamennais and the conservative *salon* of Madame Récamier
where Chateaubriand held his court. *Joseph Delorme*
was also followed by *Les Consolations* (1830) and
Sainte-Beuve's one published novel *Volupté* (1834).
The literary unorthodoxy of the young critic made him
a questionable candidate for any teaching post that
might provide him financial security. He therefore determined to do a solid work of erudition. His work on
Port-Royal brought him an invitation to lecture at the
Lausanne Academy in 1837, but the final epilogue to
the seventh volume of *Port-Royal* was written only in
1857. This monumental study has since, of course, been
partially superseded, but to Sainte-Beuve goes the
honor of reinterpreting Pascal and revivifying the
whole Jansenist struggle of the seventeenth century.

The period 1840-1848 was relatively quiet and secure. Sainte-Beuve had been appointed librarian at the
Mazarin Library, which guaranteed him a modest living, but also allowed him liberty and free time to study
and write. In 1844 he was elected to the French Academy and, ironically, was received into the august group
by his former friend Victor Hugo. In the unsettled days
of the 1848 revolution, however, a passing suggestion

of misuse of public funds (100 francs to fix a stove-pipe) piqued Sainte-Beuve. He resigned his post at the Mazarin Library and accepted an invitation to lecture at the University of Liège. The result of his Belgian stay was the study *Chateaubriand et son groupe* which shocked some people by its objectivity and truth.

On his return to Paris, Sainte-Beuve began his long and famous series of *Causeries du lundi* first in the *Constitutionnel* and later in the *Moniteur*. Appointed professor of Latin poetry at the Collège de France in 1854, he gave only two lectures because of politically inspired student manifestations. He interrupted the series, the *Lundis,* only for his teaching at the Ecole Normale from 1857 to 1861, and the series after his return, though unchanged in character, is known as *Nouveaux lundis*. In 1865, he became a senator. Though hardly a politician, he did defend Renan, speak for freedom of the press and in his last speech (May, 1868) appeal for a truly liberal education not merely in name but in fact. That evening a deputation of students brought flowers to his house as a tribute of gratitude, a fitting honor and retribution for the students who had not allowed him to discuss Vergil at the Collège de France in 1855.

Sainte-Beuve was already in ill health and though he continued his weekly column, he restricted his other activities to small functions with old and close friends during the last decade of his life. He died October 13, 1869 and was buried without religious ceremonies in the Montparnasse Cemetery about three blocks from his house in the rue du Montparnasse.

Sainte-Beuve was not lucky in love, he never married, but had many close friendships. One of the most charming stories is that the busy librarian-critic

stopped his work one afternoon each week in 1847--
1848 to read Horace with Ondine Valmore-Desbordes,
the seventeen-year-old daughter of his old friend, the
poet Marceline Valmore-Desbordes. Sainte-Beuve was
not the usual Romantic hero type physically; he always
had a great sense of inferiority about his short stocky
build and the red hair which he lost early. His correspondence, however, reveals a very kind, compassion-
ate man ready to help either by action or advice. His
quick and piercing wit was well known; *Mes Poisons,*
a private notebook published after his death, attests to
the sharp epigrammatic turn of his mind. The delicacy
and subtlety of many of his interpretations are fruitful
and suggestive almost a century after his death despite
the important shift in the critical point of view. His
motto was the English word *Truth,* and certainly if one
word were required to symbolize Sainte-Beuve's intellectual and moral attitude toward life, it would be
probity.

The first comprehensive study of Sainte-Beuve's
work was published in the *Revue de Paris* in 1838 just
about fifteen years after the critic had first begun to
write for the *Globe.* It was particularly fitting that this
study should appear in the *Revue de Paris* since Sainte-
Beuve had helped inaugurate that literary review in
1829 with one of his first *portraits.* Sainte-Beuve was
pleased with the appreciative and perceptive study by
Jean Chaudes-Aigues and wrote to thank him for it.
In his letter the critic made one comment which has
seemed to govern the publication of all subsequent
collections of his critical work. He wrote:

As for the ideas themselves, there are some at
least for which I can tell you that you expressed

my own thought exactly, for example, when you considered the *Critiques et portraits* as part of my elegiac and novelistic work rather than as formal criticism. That is exactly true, and to such a degree that if some day, in reprinting the *Critiques et portraits,* someone were to arrange them in chronological order of the subjects which I treat in them that person would commit a real blunder: the true order is the one in which I wrote them, according to my feeling and my fancy, and always in the particular mood in which I myself was at that moment.

At first sight Miss Wormeley, the translator of these volumes, would seem to have flown in the face of her author's own statement,[1] but this conclusion is not quite accurate; she has rather given a central unity to her selected translations by choosing them all from *le grand siècle,* disengaging in this manner a major pattern in Sainte-Beuve's criticism: the constant preoccupation with French national classic tradition during all the periods of his active journalistic career. Another positive advantage, at least for the Anglo-Saxon reader, is that we have here a kind of textual synthesis of Sainte-Beuve's critical and elegiac thought mingled but nevertheless clarified and emphasized by its focus on a relatively limited and unified epoch. Furthermore, despite the critic's own statement (and what critic is infallible even, or especially, about his own work), a striking consistency evidences itself in this series which can no longer be credited either to chronology nor to separate and distinct genres like the *portrait* or the *causerie.*

---

[1]   See the Collation Table starting on p. 463 of Volume I and p. 445 of Volume II for dates of the essays in this series.

The *portrait* as a form distinct from formal criticism was created and developed by Sainte-Beuve to a degree that it has been imitated by many subsequent critics and literary biographers. Normally the portrait was an extended study for a review rather than for a newspaper column. Generally too, it dealt with a writer and the totality of his work rather than with a specific book at hand to be reviewed. Writing in the context of Herder's philosophy of an organic evolution as well as during a period which sought to view the history of man synthetically, Sainte-Beuve developed his short dense essay which described the organic structure of the literary life of a writer, including the formative influences of family, friends, society, and education. The critic was also prone to set the writer into the historic perspective not possible from the close inspection of a single work. With the older author, it provided the critic an opportunity to revivify the work of a talented writer whose work risked being forgotten or misinterpreted in the press of daily events.

The *causerie*, on the other hand, belongs in the category of formal criticism which stems from a text at hand. Sainte-Beuve never forgot this text although the consideration might lead him to more general topics. His criticism also was not unfailingly judicial; it might be explicative or appreciative; it might even be "intestinal" as he once described some of his articles. The articles on older authors tended, however, to fall into the category of appreciation and explanation, for they were intended to protect and keep alive the national literary tradition as well as to comment on the new erudite editions which were being published in the nineteenth century. In principle and generally in practice, Sainte-Beuve welcomed the new textual editing which was rapidly evolving during his lifetime, but he was also pointed and, at times, even petulant about what he called the "mystique of the unedited." Such discoveries, as he explains in the introduction to the essay on the Duc de Rohan, engender enthusiastic *"rehabilitations"* or *"new"* interpretations when, in fact, they provide nothing new or at best complement the previous interpretation. In these articles on new editions of older writers, the portrait technique is not uncommon even when it is not central to the general structure of the essay. The essay on Rancé in this collection is a good example, for the major portion of it is from an essay entitled "Chauteaubriand" in the original since it was written about Chateaubriand's *Vie de Rancé*. It is in this sense that all of the essays in this collection may be called *portraits*.

Simultaneously, also, this collection of essays induces through its very form a kind of synthetic portrait of the author. As they stand, they exemplify Sainte-Beuve's thought and style from 1829 to 1858, or from almost the beginning of his career to within twelve years of his death. The approach changes from the youthful essay on Boileau through the almost over-meticulous, somewhat mannered style of the essay on La Rochefoucauld to the critic's fully developed, mature style, which is more straightforward, still precise, but less studied, as in the essay on Bossuet or the Duc de Rohan. It would perhaps be a mistake, however, to insist too much on the changes in style and approach, for the general unity of approach is equally notable and, in the end, more basic to the comprehension of the critic and his work.

The very title of the great series of critical articles, *Causeries du lundi*, evidences a dialogue concept in

the author's mind. Urbane conversation between cultivated readers was more nearly his ideal than pontifi-
cal pronouncements from any sort of arbiter of taste.
For this reason, personal commentary on the motiva-
tion of his choice or his procedure is not infrequent.
For example, Sainte-Beuve explains at the beginning
of his portrait of Madame de Longueville that his interest in her resulted from his investigations on *Port-
Royal;* indeed, the essay itself was borrowed from that
monumental work. Similarly, the introduction to the
article on La Rochefoucauld is very personal and describes discreetly but with incisive accuracy the critic's
mood in 1840 just after his final rupture with the Hugo-
lian Romantics and with Adèle Hugo herself. In the
article on Ninon de L'Enclos, he quotes Goethe's comment on the celebrated women of the eighteenth century as justification for his own interest in so many
"amiable and clever women of the past," adding that
in the seventeenth century "there was on the part of
the celebrated women who influenced it, still more
initiative and personal originality." Through this commentary, the critic and reader arrive at a joint involve-
ment in the comprehension of literature and civiliza-
tion. This was the unfailing aim of Sainte-Beuve's
study and essays.

Very early in his career, Sainte-Beuve shocked some
of his contemporaries by suggesting that the great
seventeenth-century literary figures of France should
be studied as *classics* somewhat in the manner of the
Greco-Roman classics. This statement was viewed as a
kind of impertinence on the part of a young man of
the Romantic generation who, with one sweep of his
pen, was doing away with the great traditional litera-

ture of France. The young critic was indeed Romantic in his desire for freedom and literary innovation, but he was not thereby dispensing so lightly with national literary tradition. Their aesthetic might not be his own personal code, but his effort was to understand their work in the light of their aesthetic within the intellectual climate of their time. Understanding usually implied some degree of admiration for Sainte-Beuve, but this admiration was far from being idolatry or implying any form of imitation. It was rather a completely rational, intellectual process of reading perceptively and widely in order to chart his own path more lucidly. It is hardly surprising therefore to find him returning time after time to the seventeenth century.

RUTH MULHAUSER

Cleveland, Ohio

TRANSLATOR'S NOTE

In the following volumes—taken from the *Causeries du Lundi,* the *Portraits de Femmes,* and the *Portraits Littéraires,*—some passages have been omitted ; these relate chiefly to editions that have long since passed away, or to discussions on style that cannot be made clear in English. Also, where two or more essays on the same person have appeared in the different series, they are here put together, omitting repetitions.

CONTENTS

CONTENTS

ILLUSTRATIONS

I.

Cardinal de Richelieu.

His Letters and State Papers.

I.

Cardinal de Richelieu.

His Letters and State Papers.

THE fate of Cardinal de Richelieu as a man whose pen or whose dictation produced important works is singular. As such he was long ignored or depreciated. When his "Testament Politique" appeared in 1687, men of judgment recognised the stamp of the master:

"Open his Political Testament," says La Bruyère, "digest that work: it is the picture of his mind; his whole soul is there developed; there we discover the secret of his conduct and of his actions; there we find the source and the fore-shadowing of the many and great events which appeared under his administration; there we see without difficulty that a man who thought with such virility and accuracy must have acted safely and with success, and that he who achieved such great things either never wrote, or must have written as he has done."

In spite of such testimony, well justified on the reading, Voltaire persisted in regarding that same "Testament Politique" as nothing more than a collection of futilities or commonplaces. The learned Foncemagne, who applies himself to refute Voltaire with all sorts of good and demonstrative reasons, has

3

not forgotten that of brilliancy of style and literary talent, things so essential in France! Voltaire continued to triumph apparently, or at least to cast trouble into the minds of even the least ordinary readers. Far from considering this memorable treatise and the maxims of State which it contains as emanations of the austere and serious mind and meditative genius of the cardinal, those who attributed such qualities to him regarded the work as a derogation, and the great Frederick, so fitted to appreciate him, wrote, out of complaisance to Voltaire:

> "The wisest minds may meet eclipse:
> Richelieu made his Testament,
> And Newton his Apocalypse."

As for the other works, political and historical, of Richelieu, their fate was more singular still. In 1730, appeared, under the odd title of "History of the Mother and the Son," meaning Marie de Medicis and Louis XIII, a fragment of history beginning at the death of Henri IV, which was attributed to the historian Mézeray, simply because the manuscript was found after his (Mézeray's) death among his papers. But as in more than one part of the narrative Cardinal de Richelieu spoke in his own name and in his own person, critics took upon themselves to suppose that Mézeray in his youth, out of gratitude for the cardinal's benefits, chose, in this work, to assume his personality and mask himself under Richelieu's name; and they thought to explain by this disguise the various in-

CARDINAL DE RICHELIEU
From a portrait by Champaigne

congruities of the work. Though the style, at first sight, is more pompous and flowery than that which Mézeray usually employed, which at times has a tone of the *frondeur* and the republican, there was no cause for wonder, they said, because the author for once had disguised himself as a courtier and wished to be faithful to the spirit of his part. A few good judges were not taken in by such poor reasoning; they recognised the hand of Richelieu himself in more than one passage. Nevertheless, the question was not wholly cleared up till 1823, when M. Petitot obtained permission to publish the cardinal's own Memoirs which had long lain buried in the archives of the Ministry of Foreign Affairs, and now form no less than ten volumes of the Petitot Collection.

All was then made plain: Richelieu's thoughts, of which mere fragments had hitherto appeared, now came together, his words assumed their true tone and all their authority: his style was recognised; for he had a style, such a man could not fail to have one. It was seen that in addition to the glory of doing great things he had conceived the ambition to write of them in detail and extensively, and to compose, not so much his Memoirs properly so-called, as a body of history and of annals: "I own," he said, speaking of this work of selection and dictation on which, amid so many other imperative duties, he had spent his vigils, "I own that although there is more satisfaction in furnishing the matter for history than in giving history its form, there is no little pleasure to me in representing that which was done with so much trouble."

While he was tasting the "sweetness of that toil" his illness and the weakness of his constitution, even more than the pressure of affairs, forced him to interrupt his work; it was then that he wrote the "Succinct Narrative" which forms the first chapter, or rather the introduction to the "Political Testament." This narrative is, as he says himself, a "shortened picture," a fine and noble abridged discourse, in which he relates to the king all the great actions of the king, from the time of his (Richelieu's) second entrance to the ministry in 1624 until 1641. In thus attributing everything to his master and affecting to efface himself he does not fear that posterity will be misled and fail to recognise the man who was the principal instrument of great designs so gloriously executed.

Therefore, whoever desires to-day to know and have in hand all the political and historical writings of Richelieu (I am not speaking of his controversial writings as bishop and theologian in his diocese), it is necessary to have: 1st his "Political Testament," preceded by the "Succinct Narrative." 2nd, his Memoirs printed in the Petitot Collection, and later in that of MM. Michaud and Poujoulat; and, 3rd, the collection of his Letters and State-papers, the first volume of which will appear, by the efforts of M. Avenel, in a few weeks, to be followed by four other volumes in quarto.

Richelieu usually wrote little with his own hand; he dictated; but in this sort of transmission he never allowed a secretary to write as he pleased. His secretaries, among whom one named Charpentier held first rank, were no more than copyists and transcribers. Never was any thing written in his name if he were absent. He did not sign what were called "office-letters."

"Richelieu," says M. Avenel, "had, near his person day and night, several private secretaries, but he had no *bureaux* [departments]. The secretaries of State, who were no more than head-clerks, came to take his orders and executed, each in his own office, the work agreed upon, submitted it, when necessary, to the prime-minister, but signed it themselves. Richelieu signed only what was written in his own cabinet."

Many of his letters are dated in the night; he rose when an idea seized him and called a night secretary, who wrote it instantly.

Not only did Richelieu never sign a letter he had neither written nor dictated, but this prime-minister, whose spirit chose to be everywhere present, often dictated letters, instructions and dispatches that he did not sign; these were signed by the secretaries of State or their agents. In a word, Richelieu was apt to do the work of others rather than let any one encroach upon his, or upon his absolute authority. In this immense cabinet labour the part of the secretaries was, as we see, almost nothing and purely material. That of Richelieu was not only chief, but continual and sovereign.

It is a pleasure to approach and study the great
man through these new and complete documents
which show him to us at his origin and in all the
stages of his fortune. Richelieu, born September 5,
1585, the youngest son of an ancient family of Poitou,
was at first destined to be a soldier. But one of his
brothers who was appointed to the bishopric of Luçon
having made himself a Carthusian monk, Richelieu
was obliged to take the cassock rather than let the
bishopric escape his family. Henri IV named him for
it, and negotiated the appointment through his ambassador in Rome. Richelieu was at that time only a
few months over twenty years of age; he was forced
to make many appeals before he received the pope's
sanction, and went in person to Rome, where he was
consecrated April 17, 1607. After his return we find
him in his diocese, which had long been without a
bishop; for Richelieu's brother had never resided
there, and, in fact, had never been consecrated, nor
had his predecessor resided there. The young bishop,
arriving in a region full of Protestants and where there
had long been much discord, took his episcopal functions seriously, informed himself as to his rights, and
did his duty. The town of Luçon was little more
than a village, the poor inhabitants of which were
crushed by taxes; he writes to obtain some lessening
of the burden. In these first letters of Richelieu we
are not made conscious of the heart of a pastor, but
there does appear a spirit of order and equity which

requires that justice and proportionate burdens shall exist around him. He does not fear, in one place, to compare the load laid upon the common people to that of the beasts of burden, which ought to be proportioned to their strength. "It is the same thing," he adds, "with subsidies in regard to the common people; if not moderate, even though useful to the public they will not fail to be unjust."

In all that I have to say of Richelieu I shall endeavour to speak with truth, without bias, and with no idea of disparagement; the public mind has abandoned, through experience, that idea, which tended to misconceive and undervalue in him one of the most courageous artizans of the grandeur of France. I shall nevertheless avoid the other extreme, which might go to systematic apotheosis; I shall try to restrain admiration in all that concerns him within the limits of good sense and humanity. He will help me himself to do this, if I may venture to say so, for more than one of the sayings with which he judged of other men can, if turned upon himself, show wherein lay too much passion and harshness.

This powerful being, destined to hold France at his feet and make Europe tremble, began by being very poor and in great straits. He writes as follows to a certain Mme. de Bourges in Paris, who usually did his household commissions and had lately bought the decorations of which his church was in need:

" April, 1609.

" Madame, I have received the copes you sent me, which came extremely àpropos ; they are very handsome, and have been received as such by the company to whom I owed them. . . . I am now in my barony, beloved, so they try to make me think, by every one ; but I can only tell you so now, for all beginnings are fine, as you very well know. I shall not want for occupation here, I assure you ; all is so ruined that much energy will be required to restore it. I am extremely ill-lodged ; I have no place where I can make a fire on account of smoke ; you can imagine that I do not long for the depth of winter ; and there is no remedy but patience. I can assure you that I have the worst bishopric in France, the muddiest, the most disagreeable ; I leave you to think what the bishop is. There is no place here to take a walk ; neither garden, nor alley, nor anything whatever; so that my house is a prison.

" I leave this topic to tell you that we could not find among my clothes a tunic and a white silk dalmatic that belonged to the white damask trimmings which you had made for me ; and this makes me think they were left behind. . . ."

A number of letters to Mme. de Bourges treat in this way of his household and his domestic affairs, about which he jokes rather pleasantly. In his journeys to Paris, whither he came sometimes to preach and to breathe Court air, he feels he wants an abiding place, a house of his own, for convenience and decorum, instead of merely hiring furnished rooms. He consults this same Mme. de Bourges, a good household economist.

" If you will give me good advice," he writes, " you will oblige me very much, for I am very irresolute, principally about a house, fearing the quantity of furniture that may be needed. On the other hand, being of your humour, that is to say, rather vain-glorious, I should like, as I am more at my ease, to make a better appearance, which I could do more conveniently in a house of my own. Poor nobility is quite pitiful, but there is no remedy; against fortune keep good heart."

Among these early letters, where, as I need not remark, we are still amid the language of the sixteenth
century, there are some in which Richelieu assumes
the bishop, the consoler, and, occasionally, the director
of souls. He is adequate and seemly, but little at ease
in these rôles. The letters of consolation that he ad-
dresses to persons who have lost their nearest and
dearest are over-strained, subtle, and suggest even
less the contemporary than the pretentious and rather
antiquated forerunner of Balzac.[1] To the Comtesse de
Soissons, on the occasion of the death of her husband,
he says, strangely enough and as if to persuade her
that she had gained rather than lost: " If you desire
your welfare it is better to have an advocate in heaven
than a husband on earth." On one occasion, giving
inward and wholly spiritual counsel to a devout soul
tried by discouragements and difficulties in prayer, he
attempts the language of mystical science in which he
is easily surpassed by the Fénelons and Saint-François
de Sales. We find him more in character and in the
tone that comes easily to him in the following letter,
written to one of his grand-vicars who has taken, he
thinks, too much liberty:

" 1610.

" Monsieur, I have read the letter you have written me touching the
differences between the Sieur de La Coussaye and yourself. I cannot
do otherwise than blame them, desiring that those who handle the
affairs of my diocese should live peaceably with one another. I
write the same to the Sieur de La Coussaye, and I so inform you, in order

[1] Jean-Louis de Balzac, 1594–1654; one of the creators of French
prose.

that you may each arrange to live in peace. You are both my grand-vicars, and as such you ought to have no other object than to carry things along to my satisfaction, which can be done, provided it be also to the glory of God. It seems, from your letter, that you were in bad humour when you took your pen; as for me, I like my friends so well that I desire to know only their good humour, and it seems to me that they ought not to show me any other. If a gnat stings you you ought to kill it, and not try to make those who, by the grace of God, are so far saved from such pricking, feel the sting. I know, God be thanked, how to govern myself, and I know, moreover, how those who are under me ought to govern themselves. . . . I think it right that you should warn me of disorders which may exist in my diocese; but it is necessary to do so more coolly; there being no doubt that heat would, in these days, anger those who have hot blood, like me, if they had no means of warding it off. . . ."

The stage is still narrow. Richelieu in his relations with the outside world is obliged to pay many civil-ities, practice much suppleness, and bow low before the powers of the day. But wherever he felt himself master he already applied his method and made the stamp of his character felt.

I perceive this no less in another letter addressed to a certain M. de Préau, in which, after speaking of threatened troubles in the interior of France (1612) and omens of war without, he adds, hopefully: " The wise conduct, affection and fidelity of many good servitors guarantee us from ills within. As for those without, I shall baptise them with another name if they bring us opportunity to enlarge our borders and cover our-selves with glory at the cost of the enemies of France." There we hear the instinctive cry of that soul of cour-age and virtue, which, in its ambitions, was patriotic and French above all else, and was destined in future to fuse its personal passions in the grandeur of its public purpose. There is a saying of Montesquieu which seems to show such absolute misconception that I have difficulty in comprehending how it came from so great a mind: "The most mischievous [*méchants*] citizens of France," he says in one of his "Pensées," "were Richelieu and Louvois." We will set aside Louvois, who is not in question here; but Richelieu, a bad citizen of France! To what a point must Montesquieu have been imbued with the old parliamentary spirit, or with the modern philosophic idea, on the day when that saying escaped him! A citizen is precisely what Richelieu was; a patriot, ardent for the public grandeur of the State; as much so, at the very least, as the two Pitts were great patriots and citizens of England.

We see dawning in Richelieu's Letters the first gleams of his favour at Court, without, however, learning much more about it than he tells us in his Memoirs. His first political act, properly so-called, was the harangue he pronounced in presenting the report of his Order at the closure of the States-General, February 23, 1615. He was chosen as orator, and acquitted himself with honour and applause. A tone of high authority and reason makes itself felt through the pomposity of the speech in certain places. He knew the queen, Marie de Medicis personally, and had already insinuated himself into her confidence. It was about this time that he first saw the Maréchal d' Ancre.

"I won his heart," he says, "and he formed an esteem for me the first time we conferred together. He told some of his familiars that he had a young man in hand who was capable of teaching a lesson to *tutti borboni*. The esteem lasted always; but his goodwill diminished wholly; first because he found oppositions in me which he did not expect; secondly, because he noticed that the queen's confidence leaned wholly to my side.[1] . . ."

What was the state of the kingdom when Richelieu, then thirty-one years of age, became minister for the first time? Although this first and rather obscure ministry, separated from the glorious second by an interval of seven years, lasted only five months (Oct. 31, 1616 to April 24, 1617) we already discover, by looking closely into it, the distinctive features of Richelieu's policy, the vigorous application of his principles to the same evils he was later to cure, and the dawning efficacy of the same remedies which were on the point of taking effect when the murder of Maréchal d'Ancre stopped all and threw everything into abeyance. Richelieu's great career was destined to begin twice before succeeding: "There are times," he says, energetically, "when Fortune begins but cannot complete her work."

France, after the death of Henri IV, had fallen from the most flourishing and prosperous condition and government into a miserable state of things. The queen-regent, Marie de Medicis, lazy, obstinate, and without fixed views, was still surrounded by the chief

[1] The Italian adventurer, Concini; favourite and prime-minister of the queen-regent, Marie de Medicis, assassinated at the instigation of the Duc de Luynes in 1617.

councillors of Henri IV, Villeroy, Jeannin, the chancellor Sillery, but the hand of the master was henceforth lacking to them. The princes and nobles were lifting their heads on all sides and taking arms; the Protestants seized the occasion to confederate and form a State within the State and against the State. The country had been, since 1610, beneath a continual, and in some sort a chronic Fronde, a Fronde the more dangerous because it was nearer to the League, and chiefly because the great fomenters of trouble had preserved intact their elements of power. In the royal succession, so suddenly brought about by murder, the crown conquered by Henri IV was held, as in the later Fronde, by the hand of a woman on the head of a child. Richelieu, in his Memoirs, has admirably pictured the misery of this period anterior to his coming into office, and what he calls the cowardice and corruption of hearts:

" The times were so miserable," he says, " that the ablest among the nobles were those who were most industrious in causing quarrels; and the quarrels were such, and there was so little safety in establishing anything, that the ministers were more occupied in finding the necessary means to preserve themselves than the means that were necessary to govern the State."

Thus these ministers, the queen's councillors, men trained and perfected in the old policy, now presented to imminent dangers and the growing exigencies of princes and nobles, nothing better than compromises, delays, and, finally, concessions over which they merely tried to haggle as much as possible.   On the morrow of the death of Henri IV, the queen might have seen the weakness of her councillors. It was a question of publishing a Declaration in the name of the late king immediately proclaiming her Regent. Villeroy, the boldest among them, offered to draw up the document and sign it; the chancellor Sillery, "who had a heart of wax," says Richelieu, would not seal it, giving as a reason that if he did so the Comte de Soissons would be furious with him and kill him. "He ought, on such an occasion," cries Richelieu, "to have despised his life for the safety of the State—but God does not give that grace to every man." He often recurs to this idea: that the courage which undertakes wise and just things for the public good is a special gift of God; and this is not in him a form of words; evidently he believed it. Speaking of the vain and fruitless ending of the States-General in 1614 he adds:

"The whole work of this Assembly had no other effect than to overburden the provinces with the tax to be paid to their deputies, and to show to the world that it is not enough to know evils if there is no will to remedy them; the which will God gives, when it pleases him to make the kingdom prosper, and the great corruption of the ages does not hinder."

Richelieu is not a philosopher; his lofty mind, which is, above all, a sound mind armed with a great character, pays tribute to the ideas and prejudices of his day. In many places he speaks as if he believed in omens, horoscopes, and sorcery; he is superstitious; but also he is sincerely religious; he believes in the gift of God extended over certain men destined to be

the instruments of public salvation; if the wrongs
committed against public persons seem to him of quite
another order from those committed against private
individuals, the wrongs done by those public persons
themselves seem to him graver and of heavier weight
in view of their responsibility and the far extent of
consequences. It was he who wrote, on the last
page of his Political Testament, "Many could save
themselves as private individuals who damn themselves in fact as public personages."

Let Voltaire laugh if he likes at these maxims and
see therein the trace of a small mind! For all that,
they give the only superior morality which serves as
guarantee in public personages, which saves them
from pure Machiavellianism; we rejoice when we find
the sign of this religious spirit under one form or another, this sacred sentiment of divinity invoked and
recognised by all great heads and founders of States
and leaders of peoples. In some it is but a vain and
hollow formula proclaimed on occasions and ceremonies; but in others in whom this basis of belief is
real the accent never deceives; we feel it readily.

At sight of the ruin of the kingdom and the weakness of councillors during these years of the regency, Richelieu suffered greatly, asking himself if an
avenger would not appear. The queen had no fixed
views, and let herself be led sometimes by one and
sometimes by another of her ministers, according as
she thought herself the better or the worse for the

last advice: which is, remarks Richelieu, "the worst thing in politics, where nothing is so needed to preserve reputation, strengthen friends, and terrify adversaries, as unity of mind and continuance of the same purposes and means." It was then that he began to take part himself, in the character of confidant, at first secretly, as an unseen counsellor; but, after a certain day, we are conscious, in the actions of the queen, of a persistence and vigour in which they were hitherto lacking.

She had signed the Peace of Loudun, May 3, 1616, for which the rebellious princes made her pay dearly; but what she had done for these pretended reformers and champions of the public weal had whetted rather than sated their insatiable appetites. Returning to Paris with the young king, she found herself compelled to share authority with the Prince de Condé; the mansion of the latter was besieged by the crowd of courtiers and became the true Louvre; the other Louvre being left to solitude. Richelieu, very intimate with Barbin, steward of the queen's household and a man of good judgment, who had just been appointed secretary of State, must have acted and made his influence felt through him at this decisive moment. The queen, listening to the energetic counsels then given to her, and perceiving the growing intrigues of the Prince de Condé and his allies, the Bouillons, Vendômes, and others, who, under pretext of rising against the Maréchal d'Ancre, were

conspiring against herself and her son, decided to
have the Prince de Condé arrested in the Louvre.
She chose for the execution of this order Thémines,
of whom Henri IV had said to her: "He is a man
who will recognise nothing but the quality of royalty,
and will obey nought else"—a characteristic then becoming rare indeed! Richelieu, who unravels for us
all these intrigues and paints them with more than
one stroke of Tacitus, adds that Thémines, who arrested the Prince de Condé, if he did well was fully
aware of it, for from that day he was never satisfied,
no matter what rewards the queen heaped upon him:

"She made him marshal of France, gave him one hundred and some
thousand crowns in ready money, made his eldest son captain of her
guards, gave to Laugières, his second son, the office of first equerry
to Monsieur; and yet, with all that, he still whined and complained:
so dearly do men sell the little good that is in them, and so small a
value do they put on the benefits they receive from their masters."

Richelieu the historian is full of such strokes of a
consummate moralist who has gone, by experience,
to the depths of the hearts of men.

As soon as the Prince de Condé was arrested (September 1, 1616), the whole aspect of things changed;
the crowd of courtiers who had deserted the Louvre
returned to it instantly; each desiring to show himself and testify thus to his fidelity:

"Some did it sincerely," says Richelieu, "some with intentions and
desires quite the contrary; but there were none who did not approve of
what her Majesty had done; many even declared that they envied the
luck of the Sieur de Thémines, who had had the good fortune to be

employed on the enterprise: but the fact was, the Court was at this time so corrupt that it would have been hard to find any other man capable of saving the State by his fidelity and courage."

The great seigneurs, accomplices of the Prince de Condé, seeing him taken, escaped and left Paris instantly. Pretence was made of pursuing a few, M. de Vendôme for instance; but the desire they had to escape was much greater than the desire to capture them in those sent to do so. Unfaithfulness and disloyalty were betrayed on all sides. The Prince de Condé was hardly arrested before, in order to ransom himself out of prison, he offered to reveal all and betray the secrets of his party and his cabal: "which did not show as much generosity and courage," remarks Richelieu, "as a man of his condition ought to have."

It was then that the queen saw herself in the way to form a Council of ministers decisively, having already made certain changes: for the new situation a new policy was needed. The old councillors, Villeroy and Jeannin, were set aside, or nearly so; the Keeper of the Seals, Du Vair, self-styled philosopher and a man of renown in letters, had succeeded Sillery as chancellor, in which office he made a poor figure, and was good only at shackling public business. The very day of the arrest of the Prince de Condé, all the old councillors, including Sully, reappeared at the Louvre to make representations to the queen on this *coup d' État,* of which they did not appreciate the necessity and which threw them therefore into consternation.

It was about this moment that Richelieu was called to the Council, where his friends Barbin and Mangot had preceded him. He had been employed for some time in confidential negotiations and was designated to go as ambassador extraordinary to Spain. That mission suited him well; but the proposal of the queen to enter her Council, which was brought to him by Maréchal d'Ancre, carried the day: "Besides the fact that I was not honourably permitted," he says, "to deliberate on this occasion, in which the will of a superior power seemed to me absolute, I admit that there are few young men who could refuse the splendour of an office that promised both favour and employment." On entering the Council he became, from the very first day, its most important personage. He had, as he tells us, the portfolios of War and of Foreign affairs, also precedence over his colleagues as bishop; and all that at thirty-one years of age! He was the soul of this first little ministry, composed of rather obscure men, though firmly united with one another; a vigorous and energetic Cabinet, to which nothing lacked for the accomplishment of great things but time to last, and not to have been born under the shadow of Maréchal d'Ancre's patronage, a banner that made it unpopular.

Sully, jealous and hurt, expressed himself as much scandalised. We find in his Memoirs a letter to the

young king in which a good Frenchman (a personage
whom Sully does not disavow) speaks indignantly of
seeing Maréchal d'Ancre, his wife, and Mangot, "those
three creatures with their Luçon [Richelieu] ruling the
whole kingdom, presiding at the Councils of State,
dispensing the dignities, arms, and moneys of
France." The old minister of Henri IV misconceives
and rejects the successor who was destined to maintain and enlarge the work of Henri IV.   From the
depths of his grumbling retreat facing toward the
past, Sully will never do justice to Richelieu; but, in
these first moments, the error is perhaps permissible;
for Maréchal d'Ancre still masked him.

Richelieu, in some very fine historical and moral
pages, defining for us the character of this maréchal
who was, above all else, vain and presumptuous and
who clung to appearing powerful rather than to being
so in fact, shows distinctly in what this ministry, supposed to be wholly given over to the favourite, was
not his vassal; and we are admirably made to feel
that if Luynes had not intervened, if the maréchal had
lived, a struggle between Richelieu and him for the
sole favour of the queen-mother would quickly have
come about.   Richelieu making himself more and more
useful and necessary, and affecting, as he always did
in all circumstances of which he was not the master,
to withdraw and keep aloof, the queen would have
had to choose between the two.

The great seigneurs in the provinces continued

their intrigues and their appeal to arms. One of them, the Duc de Bouillon, had the boldness to write to the king to make complaints. The king returned an answer in which, for the first time, is seen the finger, the lion's claw of Richelieu. This vigorous act of Louis XIII which "showed more of royal majesty than his past conduct," was nevertheless not received by the body of the people as it should have been, on account of Maréchal d'Ancre. That which would have been recognised as advantageous to the service of the king and the good of the State if the favourite had not been there, was taken in bad part by the people, and envenomed by the malcontents; such was the rock, the wrecking-point of Richelieu's first ministry, and he himself knew it to be so.

Nevertheless he worked to enlighten opinion; he thought of Europe and dispatched three ambassadors extraordinary, one to England, one to Holland, and M. de Schomberg to Germany. We have the Instructions that he gave to Schomberg; they form an historical summary of the situation of France as strong as it is skilful, a justification of the measures of his government, and a first tracing out of the new policy. They begin with these words:

" The chief thing that M. de Schomberg must keep before his mind is that the object of his mission to Germany is to disperse the factions that may be formed there to the prejudice of France, to put forward the name of the King as much as he can, and establish powerfully his authority."

The nobles in the provinces spring to arms for the

fourth time. The king puts forth a Declaration; and,
as words signify nothing if they are not supported by
arms, Richelieu raises and organises three armies at
once: one that marches into Champagne, a second
into Berry and the Nivernais, and a third in the Île-de-
France. Thanks to these prompt and energetic measures, to which they were not hitherto accustomed,
the nobles disperse and take refuge in towns and fortified places, where they are soon reduced to capitu-
late. Affairs were in this state, and the party of the
princes "as low" as possible, when all was changed
in the twinkling of an eye by the death of Maréchal
d'Ancre, who was killed April 24, 1617, by order of
the king at the instigation of the Duc de Luynes.
The favourite of the king caused the killing of the
favourite of the queen-mother. The ministry, of
which the maréchal was more the apparent than the
real head, Richelieu being its already efficacious inspirer, was overthown by the same blow.

Richelieu relates that he was paying a visit to a
rector of the Sorbonne when they brought him the
news of the death of the maréchal. He returned to
the Louvre after having conferred a moment with his
colleagues: "Continuing my way," he says, "I met
divers faces which having smiled upon me two
hours earlier no longer recognised me; many also who
made me feel no change for the change of fortune."

He was the only member of the ministry whom
Luynes seemed at first to spare and to wish to except

from dismissal and public vengeance. In his description of the scenes that followed the murder of the maréchal, Richelieu proves himself a great painter of history. He shows us oronically the king, whom Luynes puts upon a billiard-table, that he may be seen more easily by the guilds of the city and by the deputies from the States who came to congratulate him. "It was," says Richelieu, "like a renewal of the ancient custom of Frenchmen who carried their kings at their accession on shields around the camp." He points to Luynes as the most dangerous enemy of the Maréchal d'Ancre because he was less so of his person than of his fortunes: "He bore him the hatred of envy, which is the most malignant and most cruel of all." He makes us see the insolence which, on this death of a favourite, merely changes its object. Richelieu, who will one day be considered cruel and pitiless himself— and who is so at times, though his chief vengeances mingle with State interests — considers, àpropos of the murder of the maréchal, that it was done "through hasty advice, unjust, and of evil example, unworthy of the royal majesty and virtue of the king." He thinks it would have been enough to make him a prisoner and send him back to Italy; and he blames so sanguinary a beginning of the new government.

It is to be remarked that Richelieu, when writing, though inflexible, is never inhuman. When he shows us Marie de Medicis forced to quit the Louvre, accompanied by her servants, all with sadness painted on their faces: "There was scarcely a person," he takes pleasure in noting, "who had so little the sentiment of humanity that the sight of this almost funeral procession did not move to compassion." Speaking of the odious and even barbarous treatment inflicted on the wife of the maréchal, and of her execution after she was condemned as a sorceress to have her head cut off on the scaffold, and her body and head burned to ashes, he uses words of extreme pity:

"On leaving her prison and beholding the great multitude of people crowding to see her pass: 'How many persons,' she said, 'have gathered to watch a poor, afflicted woman go by!' And presently, seeing some one to whom she had done an ill turn with the queen, she asked his pardon; so much did the true and humble shame she felt before God for having injured him take from her all shame before men. And so marvellous an effect did the blessing of God upon her have, that, by a sudden change, all those who were present at that sad spectacle became quite other men, drowning their eyes in tears of pity for this desolate woman. . . ."

I suppress a few touches of bad taste. He ends by remarking that what he says is not the result of partiality; it is the simple truth itself that compels him to speak thus: "For there is no one, however odious, who, ending their days in public with resolution and modesty, will not change hatred to pity, and draw tears from those who, at an earlier moment, have desired to shed their blood."

I like to set these words of Richelieu, so worthy of a great soul, against what was cruèl and pitiless in his later conduct, by which he exceeded, on certain occasions, the necessities of even the most austere policy.

During his first ministry we find him, in those few months, doing all he could to break down the revolt of the princes and nobles and to re-establish the royal authority at the point from which it ought never to have fallen. We can perceive, even in that short time, his distinct intention to raise France abroad, and not suffer her to fall away from the rôle and title of "umpire of Christianity" which Henri IV had won to the crown. In his Instructions to M. de Schomberg, ambassador to Germany, and also in the letters written in the king's name to M. de Béthune, ambassador to Italy, Richelieu never ceases to claim that glory, and almost that function which belonged of right to France as being the "heart" of all Christian States. The republic of Venice was quarrelling with the Archduke of Grätz; Louis XIII, by Richelieu's advice, desired that the affair be appealed to him; and as the war in Piedmont was being prolonged in spite of all efforts on the spot to arrest it, Louis XIII also desired that the Duc de Savoie should send an envoy to Paris to negotiate with the Spanish ambassador accredited there, believing that the affair could be better settled near his own person. With this view he dispatched an ambassador to Spain to obtain the agreement of the Catholic King. When Venice, playing a double game, made terms with the Archduke of Grätz through the channel of Spain only, Louis XIII took offence; he complained of being defrauded of one of his noblest rights, that of holding the scales: "It seems," he writes, "that they [the republic of Venice], falling into voluntary ingratitude, desire, exempting themselves from gratitude to me, to deprive me of the glory that is due me for the accomplishment of so good a work by transferring it to others." In that we see the finger of Richelieu and his seal on foreign affairs during his five-months' rule in the ministry, and in the midst of civil troubles that seemed to compromise the very existence of the State. He is tenacious of showing to Europe, from the very first, what he nobly expresses in his Instructions to Schomberg: "Never vessel will resist so great a tempest with less of damage than will be seen in ours."

Richelieu, fallen from his first ministry, accompanies Queen Marie de Medicis in her exile to Blois (May, 1617). Soon, however, his presence in that little Court gives umbrage to his enemies; calumny implicates him in various intrigues, from which his common sense sufficed to keep him aloof. He himself asks the king to send him back to his diocese; he is taken at his word, and for some time we see him in his priory of Coussaye playing the bishop, even the recluse, "reduced to a little hermitage," and apparently resolved to let "time flow gently onward among books and neighbours." It was during this interval that he wrote a book of controversy against Protestants, seeming to be solely occupied with the duties of his bishopric.

In placing a certain confidence in the letters which

we have of Richelieu we must not forget that we do not possess them all; that the most important were in cipher and have not come down to us. Neither have we his secret letters, those in which he talked to his intimates from a full heart — *à cœur saoul,* as he says himself. In all that he reveals to us of his life at divers periods there is always an undercurrent of negotiations that escapes us. Suffice it therefore to discern his general line of conduct.

He was not left tranquil in his retreat very long; he was still too near the queen; calumny riddled him at Court, and he himself was the first to instigate a sort of exile; he requests that he may be ordered to some other place "where he can live without calumny, being, as he is, without fault and without just blame." Thereupon he receives an order to go to Avignon (April, 1618); he remains there nearly a year in retirement. Meantime the queen, escaping from the castle of Blois by night (February, 1619), took refuge with the Duc d'Épernon. Luynes, then ruler, feared that in obeying the influence of that old seigneur and the mischief-makers by whom she would be surrounded, she would become a great danger. It was then that Richelieu's active friends, Père Joseph, Bouthillier, and others, bestirred themselves, and fixed attention upon him as the most suitable negotiator to recall and soften the mind of the queen, to whom he had never ceased to be agreeable. Richelieu reappears in that delicate rôle, as semi-avowed agent. He leaves Avignon; is arrested on his way by some too-zealous servants of the king, who think him still in disgrace, but soon make haste to excuse themselves. He reaches Angoulême on the Wednesday of Holy Week (March 27, 1619), and there, where he thought to enter port, he found, he says, "the greater tempest." He is received with an evil eye by all the other councillors who fear his influence towards moderation and his wise counsel. The queen dissimulates; he and she understand each other. He lets us be present at some of the bickerings of the little Court. Soon he becomes the necessary man, and concludes the negotiation that reconciles the mother with the son. That treaty made, he arranges the interview which is to seal the reconciliation, at Cousières near Tours. The favourites, the Luynes, are present with an eye on everything and keeping watch over the emotions of nature between mother and son. Richelieu, nevertheless, attains his end, he fulfils his mission, and from that day the king, to reward the good service, asks the pope on his behalf for the cardinal's hat; which, however, he did not receive until three years later. Thus it was that at the very moment when Richelieu's fortunes seemed irretrievably ruined they were suddenly repaired, and henceforth insensibly rose and broadened without further check.

Nevertheless, the years that immediately followed left him still in a secondary position, in which he had need of all his insinuation, suppleness, and patience.

The Duc de Luynes triumphed at Court, and reigned throughout the kingdom. Richelieu remained attached to the queen-mother in her government of Anjou; he is the superintendent of her household, and, correctly speaking, the minister of this semi-exile; for, in spite of the meeting and the embraces at Cousières, evil passions interposed and worked at sowing fresh discord between mother and son. The Prince de Condé, whom Marie de Medicis had put in prison solely in the king's interests, was released, and that prince of the blood became her active enemy, serving all the evil purposes of Luynes. Richelieu was strongly of opinion that the queen, to thwart these intrigues, ought to go straight to Court, make Nature speak for her in the heart of the king, and boldly drive into nothingness this malignancy. But other counsellors of the queen thought otherwise, supporting their opinion with plausible reasons. Fearing to lose the confidence of his mistress, Richelieu, out of prudence, felt himself obliged to adopt their opinion, "imitating wise pilots who yield before tempests. There being no advice so judicious," he reflects, "that it may not have a bad issue, one is often obliged to follow opinions that we least approve." Even when he reveals to us the many hindrances and disappointments that barred his fortunes, Richelieu's style is never irritable and shows neither anger nor vexation.

The power and the pretensions of Luynes and his

brothers keep on increasing and rouse universal repro-
bation. Greedy of honours and possessions, and without the slightest patriotic ambition, they monopolise
all governments, offices, fortified places, and castles;
they buy up for themselves and cheapen the royal
companies and the pick of all others; the taxes levied
on the people are appropriated to these private sales:
"In a word," says Richelieu, "if the whole of France
were for sale they would buy France from France itself." Richelieu is in the Opposition, as we should
now say; he is too patriotic at this time not to be,
but he is so in a manner of his own.

The nobles and the seigneurs, whom he had formerly combated are now, it seems, rising on his side,
and in the name of the queen-mother; they surround
the latter with intrigues, and under pretence of deliv-
ering the kingdom from the favourite, they are thinking only of their private interests. Seeing them arrive
at Angers, Richelieu effaces himself and takes no part
in their deliberations. Between two papers drawn up
in the queen's name, one more moderate, more prudent, and not tending to civil war, the other bitter,
violent, in short a manifesto of hostility, he is of opinion to choose the first, all the more because they have
not force enough to support the second. He fears to
give pretext to these powerful and turbulent allies who
"after ruining the varlets" will next, out of ambition,
attack the masters. He thinks that "there is no peace
so bad that it is not better than civil war." Luynes

advances into Maine with the king's troops; all the seigneurs and captains grouped around the queen-mother at Angers make countless plans that interfere with one another. Every one prays for the queen: she has all hearts, she has even many arms, and yet she is about to be vanquished in the twinkling of an eye. "God permits it, as I think," says Richelieu, "to make it plain that the peace of States is of such great importance in his sight that he often deprives of success enterprises that would trouble it, however just and legitimate they are."

Speaking of the part taken by Richelieu at this critical moment, some men of the period accused him of having betrayed the interests of the queen-mother and the confederates. The Duc de Rohan, that fomenter of civil war, accuses him of having intentionally advised the queen to make "a trembling defence." No; Richelieu gave then, even to the men of war, the best counsel, which was not followed; but the true explanation, in my opinion, is that he was not in heart with the confederates. Richelieu remained the past and the future minister of the monarchy even under dismissal and exile; he is conscious of his coming destiny; he does not belie his future.

Nothing can be more piquant than the portrait he draws of the principal leaders in the affray and rout that goes by the name of the "Pont-de-Cé" (August 7, 1620): it was a panic. The boasters, the cowards, the brave (in small number), each and all have their

place. It is an ironical picture such as Philippe de
Commynes might have painted, and he ends it by
considerations worthy of him, worthy of the man
who remained, at all times, royalist:

" I learned on this occasion that any party composed of various bodies
having no other bond than that their excitability gives them . . . has
no great subsistence; that whatever is maintained only by precarious
authority has no great duration; that those who combat legitimate
power are semi-defeated by their imagination; thoughts come to them
that not only are they exposed to the loss of their lives in battle but,
what is worse, by the arm of the law if captured; they think of the
executioner as they face the enemy, rendering the fight very unequal;
for there is little courage stiff enough to rise above such considerations
with as much resolution as if they were not aware of them."

Such Richelieu is still at heart when he finds
himself reluctantly involved in armed revolt and sedition. It is he who, on the morrow of the defeat at
Pont-de-Cé, contributes most to healing matters and
to bring about a peace which Luynes the victor did
not, for once, abuse to his own advantage.

So long as Luynes governed the king, there was no
great place possible for Richelieu. About this time
the favourite had a passing fancy to form connection
with the queen; he seems to have even sought alliance
with Richelieu, and the niece of the one married the
nephew of the other. But the two men were incompatible, and Richelieu had then no other real security
than the goodwill and confidence of the queen-
mother. To all the hazardous advice that was given
to the latter he urged the opposition of consistent
prudence and patience. Seeing the excessive good

fortune and the poor discretion and conduct of the
adversary, he felt with his sound good sense that it
behoved them only to wait and hold fast: "It is not
in France as in other countries," thought he; "in
France the best remedy we can have is patience.
. . ." And he expresses, àpropos of our light-
mindedness, so fruitful of reverses, distressing ideas
that would be too discouraging if he himself, man of
authority and organisation, did not come erelong to
oppose and correct them by his own example. But
for those who seek to find cause against our nation in
his words let me add that, according to him, this
French levity often bears its own remedy within
itself; for, if it sometimes casts us down frightful precipices it does not leave us there, but "pulls us up
so quickly that our enemies, unable to take right
measures on such frequent variations, have no leisure
to profit by our faults."

While Richelieu takes patience and waits, war begins in the south of France against the Protestants
who have organised themselves into churches and
chosen for leader and generalissimo the Duc de Rohan
(1621). Rebellion is manifest; the king goes down
there in person, full of courage; but Luynes ill knows
how to prepare the ground and afford him occasions
for acting. Before Montauban, for instance, Luynes
relies too much on information he obtains from a
traitor. He plans the advance of the king, who is
repulsed: "It is well," says Richelieu, 'not to neglect

small advantages; but it is dangerous to depend upon them, especially for a great prince who ought rather to win than to filch victories." How noble and how well said that is! Richelieu has his system of the way a devoted prime-minister ought to bring forward and put in relief a courageous king; he suffers in seeing that Luynes knows nothing of that art, nor of the jealousy for the honour of his master's arms that he ought to have.

If Luynes had lived, Richelieu's fortunes would have been long delayed, perhaps for ever. When he disappears, carried off by a sudden illness (December 14, 1621), in the midst of this very campaign which he had undertaken without ability to bring it to an end, Richelieu, in describing his death, his character and his person, has flashes of colour and passion such as Saint-Simon, a century later, might have given. Luynes, in the midst of his other defects, had one which, in France, would spoil even the best qualities, he was not personally brave. At the siege of Montauban, Constable of France as he was, he never approached the town within cannon-shot. He amused himself by sealing, filling the office of Keeper of the Seals, while others fought: a good Keeper of the Seals in war-time, people said, and a good constable in times of peace. "At the height of his cowardice," cries Richelieu, "he never ceased to talk as if he were riddled with wounds and covered with the blood of the enemy . . . " "The height of his cowardice" is one of those involuntary expressions which characterise a great and brave historian.

The whole portrait of Luynes is one of extreme beauty; it should be read as a whole; I can note only a few salient points which reflect the character of Richelieu himself. He is bent on showing Luynes as little fitted for the height to which favour had lifted him; a height that merely made him giddy and insolent: "Such minds," he says, "are capable of every fault; especially when men come, as this one did, to favour without having passed through public offices; men who see themselves suddenly above rather than in public affairs, and are masters of the Council without ever having entered it."

"He had," he says again, "a mediocre and timid mind, little faith, no generosity; too feeble to stand firm under the rush of great fortune . . . He wished to be Prince of Orange, Count of Avignon, Duke of Albert,[1] King of Austrasia,[2] and would not have refused more had he seen his way to it. Flattery carried him to such a point that he thought all the laudations bestowed upon him were true, and that the grandeur he attained was the least of his merits. . . . He was full of fine words and promises that he never kept faithfully; when he gave his most positive word persons felt the most certain that he would not keep it; and when he promised his affection it was then that its object had reason to doubt it: so faithless was he without shame, measuring honour solely by utility."

Richelieu reproaches Luynes for seeking to apply to France the narrow and tyrannical policy that is practicable only in the lesser provinces of Italy, where all

[1] Ancre in the department of the Somme.
[2] Eastern part of the empire of the Merovingian kings:—TR.

the subjects are immediately under a hand they fear:
" It is not the same in France," he says, "a great,
spacious country, parted by many rivers, with provinces very far from the seat of the king." In this
whole picture Richelieu indirectly reveals to us his
private thoughts; in representing to us the odious
favourite it is evident that he is feeling how he himself would differ from him. Richelieu, for example,
does not think himself tyrannical in the same manner
as the predecessor whom he scathes:

> " He, on the contrary," he says, " having the power in hand, scorned
> to gratify any one, believing that it sufficed him to hold their persons by
> force, and that he had no need to attach their hearts. But in that he
> was greatly mistaken; for it is impossible that a Government can exist
> under which none are satisfied and all are treated with violence. Se-
> verity is very dangerous where no one is content; laxity where there is no
> satisfaction is dangerous also; the only means by which it can exist is
> by uniting severity with just satisfaction to those who are governed;
> which will end in the punishment of the bad and the reward of the
> good."

Richelieu's theory is in those words; it is true, as he
tells us elsewhere, that where it is absolutely necessary
to choose, he considers punishment more necessary
than reward, and he puts it in the front rank.

Machiavelli said: " It is not the violence that repairs
but the violence that destroys which should be condemned." It is best, however, that in all that is permanent, all that is founded to last, the idea of violence
should fade away; and Richelieu, in his government,
never attained to this course of regular, almost impas-
sive, action. He was certainly of the race of royal

souls, but he was not born king.   It was the resistance and effort he had to make to maintain the royalty
he held as a loan that made him sometimes tyrannical in
action and manner.   Montesquieu said of Louis XIV:
"He had a soul that was greater than his mind."   In
Richelieu the mind was as great as the soul and
seemed to fill it but never to overflow it.

Richelieu does not enter the ministry immediately on
the death of Luynes; the ministers at Court dread him,
knowing that he is full of ideas and of force of judgment; they retard as much as they can the moment
when the king will take particular notice of him, fearing to see him at once at the head of affairs: "I have
had this misfortune," he says, "that those who had
power in the State have always wished me ill, not for
any harm that I had done them, but for the good they
believed was in me."   Do what they would, however, in vain did they oppose fate and sink deeper
daily into wastefulness and blunders; the moment approaches—it has come—and Richelieu henceforth is
inevitable.

We will leave him to reign.   But it is essential, that
I may not fall below my own idea, to say a few more
words about that Political Testament in which he laid
down, in a rather sententious form, the summing up
of his experience and the ideal of his doctrine.

Among the objections that Voltaire raised against
the authenticity of that work, there is one, among
others, that strikes me by its weakness and even its

misconception: "Admit," he says, addressing M. de
Foncemagne, "admit that after all you do not believe
there is a single word from the cardinal in this Testament: in good faith, do you think that Sir Robert
Walpole would ever have thought of writing a political catechism for George I?" But Richelieu is
precisely the contrary of Robert Walpole: he is a
man who believes in God, in the nature of kings, in a
certain moral grandeur in public affairs, in virtue belonging to each Order of the State—lofty rectitude in
the Clergy, generosity and purity of heart in the
Nobles, integrity and gravity in the Parliaments; all
this is what he desires at any cost to maintain or restore. Richelieu likes and prefers honest men· in
what memorable terms does he speak in his Memoirs
of the heroic gravity of Achille de Harlay and of the
prud'homie of President Jeannin!

In the Political Testament there is a remarkable
chapter entitled: "On Letters"; that is to say, on
classical literature and on education. In it Richelieu
explains his ideas about a wise administration and
dispensation of literature, and, considering the date at
which he wrote, it proves his lofty foresight. One
might really think he had the eighteenth century and
something of the nineteenth before his eyes.[1] He
cannot admit that in a State every one, without difference, should be brought up to be learned. "Just as a
body which had eyes in every part of it would be a

[1] The French Academy was founded by Richelieu in 1635:—Tr.

monster," he says, "so would a State be if all its subjects were learned men; we should see little obedience,
while pride and presumption would be common."
And again: " If Letters were degraded to all sorts of
minds, we should see more men capable of forming
doubts than of solving them, and many would be
more fitted to oppose truths than defend them." He
cites in support of his opinion Cardinal Du Perron, that
friend of fine literature, who would have liked to see
less colleges established in France on condition that
they were better, supplied with excellent professors,
engaged with worthy studies only, fit to preserve in
its purity the fire of the temple. The rest of the
young manhood would naturally go, he thought, to
the mechanical arts, to agriculture, commerce, the
army; whereas by applying them all indifferently to
studies "without the capacity of their minds being
first examined, nearly all remain with a mediocre tinge
of Letters and fill France with disputers [*chicaneurs*]."
This opinion of Richelieu, coming after the inundation
of the sixteenth century and before the deluge of the
eighteenth, is Bonald's legislation unadulterated; and,
on whichever side we look at it, expressed at that
time and with that precision, it bears witness to the
profound insight of a statesman.

This rôle of statesman, which, at every social crisis,
is the chief and the most actual, is not the only
rôle; two forces in conflict govern the world. While
Richelieu was expressing these forecasts and fears,

Descartes was preparing free access for all minds not only to Letters but to the Sciences by teaching mathematical doubt.   There is much to meditate upon in those two names.

On superficial reading, the Political Testament may seem to be composed of rather trite and commonplace maxims: but read it carefully, and you will always find the statesman and the experienced moralist.   In all the reforms that he proposes, Richelieu shows himself full of moderation; he takes account of accomplished facts; and even in correcting evils he desires to proceed with gentleness and caution.   He is one of those architects who prefer to remedy the faults of an old building, and bring it by their art to satisfactory symmetry, rather than pull it down on pretence of building another quite perfect and complete.   However ardent may have been Richelieu's nature and his fire of ambition, it remains evident that his mind in its foundation was essentially just and temperate.   In his moral descriptions, and in the examination of conditions that he exacts from men chosen to be political councillors, he certainly had in view this one or that one of those whom he had known; and his observations are so just and strong that merely in transcribing them here it seems as though we could put the right names beneath both virtues and defects:

"The greatest minds," says Richelieu, "may be more dangerous than useful in the management of affairs; if they have not more lead than quicksilver, they are worth nothing to the State."

" Some are fertile in invention and abundant in thoughts, but so variable in their designs that those of evening and those of morning are always different; and such men have so little persistency in their resolutions that they change the good ones as often as the bad ones and are constant to none."

" I can say with truth, knowing it from experience, that the levity of some men is not less dangerous in the administration of public affairs than the malice of others. There is much to fear from minds whose vivacity is accompanied with little judgment, and, even if those who excel in judgment have no great force they may nevertheless be useful to the State."

" Presumption is one of the great vices that men may have in public office; if humility is not required of those who are called upon to lead States, modesty is absolutely necessary."

" Without modesty great minds are so in love with their opinions that they condemn all others, better though they be; the pride of their natural characters joined to their authority soon renders them intolerable."

Such are the counsels, or rather the specifications of experience given by a man who did not pass for modest, but who certainly was still less presumptuous. In reading carefully Richelieu's State maxims, a doubt has possessed me at times: I ask myself whether, in the historical judgment formed upon him, too much of the unpopularity that easily attaches to strong powers in periods of public relaxing, has not been allowed to enter; and whether, from afar, we do not now judge him, even in his glory, too much through the imputations of the enemies who survived him. Richelieu was vindictive; was he as much so as was said of him? He certainly did not think so when he said: "Those who are vindictive by nature, who follow their passions rather than reason, cannot be considered to have the requisite integrity for the management of the State. If a man is subject to revenge, to put him in authority is to put a sword in the hand of a madman."

Such words show that the mind of Richelieu was far from tending to violent extremes. I leave these divers problems, these apparent contradictions between some of his thoughts and his acts, for future historians to agitate; the fame of Richelieu (and fame, he said, is the sole payment of great souls) can only increase with the years and the centuries; he is of those who have most contributed to give consistency and unity to a great nation which, in itself, has too little of them; he is, under that head, one of the most glorious political artisans that ever existed, and the more the generations are battered by revolutions and ripened by experience the more will they approach his memory with circumspection and respect.

II.

The Duc de Rohan.

Ibenri, Duc de Roban.

The Protestant Leader.

THE sixteenth century, which produced so great a number of good captains and writers of the sword, had, as it were, a last scion in the Duc de Rohan, who, under that double aspect, made himself illustrious during the first third of the following century. He is the last great man the Reformed religion produced in France; and it is the right of the historians of that party to study him with complacency and peculiar admiration. For us, who content ourselves with feeling his force, his merit — merit always thwarted and obscured by certain shadows — he attracts us chiefly as a writer, and it is on that side that I wish to render account of him to myself in presence of my readers, adding nothing to the idea, very lofty already, that we ought to form of him, and exaggerating nothing.

The fact is, we are at the present time in the habit of exaggerating many things. The study of the past, where great talents have lighted beacons that attract

all sorts of minds, is becoming a fashionable enthusiasm and a snare.   It is time for criticism, if it still dares
to be critical, to lay upon this enthusiasm certain restrictions and to remind it of some salutary rules.   In
France, we do things too often by fits and starts; the
fever of the present day is to rehabilitate all that comes
to hand or within the reach of every one.   A few old
papers found, which often, if read carefully (but nothing is more difficult than to read carefully, especially if
the words are not in print), tell us nothing more than
we knew before; a few unpublished documents which,
in every case, ought to combine with notions already
acquired and positive, these are the pretexts for an upsetting; accepted judgments are reversed, reputations
are made anew, we all blow our trumpets for the discoveries we think we have made, and in our eagerness to succeed we readily grant all to our neighbour
so that in return he may grant all to us.   I see many
hod-carriers who pretend to be architects, and copyists
saying to themselves: "I, too, am a painter."—But
this is not the time and place to treat of so grave
and delicate a question.   Happily the Duc de Rohan is
not in need of rehabilitation; he needs only to be
studied, and we have only to study him.

He came of a proud, strong race, descended from the
ancient dukes and kings of Brittany, allied by descent
and marriage with the principal sovereign families of
Europe.   "I shall content myself," writes one of his
earliest biographers, "by merely saying one rather

fine and rather peculiar thing: to whatever part of Europe he went he was related to those who reigned there." We all know the speech of his sister, replying to a gallant declaration from Henri IV, "I am too poor to be your wife, and too well-born to be your mistress." [1]

Born at the castle of Blein in Brittany in 1579, Henri de Rohan, the eldest of his family, was brought up with great care by his widowed mother, Catherine de Parthenay, who fixed upon him from childhood her pride and hopes. He was proficient in all exercises that made part of the education of a noble and a man of war; and he likewise applied himself to things of the mind, especially history geography, and mathematics, which he said was the true science of princes. It was told that he neglected the ancient languages, Latin and Greek, being more eager after things than words. However that may be, it would not have injured him to know Latin, fond as he was of studying ancient authors and of annotating Cæsar, of whom he was to make, in his leisure hours, a sort of breviary. He read also, like Henri IV, Amyot's translation of Plutarch, and kindled with enthusiasm for the Greek and Roman heroes; Epaminondas and Scipio being his models. In short, he received from his excellent mother a hardy and virile education, which his own

[1] It is singular that Sainte-Beuve does not here mention the proud motto of the Rohans: *Roi ne peux, prince ne veux, Rohan je suis*— "King I cannot [be], prince I will not [be], Rohan I am."—TR.

nature welcomed and the austerity of his religious communion confirmed: his youth was ardent, frugal, and serious.

Henri IV distinguished him among all the young nobles and loved him. As Vicomte de Rohan, he made his first campaign under the king's eye at the siege of Amiens, when sixteen years of age. This was his first school of war. The peace of Vervins (1598), which was to give France years of repose and a national felicity long unknown, made the warlike zeal of the young man useless, and he resolved to travel. His first idea was to push on to the East and see the empire of the Turks: "not from superstition," he says, like most of those who go to visit Jerusalem, but to instruct himself during the active years of his novitiate and to study the diversities of peoples and countries. Circumstances thwarted this first intention, and he fell back on travelling through European Christendom (1600–1601). He has left a narrative of his journey, dedicated to his mother, and written to preserve his own recollections and to please his friends. This *coup-d'œil* of a tourist of twenty years of age through France, Germany, Italy, Holland, and Great Britain, shows plainly the qualities and the solid inclinations of a mind that was preparing itself to play a great part. He notes everywhere, as a future commander and statesman, the site of fortresses, fortifications, commerce, the genius of nations, the form of governments. For a man who was said to have no

taste for classical study, he takes such interest in an-
tiquities and quotes so much Latin that we must
believe his first biographer exaggerated his repugnance
and his ignorance in that respect.

Venice impressed him keenly by its originality of
aspect, its arsenal, its fine police, its palaces, even its
pictures and its fantastic magnificences.

"In a word," he says, "if I tried to note down all that is worthy
of it paper would fail me : content thyself, therefore, my Memory, in
remembering that having seen Venice thou hast seen one of the collections of the marvels of the world, from which I depart as enrap-
tured and content at having seen it as I am sad at having stayed so
short a time ; for it deserves, not three or four weeks but a century to
study it to the level of its merits."

He stays longer in Florence and from there makes a
trip to Rome and Naples. Though he stayed but a
week in Rome, and seems to have ransacked at full
speed her curiosities and ruins, he is not too unjust or
too calvinistic in his remarks upon her.

But after Venice he finds nothing more interesting
nor more admirable than Amsterdam and the government of the United Provinces; he prefers the latter to
that of Venice. He likes Holland, even that which is
rather sad about her, even her difficulties, even that
long war she had successfully maintained against
powerful Spain for her independence as a country.
Holland, under the illustrious princes of Nassau, was
always the ideal land of Reformed religionists. He
ends his journeyings in England and Scotland where,
more even than elsewhere he is received with

distinction and hospitality by the sovereigns of the two
countries.   Queen Elizabeth calls him her "Knight";
and James VI, treating him as a cousin, invited him
to be godfather to his son, just born, afterwards the
unfortunate Charles I of England.   In concluding his
narrative, Rohan draws a species of parallel between
the genius of the different peoples and their government.   What he says of the good qualities and defects of the French nation in comparison with the
English shows him to be a judicious and impartial
observer.   As for the nobility and aristocracy of France,
he considers them (without enough reason perhaps)
far more fortunate than those across the Channel:
"As much," he says, "because the latter pay taxes like
the people, as for the rigour of the law, which is so
constantly exercised against them that some hold it as
an honour, and rest the grandeur of their families on the
number of their forbears who have had their heads cut
off; which is very rare among us."   Here speaks the
young man, and before the days of Richelieu.   He
sees only the agreeable advantages he then enjoyed:
"the privileges of the nobility in France, its liberty,
the familiarity with which the king treats it, in place
of the superstitious reverence that the English pay to
their king"—all things well fitted to seduce even so
solid a mind as that of young Rohan.   It was not
until the day of Louis XIV that the fatal levelling of the
nobility was really felt; it was permissible amid the
gracious sallies and smiles of Henri IV to mistake its

actual position. Nevertheless, one year later, the head of Biron was to fall.

Henri IV had a true friendship for young Rohan; in him he saw a pupil, a future lieutenant for his military projects; doubtless he also discerned a head capable of upholding and leading the Reformed party in future years, and of opposing his own better views to the perpetual intrigues of the Maréchal de Bouillon. He desires to confirm him in grandeur and makes him duke and peer (1602): his first idea was to marry him to a princess of Sweden, but this project did not take shape. Rohan married the daughter of Sully becoming the son-in-law of the man who was daily gaining more importance in the State and more credit with its master. Rohan himself received the office of colonel-general of the Swiss Guard. He served in this capacity in 1610, and was one of the principal leaders in the army that awaited Henri IV for that great and mysterious enterprise of which, to all appearance, the siege of Juliers was to be the signal. He was thirty-one years of age, and the noblest and most brilliant career lay open before him; when suddenly the knife of Ravaillac, taking from France a great king, took also from all generous hearts their true guide.

"If ever," says Rohan, "I had reason to join my regrets to those of France, it was at the unhappy death of Henri the Great, so full of gloom and fatal results for us ; yet for him it may, perhaps, be reckoned, from a worldly point of view, as fortunate. . . . After his accession to the throne (1589) he employed eight years in bringing the kingdom to obedience ; and these years, though toilsome, were the happiest of his life ; for, in augmenting his reputation he augmented his State : the true happiness of a magnanimous prince does not consist in long possessing a great empire, which may serve to plunge him into pleasures only, but in having from a little State made a great State, and satisfied not his body but his spirit. One often sleeps worse among delights on good mattresses than on gabions, and there is no such rest as that which is acquired through labour."

Rohan thinks (and this judgment is characteristic of him) that those eight laborious and victorious years— victory so contested and bought by such perils and vigils — were happier to Henri IV than the twelve years of peace and felicity, during which he governed his kingdom without further struggle. Rohan is, in his way, a hero, but a thwarted hero, who will always have a burden to bear upon his shoulders; one might almost think from those words of his that he found more pleasure than resignation in bearing it; he loved effort.

He foresees all the evils that will follow the king's death, all the ambitions that already are whetting their appetites.

" In his lifetime he [Henri IV] restrained evil-doers by his authority; by his death all fear in evil-doing is removed, liberty seems given to worthless men. The still recent memory of his name bears with it some respect, but every day that carries us away from it is a sure step into the path of disobedience. Those who witnessed the reign of Charles IX, with the consequent evils that France suffered after it, can easily judge of the danger she is now in. . . . I regret in the loss of our invincible King, that of France. I mourn his person, I deplore the lost opportunities, and I sigh in the depths of my heart over the manner of his death. Experience will teach us in a short time the legitimate cause we have to regret and mourn him. The people already shudder and seem to foresee their misery; the cities

are guarded as if they expected a siege; the nobles look for safety
to the most important in their own body, but find them all dis-
united; there is every occasion for fear and none for security. In
short, one must either not be a Frenchman, or regret the loss of the
happiness of France. I mourn in him the loss of his courtesy, his
familiarity, his good humour, his pleasant conversation. The honour
that he did me, the good cheer with which he favoured me, the
admittance that he gave me to his most private places, oblige me
not only to mourn him but also to no longer like myself where
I was accustomed to see him. I mourn for the noblest and most
glorious enterprise that was ever spoken of . . . an opportunity
I shall never see again; certainly not under so great a captain, nor
with the same desire on my part to serve it and learn my profession. . . . Is it not, for me, a subject of great regret to lose
the only opportunity that ever came to me to prove to my king —
and O God, what a king! — my courage, my affection, my fidelity?
Surely when I think of it my heart breaks. A lance-thrust given in
his presence would have pleased me more than now to win a battle.
I should have more esteemed one word of praise from him in this
profession, of which he was the greatest master in his time, than
those of all other living captains. . . . I part my life in two, and
call the first, that which I have now lived, happy, because it
served the great Henri, and that which I have to live unhappy,
employing it in regretting, mourning, complaining, and sighing."

Rohan did not pass the rest of his life mourning
and sighing, nor even in serving inviolably (as he
vows to do at the end of this paper) France, the
young king and his mother. But he had good reason
to consider his career as cut in two by King Henri's
death. Instead of the way lying open before him,
that of a great captain of generous and loyal Frenchmen, beneath the great man of whom he would have
been the illustrious lieutenant and second, he was
henceforth to find himself engaged, by force of circumstances, in a life of faction, of struggle in all

directions, of disputes at every step, wrangles with his own people and with the envious orators of his own party, in rebellion before the armies and the person of the king, and continually in alliance with foreigners. He was now to train and consume his faculties as an able statesman and a skilful soldier on manœuvres in which selfish interests and personal ambitions made, with the names, perpetually invoked, of God and conscience, a most equivocal mixture that even those assiduously given to it found difficulty in distinguishing apart.

His *Mémoires*, which cover, from his point of view, the whole history of France from the death of Henri IV to the end of the third war against the Reformers, when La Rochelle fell (1610–1629), exhibit the complication of events and the obstructions to the writer. The first religious civil war seems to have been begun, in 1621, against Rohan's will, although he became its instrument and most energetic champion. There happened to him that which so often happens to leaders of party : it is the parties and the Assemblies that lead them. The Assembly of Protestants, convoked at La Rochelle, believing that the guarantees to their Churches were threatened, even by the conditions of the Edict of Nantes, and excited by the Vicomte de Favas, pushed forward to a rupture. Rohan's prudence made him see the peril ; the point of honour and the instinct of a soldier made him brave it. Most of the nobles of the Reformed religion, who seemed at first to take the same course, made terms, little by little, and withdrew. Rohan, with his brother Soubise, was left to bear the brunt of the defence. His governments in Poitou fell into the power of the royal armies. He organised the resistance in the South, and succeeded in throwing succour into Montauban, in spite of the vicinity of the two royal armies. His plan was to act in the true military manner: to dismantle the small places he could not hold, and to fortify the large ones, Nîmes, Montpellier, Uzès: "We had," he says, "a sufficient number of men to make a lively resistance; but the shortsightedness of the people and the private interests of the governors of the towns caused my advice to be rejected, for which they afterwards repented sorely."

Leader of a league, and that a religious league, Rohan had to struggle against all the disadvantages of that position: fanatical forebodings and denunciations from within, popular violence, excesses and crimes to punish, self-willed and headstrong troops, difficult to collect or retain under the flag. He got along as best he could, sometimes for three months, with unpaid troops, holding his own against the armies of the enemy, laying several sieges; but, after all, being forced to desist from what he was on the point of attaining, "as much through the ill-humour of his colonels as because the harvests were beginning, which is a time when the poor of lower Languedoc earn much money."

These are but glimpses, but they give an idea of the
nature of the genius and the firmness required to make
as good a show as Rohan did in such a style of war;
I leave it to others to admire him for it. Great
occasions were lacking, but he ennobled as much as
he could the lesser ones. There is one place in his
narrative where the Duc de Luynes (the favourite in
power, who had married his cousin), asks for a con-
ference with him at a league from Montauban; Rohan
trusts himself to him, and gives us the details of the
interview and of their speeches, — that of Luynes
and his own reply :

> "I should be my own enemy," says Rohan to Luynes, "if I did not
> desire the good graces of my King and your friendship I shall never
> refuse the gifts and honours of my master, nor your good offices as
> an ally. I have fully considered the peril in which I am; but I ask
> you to also consider your own. You are universally hated, because
> you alone possess that which every man desires to have. The ruin of
> those of the Reformed religion is not so near that malcontents will not
> have time to form parties. Reflect that you have already harvested
> all that promises, mingled with threats, can ever obtain for you, and
> that all who now remain to us are fighting for the religion they
> believe in. . . ."

He ends by refusing to lend himself to any personal
conclusion that would separate him from the general
interests. For these religious wars, having once begun, even against his will, it is to Rohan's honour
that he never put his hand to private negotiations,
nor sacrificed his party. It is for this, as much as for
his talents as a commander, that he is distinguished
from the other seigneurs who, sooner or later, deserted

their party, and he deserves that the French Protestant cause shall remain for ever identified with his name.

After the death of Luynes, and after many similar parleys, mingled with various bold attacks, Rohan, who sees the people to be weary of war, and that forage for his much-diminished cavalry will last only eight days longer, and who, moreover, has lost all hope of succour from foreign co-religionists, confers with the new connétable, Lesdiguières, to draw up a treaty (October, 1622) which saved and maintained the principal points necessary to the Reformed party, and in which his own interests were not altogether forgotten. After which, he is not only pardoned by the king, but he has a dazzling moment of favour at Court. Richelieu, then approaching power with slow step, had not yet reached it; when he did so, pacifications were conducted differently.

But this peace, obtained by bargaining, was ill-kept. The Duc de Rohan was forced to submit at Montpellier to an affront from the governor, M. de Valençay, and to a species of imprisonment. Besides which, he had to defend himself in his own party against censors who, for the most part, had kept their arms folded during the war, and to "justify his good intentions blamed and his best actions calumniated." We begin now to see the thankless and difficult part he had to play, which was destined to become far more so in his two following wars, with Richelieu in power.

There is a race of brilliant, favoured warriors and
fortunate heroes: Rohan is not of it. He is of those
to whom adversity serves as a continual school, and
even as a strengthener; men who snatch glory bit by
bit, in fragments only. He is not of that group of
Captains — the Condés, the Luxembourgs, the Villars,
the Saxes — of whom we may say that fortune smiled
upon them like Venus, like a woman. He is of the
race of grave men, thwarted men, morose men; whose
very brilliancy is darkened and sombred; who have
more merit than opportunity or luck, esteemed though
often defeated; and who do the utmost that they can
with a dismembered and rebellious cause; he is, in
short, of the race of the Colignys, and of William of
Orange; less French, perhaps, than foreign in physi-
ognomy. In place of the lightning-flash of the French
nature, the Reform has placed upon his brow its
thoughtful seal, its frown, proclaiming less the inspired
warrior than the reasoning soldier.

We may follow and study closely the narrative that
M. de Rohan has written of the religious civil wars
under Louis XIII and the noted part that he played in
them, but we cannot, even by placing ourselves at the
most neutral point of view and avoiding all questions
of the Church, —we cannot, I say, take a strong interest
in him, or desire at any moment his success and the
triumph of his arms. He is definitively against France;
he fights against the nation; he conspires against its
grandeur, and makes common cause with the foreigner.

I desire, in this rapid outline and while stating
the principal facts, to shock no true and noble feeling,
to slight no claim of the human conscience; and yet I
must maintain the line which is ever the most direct,
the only French line, that of the broad and royal road.
The question, so sacred to us, of tolerance and respect
for all convictions and professions of sincere faith
compatible with social order, had in that day not been
evolved. A few men who had enough wisdom and
firmness of judgment to understand it and to forestall
its solutions, spoke to deaf ears; and when they tried,
like l'Hôpital, to introduce moderation publicly by
edicts, they merely lent immediate arms to passions.
In that heated atmosphere, which had not been sufficiently worked over in every direction, which had
not yet vented all its storms, and where the numerous currents of indifference had not as yet worked
their way, how could there be tolerance? Satisfaction, full and exclusive, dominion, the upper hand,
was what they wanted.

Henri IV was the only man who was able to calm
this spirit; he did it by his skill, his justice, his force
so wisely tempered by dexterity. He died too soon;
and when he was gone it was difficult indeed for the
ill-appeased fermentations, stirred up afresh by the
air without, not to burst once more into flames.
The Duc de Rohan felt, from the moment of that
death, that his party was released from tutelage;
the Reformers lost with Henri IV their guardian, and

also the powerful hand that restrained them. Their
policy ought to have been to fortify themselves in
the places of safety they had preserved, and to recover others that they had lost; in a word, in order
to make themselves respected they ought to have
made themselves more feared than ever.

" I know," said Rohan to the Assembly of Saumur (1611), " they
will oppose us if we ask more than we possessed in the time of
the late king; I know that we ought, in order to insure peace
during the infancy of this reign, to content ourselves with the same
treatment. To that it may be answered that the change of things
causes apprehension. . . . How many alarms have we not received since the unhappy day of the parricide of our Henri the
Great! The law of States changes with the times; no one can give
positive maxims; what is useful to one king is hurtful to another."

The princes of the blood, the Condés, by their conversion to Catholicism had not, Rohan thought, weakened the position of the Reformers; for those princes,
if they supported the party, had to be supported by it,
and often carried on their own affairs to its injury.
What is certain is that, in default of the princes,
it was the higher nobles who took their place, who
took the initiative and the command of the armed
rebels; and the house of Rohan was in the front rank
of this active rôle. It gave itself to the common
cause with a devotion that cannot be contested;
neither the Maréchal de Bouillon, whose career was
ending and who had long been only a consulting
power, nor the old Lesdiguières, who was thinking
of being converted and returning to his former breth-

ren, nor the Trémouilles, the La Forces, the Châtillons, whose resolutions were never long-breathed,—not one of these attempted in the new uprising to dispute the supremacy of the Rohans.

Without here speaking of his mother, a strong woman, of *vieille roche*, the inspirer and soul of all resistance, to whom we shall presently return; without speaking of his wife, — the daughter of Sully, a dainty and charming beauty, the most volatile of wives, but faithful politically and an active and devoted auxiliary,—Rohan had for his second a brother, Benjamin de Rohan, known under the name of Soubise, a sailor, high admiral of the Reformed Church just as Rohan was the generalissimo ashore and in the mountains. During the first war, of 1621, Rohan, not willing to let himself be shut up in his town of Saint-Jean d'Angely, left that place in charge of Soubise, who held out against the army of the king, received with doffed hat the royal summons to surrender, and replied with these words in writing, which have come down to us: "I am the very humble servant of the king, but the execution of his commands is not within my power. [Signed:] Benjamin de Rohan." Forced to surrender after a siege of twenty-four days in virtue of a capitulation which took the form of letters of pardon, Soubise, although in issuing from the town he had asked forgiveness of the king on his knees, went straight into the same war that same year and continued the work

of resistance and rebellion, in which he never slack-
ened. He thought he had in the depths of his con-
conscience (such are the sophistries of the spirit of
faction) that which released him from the engage-
ment he had taken and absolved him in the last
resort. Taking refuge in England, during the truces,
returning with English vessels, which he strove to
take into the port of La Rochelle, leader and pilot
of foreigners to our shores, his whole conduct in
those years casts a sorry light on the most vulner-
able side of the policy of Rohan, that elder brother
with whom he was so fully in accord, so unanimous,
planning in concert.with him at all times, and willing
to be disavowed for appearance' sake when the occasion demanded. Soubise, unsubdued and unsub-
duable, in whom the idea of duty towards the sovereign
of France did not exist, determining, in the last extremity, to make a piratical war rather than submit
to his king, represents very well the Frenchman who
forgets himself and who is to a certain point denat-
uralised, or, at least (for I would not say an unjust
thing of a vanquished man), denationalised.

M. de Rohan had more prudence: prudence and
obstinacy are the two distinctive traits of his character. He claims, through it all, to remain a good
Frenchman; he has always the air of taking arms
against his will, in self-defence, and because he could
not in honour do otherwise without failing in his
duty to the Reformed Church. But, arms once taken,

he never lays them down until there are no means left to prolong the struggle; and there are no expedients he does not employ to force his people to imitate him and follow him to the end. His Memoirs, very good to read, are far from being a complete narrative to which we can trust implicitly; he conceals where it suits him to do so. Orator, man of discussion and persuasion as much as he was a warrior, a whole very important side of his talent and of the part he played has disappeared from sight. In his harangue before the town-council of Montauban during the first war, he said: "I beg you to believe that I will never abandon you, no matter what happens. When there are but two persons left to the Religion, I shall be one of the two." He kept that promise throughout the wars and renounced it only when all had failed him. No scruple withheld him from making terms either with the King of England (that was natural) or with foreign co-religionists, with the Duc de Savoie, or even with the King of Spain, whose succour he had long hoped for, expecting a subsidy from him as a last resource. The Spanish doubloons and the *Catholicon*, the subject of so much sarcasm against the League, would have seemed to Rohan purified by passing through his hands.

A double reading is interesting to make here that of the Memoirs of Rohan in comparison with the Memoirs of Richelieu. What a different policy!

what a conflicting game ! what opposing views
and sentiments, reflected in their very manner of
speech and expression!   Let us guard against forgetting that those who did not succeed have against
them many equivocal appearances and beginnings,
which might have quite another air had the issue
been otherwise: a ray of sunshine falling at the right
moment changes the landscape.   " But because,"
says Rohan somewhere, " histories are made by the
victorious only, we usually find none esteemed but the
children of fortune." That is true.   Nevertheless, it is
Richelieu who is right in this struggle, who has on his
conscience the great cause he serves, the noble monarchy he continues, the incomparable France he is
perfecting.   Words and language tell it; through images his thoughts gleam; Rohan envelops himself
where Richelieu develops.

It was not until the second civil war that Rohan
came face to face with the supremacy of the haughty
cardinal, in whom, up to that time, he had seen only
one favourite the more:

" To that man's favour," he says, speaking of the Marquis de
La Vieuville, " succeeded that of Cardinal de Richelieu, introduced
by La Vieuville into public affairs; that is how all those favourites
serve one another faithfully.   .   .   .   The support that the Cardinal
gets from the queen-mother [Marie de Medicis] has made his favour last
much longer than that of others, and has also made him more insolent."

Rohan seems to have been some time in perceiving
that he had encountered in Richelieu his great and
fatal adversary.

The second war was begun by Soubise, who gave the signal for it (January, 1625) by an audacious act. Feeling that La Rochelle, that bulwark of the Protestant cause, was becoming more and more blockaded by Fort Louis and from the direction of the islands of Ré and Oléron, and that the city would stifle if it did not have free communication with the sea, Soubise went to Blavet (Port Louis), seized a number of large vessels that were being equipped, and, after various adventures, succeeded in bringing away his prizes. Master of the sea, he gave hope and courage to the Rochelle people, who at first had pretended to disavow him. Rohan, though concurring with him on every point, had hitherto not chosen to take up arms, even lending himself to a semblance of negotiation with the Court; he now began to declare himself, "constrained to do so," he says, "to show that it was not his inability, as people imagined, that prevented it, but his desire to pacify all things."

He had already gone through many of the towns, accompanied by a great number of ministers, haranguing, saying prayers, and having a Bible carried before him, faithful to his double rôle of Captain and servant of the Religion. On the 1st of May, 1625, he began his armed enterprises, failed in his attack on Lavaur, but made all the towns on his way declare themselves. Usually, he had only to show himself to give courage to his allies within the walls, to the "good inhabitants" who swept in the others; for sheriffs and magistrates, more circumspect and always men of middle courses, needed to have the people in the streets take part and force their hand. Castres and Montauban were his principal points of support. The Cévennes were favourable to him, and thence he drew his soldiers. The whole was done with accompaniment of assemblies, and the holding of conferences, as befitted a republican enterprise, which rests not only on the consent but the emotion of the people.

Maréchal de Thémines commanded the army of the king; he appeared before Castres, where the Duchesse de Rohan, who had left her husband, with a Council or committee of the Assembly, took upon herself (her councillors being perplexed), to issue orders, and rising, by force of circumstance, above her usual self, that mundane but courageous little person sufficed for all. The maréchal, who had the advantage in numbers, held the country, ravaged the low lands and seized Saint-Paul; the only rather notable action that Rohan in his Memoirs attributes to him; diminishing it however, as much as he can, and representing it as more easy than perhaps it was. On the other hand, Rohan takes delight in extolling the heroic action of seven soldiers of Foix, who, being shut up in a paltry little town near Carlat, stopped the maréchal and his whole army for two days, and after killing forty of his men, made their escape to the number of four; three of the seven, all near relatives, choosing to

remain and be sacrificed because one of them was
wounded and unable to get away: "The four others,"
says Rohan, "at the solicitation of the three, under
cover of the night, and after embracing one another,
fled; and the three that were left stood at the gate,
loaded their arquebuses, awaited patiently the coming
of daylight, and received their enemies valiantly and,
after killing several, died free men." That is the sole
flash of emotion in Rohan's narrative; he wanted to
secure to the names of those brave soldiers an im-
mortality of which he has not proved the dispenser;
for certain special echoes, which are not found twice,
have alone given us the glorious names that immor-
talise Thermopylæ.

After this, he is obliged to relate the defeat of
Soubise in a conflict with the forces of the king at the
island of Ré, his resistance more or less desperate, and
his flight to England with what vessels he could save.
A peace was then bargained for and concluded; Richelieu, now at the beginning of his great designs, did
not make it too difficult, and the ambassadors from
England and Holland, two powers then allied to
France, imperiously advised the Reformers to accept
it. Rohan in his Memoirs has an air of triumphing
more than is becoming. He complains, however, of
everybody:

"This is what took place," he says as he concludes, "in that second
war, where Rohan and Soubise had against them all the chief nobles
of the Religion in France, either from jealousy or want of zeal, all

the kings on account of their avarice, and most of the principal men
in the towns, won over by the enticements of the Court. . . .When
we are no longer men of property God will assist us more powerfully."

By this peace the Reformers obtained what to their
eyes was the essential thing, namely: the maintenance
of the new fortifications which they had constructed
in nearly all the small towns of the South of France;
in other words, facilities for renewing the war.

From this period of his narrative we may note
Rohan's frequent complaints of the versatility, the
impatience, the lack of justice in the common people,
the ingratitude "which is the usual reward for services done to them," and their temper "that leads
them to be as insolent in prosperity as they were
cringing in adversity." He says this again and again
in a score of places. "He who has to do with a
people who find nothing difficult in undertaking an
enterprize but in its execution foresee and provide for
nothing, is greatly hindered." He wishes that those
who come after him "may have as much affection,
fidelity, and patience as he has had, and meet with
peoples more faithful, more zealous, and less miserly."
That proud soul, that energetic Captain, born to command, that aristocratic nature, ambitious of great designs
but shackled at every step, must have suffered much!

Another point must here be mentioned, though
rather delicate and one it seems strange to dwell upon
in speaking of a great warrior who died of wounds
received in battle. Rohan, and also his brother Sou-

bise, have been accused of sparing themselves in
military engagements and of not always putting themselves at the head of their troops or into the thick of
the battle, sword in hand. At Ré, at the most decisive moment of the effort against the king's troops
Soubise appears to have not done with his person and
his arm what he might have done; and at Viane,
while Maréchal Thémines was attacking and burning
a suburb, driving out the troops who opposed him,
the Duc de Rohan was seen on a bastion of the town,
"whence he was observing the action cane in hand."
Nevertheless, to neither should be offered the insult of
asking whether they were brave or not brave. They
were the leaders of the party; they were bound to
preserve themselves for the Cause; moreover, as
others have judiciously remarked, they had to fear,
not to die the death of a soldier, sword in hand, but
to be taken prisoners and finish their days as rebels
on a scaffold.

Let us now open the Memoirs of Richelieu where
he speaks of the same circumstances. The tone is
different, the mists clear away, the flags are hoisted;
we feel at every step the advantage of defined situations and of a genius that treads its native way. The
XVIth book of the Cardinal's Memoirs thus describes
the opening of the second civil war:

"This year (1625) saw at its beginning the outbreak of an infamous
rebellion of our heretics, which was plotted by Soubise, from whom
no one looked for such treachery.

"He was noted among the rebels as having been the first who dared present himself to forbid an entrance into one of his towns to the king

"Coming out of Saint-Jean-d'Angely by capitulation, he swore never to take up arms again against His Majesty.

"In defiance of his oath he did not refrain, shortly after, from seizing the dunes of Olonne; but seeing that the king was about to swoop down upon him, he retired to La Rochelle, like those timid birds who hide in the hollows of a rock when an eagle pursues them. There he was pardoned a second time by His Majesty.

"But, as the gratitude of infidels is as faithless as themselves, these favours descended so little into his heart that no sentiment or memory of them remained, and his rebellion, as fruitful as the Hydra, was born again.

"He set fire to the kingdom while the king was engaged in the defence of his allies, as Eratostratus set fire to the temple of Diana while she was giving her attention to promote the birth of Alexander. . . ."

Let us not ask of Richelieu the correct and sober taste that belongs to Rohan: Richelieu has imagination and he shows it; he has literature and he affects it. His style loves the plumed hat, and the plumed hat does not misbecome him, any more than it does the nation that he guides and represents. His bad taste has something in common with that of Château-briand; it is a bad taste which seduces and, at moments, carries us away far more than cold reason; it waves the oriflamme.

While Richelieu, already strong in the confidence of Louis XIII, was preparing his grand European design — the lowering of the power of Spain and the house of Austria — for which he expected to use a new and close alliance with England, he found himself

suddenly stopped short by this uprising in the interior
which cut in two the kingdom.

"This revolt," he says, energetically, " came so unseasonably for
the King, at a time when he had many affairs with foreign countries,
that most of his Council lost their heads so that sometimes they
wanted him to make an ignominious peace with Spain, and sometimes they were willing to grant the Huguenots more than they
demanded.
" The cardinal, on the contrary, looking with a firm heart on all
this tempest, said to the King. . . ."

Here follows one of those indirect, expounding discourses, such as the cardinal likes to put on paper, in
which he develops all considerations in every direction, not without a certain complacency and an ear
to his own words, but with clearness, loftiness,
breadth, and accuracy. His conclusion is that "so
long as the Huguenots have a foothold in France the
king will never be master within the Kingdom or be
able to undertake any glorious action without"; that
there is no way of doing two important things at
once; that the internal evil, be it least in itself, is the
worst now, and the one to be looked to before all
else. He had the idea, very bold and original, to
make use for that purpose of the help of allies, and
those the very ones who belonged to the Religion of
the rebels; for France at that time had no navy; she
had not even a single ship to oppose to Soubise, now
triumphant on the seas since his capture of vessels.
Richelieu resolutely insisted that the number of auxiliary ships which the king was compelled to obtain

for these new wars must be exacted from the English
and Dutch,—twenty from Holland, seven or eight
from England; he also desired to stipulate, so as to
make sure that these vessels should operate efficaciously
and not against the object for which they were obtained, that French captains should be put on board,
and French crews, either wholly or in part. In advising the king to make, imperiously and even with
threats (if necessary), these rather singular demands
on his Protestant allies to defeat his Protestant subjects, the cardinal, whose instinct told him that all
could be obtained, knew very well that he was running a great risk with his master in case of refusal:

" Had he considered himself," he says, with a feeling of noble pride,
" he might not have taken this course which, being the best for
public interests, was not the safest for those who proposed it; but,
knowing that the first condition for him who takes part in the government of States is to give himself wholly to the public and not to
think of himself, he passed over all considerations that might stop him,
liking better to ruin himself than to fail in any necessary thing to save
the State, of which it may be said that the base and cowardly proceedings of the late ministers had changed and tarnished its whole
face."

This naval armament, so boldly collected, to which
England contributed by vessels only, and Holland by
ships and men, had all the success and effect that
Richelieu expected to get from it. In short, and as
we have already seen by Rohan's narrative, after the
defeat of Soubise at the island of Ré, peace was
made, but not altogether such as Rohan desired. The
cardinal, no doubt, knowing, as he says, that " pru-

dent policy consists in taking the most advantageous occasion that can be had to do what we wish," and feeling that the great and various affairs the king then had upon his hands demanded more or less delay, dissimulated and allowed the Reform party to believe that he was not their adversary: "For peace being made," he says, "there was means of waiting for a more convenient time to reduce them to the terms all subjects should be under in a State; that is to say, that no separate body shall be formed within it independent of the will of the sovereign." At any rate, by this treaty of February 5, 1626, the king, already more a king than before, gave peace to his subjects, but did not receive it; on the side of La Rochelle he expressly reserved Fort Louis, as a citadel taken from the town, and the islands of Ré and Oléron, two other fortified places, "which did not make a bad circumvallation."

Rohan in his Memoirs (intended in a way to be read as an apology) asserts that he was satisfied with this provisional peace. His letters and confidential missives, some of which were intercepted and conveyed to the cardinal, show much less satisfaction, and this treaty, so disadvantageous to the Protestants, "threw the two brothers into such despair," says Richelieu, "that Mme. de Rohan, not knowing what other advice to give Soubise, tried to persuade him, in an intercepted letter, to join the Moorish corsairs and retire to the Barbary coast" rather than resign himself

to the law of the victor. It is worth while to read
how Richelieu exclaims, not as a politician only, but
as a theologian and fervent Catholic, at the thought of
such advice.

Such a state of things, in which one part of the
nation was engaged in curbing the other part, which,
in turn, held it in check, could not last without the
greatest detriment to the monarchy and to France,
which, in face of Europe and of the general recon-
stitution of modern political forces then going on,
needed unity and collected strength within its borders.
The honour of Richelieu is that he felt this with
ardent energy and an indomitable genius for execution: the misfortune of Rohan (that of his position) is
not to have been able to feel it; to have been the
natural and as if necessary ally of the foreigner, of whoever was then the enemy of his country; to have
continued to think upon it as an old-fashioned feudal
seigneur become a republican by chance who, stirred
by a peculiar religious conviction, used all means
of defence, unaware of what he was about to shock
in the breast of that other moral and religious sentiment, the patriotic sentiment, then on the point of
becoming universal.

The third war began in 1627; it is useless to seek
for the pretexts or the causes, which each party
bandied with the other; it was certain to break forth;
the peace of 1626 having been submitted to by one
side and conceded by the other with all sorts of men-

tal reservations on both sides and stress of necessity. A great cabal was formed at Court of which Monsieur, the king's brother, was the ostensible head. England, this time, appeared as an enemy; a gentleman was sent by the King of Great Britain to solicit the Duc de Rohan from whom, says the latter, "the desertions and unfaithfulness he had met with in the two preceding wars had taken all desire to renew the game." Nevertheless, he dared not assume the responsibility of a refusal, and he joined the party with that sense of difficulty and non-success which constituted his fate. "I considered what a burden I was taking on my shoulders for the third time; I reminded myself of the inconstancy of our people, of the unfaithfulness of the principal men, of the compact parties that the king had in all our communities, the poverty of the country, the avarice of the towns, and, above all, the irreligion of every one."

By "irreligion" we must understand merely the weakening of that exalted religious principle, unknown till the sixteenth century, which drove its adherents to every sacrifice of life and fortune for the faith; a weakening derived already from the modern spirit, in virtue of which many estimable Reformers preferred commerce to war. This was not the reckoning of Rohan and the feudal chiefs. Such weakening, or gradual relaxing (as much in morals as in beliefs), made itself more and more felt after the decapitation of the party by Richelieu; and this condition of minds, wisely appreciated by Mazarin in what he called "the little flock," must have been still further understood by Louis XIV, who followed the idea and the practice, where possible, of tolerance.

After the perplexities and diversities of mind which M. de Rohan himself acknowledges that he had at the beginning of the third war we can understand the severe and angry judgment that Richelieu pronounced upon him:

"That miserable Soubise," he cries with indignation (for he never separates the two brothers), "whose misfortune, capacity, and courage are equally decried, having no other art to cover his past shames than to prepare for fresh ones, is soliciting in England. The Sieur de Rohan, more fitted to be an attorney in a law court than leader of a party, the benefits of which must be procured by courage in war and by frankness and ingenuousness in peace . . . continues his practices, and by a thousand factions makes known to every one that he is doing as much during peace to bring on war, as he did during war to bring peace. In peace, his mind has no repose, just as in war his person was little risked. He keeps up intelligence with all the factious within the kingdom and all the mischief-makers without."

Let us here allow for passion's share in these words and free the thought from the insult. Richelieu was the first to show that at heart he judged better of Rohan when, later, he intrusted him with an army corps to enter the Valtelline, and in a letter he then addressed to the victorious general he said: "He would always very willingly be his surety with the king that he [Rohan] would preserve all the acquired advantages and lose no occasion to increase them." But, in this moment of cruel war, they are two spirits, two rival

and antagonistic souls, struggling against each other,
and all the defects, all the complications, all the entanglements in the conduct and rôle of Rohan were
uppermost in the cardinal's mind; he imputes them to
his character, he expresses them with exaggeration,
with injustice, no doubt, but also with discernment of
the weak point and in terms unforgettable.   The hour
was decisive for the very fortune and grandeur of
Richelieu himself.   To suppose that he would have
embarked on his great designs for foreign combina-
tions leaving La Rochelle open to the English, and in
communication with the Cévennes ill-subdued, and
with Languedoc half-rebellious, is not to know him.
Rohan, the ablest and most tenacious of the two leaders who were seeking to maintain a sort of federal
republic in the heart of the kingdom, was not his least
stumbling-block.   The latter had promised the King
of England to take up arms again whenever the English army should make its descent on the island of Ré,
and he kept his word.

It is not for me to try to write the history of those
memorable exploits in the much-disputed channels, or
of that siege of La Rochelle and the taking of the place
after more than a year's blockade and three naval expe-
ditions of Englishmen powerless to succour it.   The
constancy, the obstinacy, the intrepid faith of Richelieu
in his own wise counsel and in the fortune of France
triumphed over all, even the elements.   On the other
hand, the heroism and moral resignation of the besieged

and famished population exceeds all that is known of the longest and most trying sieges. This two-fold, conflicting sentiment, as strong in the besieged as in the besiegers, is pictured with fidelity in the pages of Richelieu and Rohan alike; the latter, who at the time was carrying on the campaign in the South and limited to holding the king's troops occupied by a series of skirmishes and small affairs, felt but too well that the brunt of the action was taking place where he was not, and that the fate of the Cause was being decided without him.

Richelieu's ardour in this perilous enterprise, the eagerness that he feels in the affair, and which consumes him, break forth in a thousand fiery flashes in his narrative:

"Nevertheless," he says in one place, "though the Cardinal employed all the mind that God had given him in making the siege of La Rochelle redound to the divine glory and the good of the State, working harder than the bodily strength that God had bestowed upon him warranted, one would have said that the wind and the seas, friends of the English and the Isles, forced themselves into the encounter and opposed his designs."

To take La Rochelle before all else, promptly and without mercy this time, such was his fixed idea; it was, according to him, the best remedy for every-thing; and all means, all imaginable inventions must be employed, not omitting a single one, to bring it about, because "on the taking of La Rochelle depends the safety of the State, the repose of France, the welfare and authority of the King for ever."

Should there be a State within the State, a natural and permanent ally of the foreigner among us, a port and an open door on the flank of the kingdom? that was the supreme question. He vowed himself to settle it with a zeal as chivalrous as it was politic. The spirit of a crusade was in his ardour. The keys of La Rochelle, when he held them, were worth in his eyes those of the Cabinets which he could not force until then, nor drag as he wished into the sphere of action of the noblest monarchy in the world. Such were the noble and frank thoughts that he put in action and pursued beneath his purple; while Rohan in his Cévennes, not daring to risk all in a headlong venture (as the great Vendéens were to do in their day), exhausts himself in hurrying from town to town, endeavouring to organise in France a *counter-France*. The disproportion of the two rôles is seen at a glance, and it is so crushing for him who does not play the nobler part that it would be unjust to dwell too much upon it.

The conscience of the vanquished, however, when sincere feelings and true beliefs are behind it, and also a portion of the right involved, has inward strength, deep, invisible springs, of which we must speak only with respect. Something of that austere and sad-dened sentiment is reflected in the following words, in which M. de Rohan, after relating the surrender of La Rochelle (October 28, 1628), adds in the tone of firmness and pride that becomes him:

" The mother of the Duc de Rohan and his sister [Anne de Rohan, unmarried], refused to be named personally in the capitulation, in order that no one could attribute the surrender to their persuasion in that respect ; believing, however, that they would share like all the others in it. But as the interpretation of capitulations is made by the victors, the Council of the king decided that they were not included, inasmuch as they were not named : unexampled rigour! that a person of her rank, seventy years old (*and over*), coming out from a siege during which she and her daughter had lived for three months on horse-flesh and four to five ounces of bread per day, should be held captives without the exercise of their religion, and so closely that they had but one servant to wait upon them. This, nevertheless, did not shake their courage or their accustomed zeal for the welfare of their party ; and the mother sent word to the Duc de Rohan, her son, that he must not give heed to her letters, for she might be made to write them by force, and that no consideration for her miserable condition ought to make him relax to the injury of his party, no matter what evils they might make her suffer. Truly a Christian resolution, that did not belie the whole course of her life, which, having been a tissue of continual afflictions [her first husband was massacred on the Saint-Bartholomew], had so fortified her with the assistance of God, that she has the benediction of all right-minded persons, and will be to posterity an illustrious example of unexampled virtue and wonderful piety. See how that poor city, formerly the retreat and delight of King Henri IV, has since become the wrath and the boas* of his son. Louis XIII. It has been attacked by Frenchmen and abandoned by Englishmen ; it was buried in a bitter and pitiless famine, yet in the end has acquired by its constancy a longer life in fame through centuries to come than those who prosper to-day in this present century."

Here again the Memoirs of Richelieu throw the light of a direct reflection on those of Rohan. In them we find that, during the siege, Mme. de Rohan in a letter which was intercepted, proposed to her son a motto, which she said was that of the Queen of Navarre (no doubt Jeanne d'Albret, Henri IV's mother): *Paix assurée victoire entière, et mort honnête !* ("Assured

peace, complete victory, honourable death!") Sent a
prisoner to Niort, they tried to work upon her during
the following year to make her write to her son and
induce him to return to his duty; they put forward
third parties, who, without using the name of the king,
exhorted her, as if from themselves, and as if they
were moved solely by consideration for her interests
and those of her children:

" But that woman, malignant to the last degree," says Richelieu,
" would not even condescend to send messages to her son, by letter,
giving as a pretext that such means were not sufficiently powerful and
that it was necessary that she should go herself, which His Majesty
refused, knowing that she desired it only to make the evil more
irremediable, and to strengthen her son and those of his party in
rebellion to the last extremity."

Such was the invincible mother who bore in defence
of her faith the soul of the Portias, the Cornelias, and
the ancient Romans.   She it was who could not bring
herself to approve of Henri IV as king, and who resisted, under his reign, the fortune he was desirous of
bestowing on her son.

Our reservations thus made against the methods
and the object of the Duc de Rohan, we have the right
to call attention to his firmness and constancy.   The
capture of La Rochelle, which seemed as if it must
surely take all hope from the party, was to Rohan a
reason for redoubling his efforts and his zeal.   He was
of those whom adversity inspires.   Prince Thomas of
Savoie having sent him word that if he were in the
same humour as in the past, and would come nearer

to him, he, Prince Thomas, would make a diversion
into Dauphiné, Rohan replied that he was "in better
humour than ever," and ready to march at the first
news he should receive of the prince. The politician
and the statesman in him (for he was a statesman)
contributed at that moment to sustain and embolden
the soldier.   He told himself that the King of England,
after his contracted engagements, could not in honour
abandon the Reformers, and that he would bestir himself to support them in war, or, if there were a peace,
to have them included therein. He believed that
Louis XIII, then about to cross the Alps, had occupation enough in the direction of Savoie and Italy, and
other rocks to scale than those of La Rochelle; that
Spain's interest in fomenting divisions in the heart of
France would lead her before long to assist the Reformers with her gold. At an Assembly convoked at
Nîmes, he made his belligerent resolutions prevail,
reviving the courage of his adherents.   Nothing short
of the glories of the Pass of Suza, where it may be
said of Louis XIII as of Cæsar, "he came, he saw,
he conquered," could convince him of his mistake.

Even then, Rohan would not admit himself cast
down; he did not believe, after the victory of Suza,
in the peace of Italy, in a solid peace that would
allow the king to turn with all vigour upon him. He
was not enlightened on the gravity of the situation
until he saw the king in person seize Privas, and the
King of England at the same moment sign a peace

that did not include the Protestants.   This last news, together with the taking of Privas and the severities there exercised on the vanquished, made him, at last, begin "to lower his horns," says Richelieu; and then, foreseeing the coming end of the struggle, he brought forth all his resources and expedients, he redoubled in activity and multiplied fine skirmishes to end at least decently, to be reckoned with to the very last, and thus obtain as many guarantees as he could for the bulk of his party.   There were no less than six royal armies, in all more than fifty thousand men and fifty cannon, acting against various places in the South at the same time.   From all sides came a cry for succour; many places weakened and capitulated; Rohan threw himself on all sides, where he could.   He excelled in a war of that kind; at any rate he did enough to compel consent to negotiations for a general peace.   "I let the Court (meaning the king's headquarters) know that I would gaily die with the greater part of my people rather than not obtain a general peace; I told them it was dangerous to take all hope of safety from persons with arms in their hand, and that I would never negotiate for myself only. . . ."

The king listened with pleasure to the propositions; but the cardinal confesses in his Memoirs that he hesitated long at this time as to the advice he should give his master; everything convinced him they would soon get the better of the rebels and their

leader by force (which was much more to his taste),
and the latter would then be reduced, after their in-
fallibly approaching defeat, to cry for mercy. Prudence, however, carried the day against temper;
and the idea that Rohan was for once sincere in his
proposals for peace induced the cardinal to consent
to negotiate. Finally, the edicts conformed in all
essential things to what we now call tolerance; but
the bastions and fortifications of the rebellious cities,
those in the Cévennes in particular, which during
the war had been seized with a species of mania
and had, one and all, fortified themselves *à la
Huguenote,* as was then said, were ordered to be
rased at the expense and by the hand of the very
inhabitants who had built them. From that day
forth a belt of little republics across France no longer
existed: there was but one France with subjects under
one king.

The era of war and of rivalry with mailed hand
was over; a new régime began, a régime that ought
to have been one of civil policy, legality, firm reason,
gentle action, and of conquest by speech only. Richelieu, keen as he was on religion, shows that he
was not far from understanding the matter thus in
idea; but, on both sides, how new they were at this
new state of things! how slow and laborious was
the transition that now took place! and before it
was fairly established in our modern order, what
changes, what waverings, what errors still!

The Duc de Rohan, by an article of the treaty, or rather of the "grace" (that was the title given to it), obtained in all that concerned himself a general royal pardon and forgetting of the past; he also obtained the return of his property and 100,000 crowns as indemnity for the losses he had incurred (he owed more than 80,000) and he was made to leave the kingdom. He wrote to the king, who was then at Nîmes, asking that a man of rank, authorised by His Majesty, should conduct him to Venice, the place appointed for his retreat, fearing, or pretending to fear some danger on the road from the Italian princes; he probably desired to shelter himself in this way from all suspicion of further intrigues.   They gave him M. de La Vallette to accompany him, and he embarked at Toulon, July 20, 1629.

Venice was a place of predilection for Rohan; we have seen how he was struck and as if in love with it in his youth.   During the last war he had negotiated with Venice through his wife, who was there in company with the Duc de Candale, recently converted by her to calvinism, and who served her as attendant. The Duchesse de Rohan and her daughter had offered to remain as hostages to give security to Venice that the money furnished should be duly employed as stipulated.   The policy of Venice suited Rohan, always full of reflections and views, and, in the matter of a republic, much more likely to accommodate himself to one of an aristocracy than to one of burgher or popular

councils. He was appointed general of the troops of
the republic, with a pension and all sorts of honours.

He passed the first period of his retirement (1630)
in composing his Memoirs on the religious wars,
which were not published until later (1644) under the
supervision of Sorbière. During a stay he made at
Padua he wrote " The Perfect Captain, otherwise an
Abridgment of the Wars of the Gauls and the Commen-
taries of Cæsar, with some Remarks"; this he dedicated
to Louis XII. Another work: " For the Interests of
Princes and States in Christianity," dedicated to Cardinal Richelieu, seems to have been composed during a
visit of some months to Paris in 1634. These writings,
which were not printed until about the time of his
death, no doubt reached their destination much earlier
in manuscript; they were the visiting-cards the Duc de
Rohan sent to Court to show that he was still capable
of action, and to prove he was no longer an enemy.
These works, much liked when they appeared, the
second of which was translated into Latin, are of little
worth to-day and are not attractive to read.

But a new career was now to begin for Rohan. The
king, by the advice of Cardinal Richelieu, believed
him the right man to conduct his affairs beyond the
Alps, on account of his various qualities as negotiator,
as captain, greatly in renown with foreigners, able to
act as if for himself, his actions not to be acknowledged
until the right time came. The Grisons, allied with
the Swiss cantons, possessed in Italy the Valtelline, a

country of importance from a military point of view, inasmuch as it forms a passage between Germany and the Milanais, and might serve as a junction between the two arms of the House of Austria. Spain had done her best to get possession of it and had succeeded, the Valtelline having revolted, hoping to get free from the yoke. The Imperials thus found the way open for a descent upon Italy: they built forts to maintain it.

The Grisons complained of France (at all times their protector) because, by a treaty with Spain, she had seemed to acquiesce in the situation as it now was. France, on her side, had an interest in the Grisons again becoming masters of the Valtelline and of the keys to the passage. It was important to find a personage to push them on and guide them; "adroit in managing a populace, and agreeable to the Grisons (most of whom were Protestants)"; fitted to "recover this people little by little, and re-engrave on their minds the devotion they were beginning to lose for Frenchmen, and one who was of such weight that he would be regarded in that country as voucher and surety for his master," without the name of that master being too much put forward at first. Above all, it was necessary to find some one in whom the republic of Venice could place confidence, and whom she esteemed.

Rohan was the living embodiment of the very complex man who was needed at that moment in that country. The king wrote to him, and made his

ambassador, M' Avaux, urge him. Rohan was pleased
to see that they were placing confidence in him, and
that coming services might hasten forgetfulness of
the past. He did not leave Venice without making
sure of the Senate's agreement with the mission on
which he was about to embark. Reaching Coire,
the capital of the Grisons, December 4, 1631, he was
very well received and soon declared general of the
three Leagues. It seemed as if he had only to act;
but it was not until the spring of 1635, that is to say,
after three years of delay and ambiguities of all kinds,
and when France at last decided openly for war, that
Rohan had the chance to distinguish himself. He
was sent at first into Upper Alsace, where he held
his own against Duke Charles of Lorraine; but his
real object, which it was important to mask to the
end, was to take possession of the Valtelline. The
manner in which he crossed Switzerland without
notifying the Cantons until the moment came — having already entered that country before it was evident that he meant to go through it; the rapidity
and precision of his march, the accuracy of his plans
and calculations, all were in keeping with his reputation for skill. His army entered the Valtelline April
24, 1635, and the campaign opened under happy
auspices. . . .[1]

[1] Then follows a rather minute account of that local war, which has
so little historical interest in the present day that it is here omitted :
— Tr.

The last battle of the campaign, that of Morbegno, the most glorious of the four that Rohan fought, crowned to his honour this fine campaign of 1635, in which, thanks to him, the king's arms, less fortunate in all other places, obtained in the Valtelline a steady success. It seemed as though he was about to triumph over fate, that he did so by force of merit, and that fortune at last would smile upon him. Let him obtain a little aid from France, reinforce him with infantry and cavalry to guard the passes, above all, succour him with money, that sinew of war, more needful than ever in the country of the Grisons, let the Duc de Savoie stand ready to back him, and Rohan, at the head of 4000 foot soldiers and 500 cavalry, his ideal of a small army, would have entered the Milanais with plans matured, seized Lecco and Como, made himself master of the whole lake, destroyed the fort of Fuentes, which is the gateway to the Valtelline, and condemned the Germans to have no other road than the pass of the Saint-Gothard by which to enter Italy.

Glorious and too fleeting moment! the secretary of War, des Noyers, writing to d' Eméry, ambassador of France to Savoie, says that it was "indeed a wonderful thing how M. le Duc de Rohan with a handful of soldiers, without cannon or ammunition, did, each day, some signal action and carried terror everywhere, while the army of the Federals, so flourishing, so well fed and well paid, remained inactive." A little more and history might have cited him as a model of good fortune. The *Gazette* was filled with bulletins of his exploits.

But the thwarting star that so many times already had crossed and darkened Rohan's career, baffled him again; once more we meet its malign influence which from this time never ceases. The Duc de Savoie, in spite of the victory of the Ticino, did not take a single step toward Rohan, who had then advanced to Lecco (June 2, 1636), and the well laid plans of the latter failed. Believing that he had done enough to acquire honour, he was unwilling to risk more, according to his maxim that "it is better not to go too fast and know where one is going, than be obliged to retreat ignominiously or perish." He returned to the Valtelline, where the difficulties of his situation, without money and in presence of mutinous populations returned upon him. He sent his private secretary and confidant, Priolo, to represent them strongly at Court; but he himself fell seriously ill at Sondrio of an illness diagnosed as a "profound lethargy," so that the rumour of his death was noised about, in his own army, who mourned him, and in that of the enemy, who rejoiced.

On his revival, and after his convalescence, either because Rohan was not altogether the same man, or that matters were growing worse, he saw no means of reconciling the orders he had received from the king with imperious necessities that pressed him on all

sides. Pestilence and famine ravaged his troops; the
Grison colonels and captains, angry at receiving no
pay, quitted their posts; the Council of the Leagues
thought of new alliances: no money, no Grisons:
"Not a week passes," writes Rohan to M. des
Noyers, "since the month of July, that I have not
written you about the state of this country, and I am
not even told that you have received my letters, which
makes me suppose you have never taken the trouble
to read them."

These bitter complaints from the depths of the Valtelline reached Paris just as the Spaniards took Corbie
and threatened the capital; we can easily conceive,
therefore, that they were scarcely heeded.   He had no
sooner recovered, than he wrote to Richelieu, thanking
him for the interest he had shown for him in his illness:

" As for me, monsieur," he says, " I shall hold out as long as I can,
according to what I promised you; but it is intolerable to me to see
that which I have so far preserved about to perish.   In God's name
take care that a person who breathes only for your service, may not
see the reputation of the king's arms blasted in a region where, until
now, he has maintained them glorious; I would rather have died of
my illness than see that."

I could not avoid being tedious in dwelling at such
length on the details of this sad affair, so brilliantly
begun, so badly finished, and in trying to find the clue
to the "labyrinth" into which the Duc de Rohan
found himself plunged without resource.   On Richelieu's part and on his we find nothing but conflicting

recriminations, so grave, so definite, that doubt alone at this distance of time remains to us: Richelieu reproaches Rohan for having increased the discontent of the Grisons by his bad government, his extortions, and his illicit profits, of which he goes so far as to name the intermediaries and agents; and, in stigmatising in the harshest terms the final capitulation of March 26, 1637, which was consummated May 5, by which, yielding to the revolted Grisons, Rohan returned to them the Valtelline, contrary to the king's orders, Richelieu also accuses him of having been seized with a "panic terror":

"It is certain," says the Cardinal, "that he had, until then, borne gloriously to a high point the affairs of the King in the Valtelline; but his last act not only ruined in an instant all that he had well done in preceding years, but brought more dishonour to the arms of His Majesty than all the past had given them glory. This shame was such that it could never be repaired and, whatever excuse he might offer for his fault, the most favorable name it received from even those who were most friendly to him was that of a lack of courage."

The Duc de Rohan in his "Apologies" seems to have strong reasons to refute so harsh a condemnation. He ought to know better than any one the points of difficulty. The affair, according to him, was desperate, and to continue it longer was impossible without exposing himself to disaster. The Comte de Guébriant, sent at the last moment to the spot, seems to have been of Rohan's opinion. On the other hand, M. de Lèques, one of the latter's best lieutenants, was of a contrary opinion, and wished to try force, having no doubt it would succeed. I say again, it is best to doubt and abstain from judging; my only conclusion is that one of the traits in Rohan's character was circumspection, even in his courage; that is to say, a disposition that is a very little French. He was not a man to risk all for all. He thought of too many things at once.

After this, Rohan, although he still held the position of general of the king's army, retired to Geneva and refused to lead the army back through Franche-Comté; he distrusted the cardinal, whose orders he had failed to follow. In this, the Duc de Rohan paid the penalty of his past; in vain had he behaved during these last years with all possible loyalty and lustre, his conscience was not clear, nor his memory free; he attributed to others designs that those suspicions on his part may, perhaps, have suggested; and he could only see France from a distance through a sombre vista of the Bastille and a scaffold. He always remembered that the Parliament of Toulouse had condemned him to be drawn and quartered by four horses and hung in effigy.

Moreover, he belonged, through his female relatives, to the party of the *dames brouillonnes de la Cour—* the mischief-making ladies of the Court, as Richelieu called them (thinking of the Duchesse de Chevreuse); and he no doubt feared to be implicated in their intrigues more than he wished. Certainly, pretexts against him would not have been lacking.

It was while he was in this suspicious frame of mind

that he received a letter from the king commanding
him to retire to Venice; he thought it a trap. For
greater safety, and distrusting even a group of horse-
men who were seen about Versoix at the time, he
crossed the lake of Geneva, passed through Switzerland on the Berne side and joined the army of the Duke
of Weimar, then besieging Rheinfeldt.   Jean de Welt
was preparing to succour the place and a battle was on
the eve of taking place.   Rohan decided with a sort of
joy to make himself a simple soldier and fight hand to
hand—he who until then had fought so long with his
head.   Fighting valiantly on the right wing (February
28, 1638) he received two musket balls, one in the
foot, the other in the shoulder, and was instantly made
prisoner, but rescued before the close of the day.   He
died of his wounds, April 13, 1638, at the abbey of
Königsfelden, in the canton of Berne.   His body was
buried with great pomp in the church of Saint Peter
at Geneva.   During the interval between his wound
and his death, he received a letter from the king expressing interest in his condition.

The Duc de Rohan was small in height, and, it is
said, ill-looking.   The portraits that we have of him
indicate a haughty mien.   He had from childhood a
lock of white hair which was held to be a family distinction.   Though so often maltreated by fate, leading none of his enterprises to final success, he has,
nevertheless, left an illustrious idea of himself.   It was
said of Turenne that ''he had in all things certain ob-

scurities that were never cleared up except on special occasions, but which never were cleared up except to his honour." M. de Rohan often stopped at two-thirds of his way; and he did not, to our eyes, triumph over all the obscurities that resulted from the many recesses in his character quite as much as they did from the conspiring of circumstances. Two or three times he was obliged to begin his career over again; he had not that celerity of ardour, that suddenness of decision that carries a man flying to his end. Still, he was incontestably a great personage; negotiator in camp, man of the sword in council, man of the pen and of noble words. It has been said of his prose, that it savoured of his rank and his quality; it is, above all, excellent in sense, very sound and judicious. We can see that in daily practice he must have had great vivacity of mind and eloquence. There is a letter from him to the Prince de Condé (November, 1628), in reply to an insulting letter from that versatile prince, which is a masterpiece of vigour and irony. Skilful captain rather than great general, his measure in that respect is difficult to take, and I should prefer to leave it to the men of his profession. To express it in modern fashion, which is always hazardous in view of the extreme difference of methods in use in different centuries, he gives me the impression of having been, as a soldier, something between Gouvion Saint-Cyr and Macdonald, nearer to the former because of his thoughts.

However that may be, he is, by the rare conjunction of his merits, one of the original figures in our history; and when, to distinguish him from others of his name, and to characterise him (the last male of his race), some people continue from habit to call him "the great Duc de Rohan," there is nothing to wonder at. In studying him closely and without bias in his labours and his vicissitudes, I doubt whether that term would come to-day to the lips of any one; but, finding it consecrated we accept it, we respect it, we see the completion and, as it were, the ideal reflection of his great qualities in the imagination of his contemporaries; an exaggeration natural enough, which does justice, perhaps, to many things that have escaped us in that far distance, and for which no claim has been made.

III.

Cardinal Mazarin.

III.

Cardinal Mazarin

And his Nieces.

TO Cardinal Mazarin, so fortunate in all things
during his lifetime, a very great misfortune
happened soon after his death: that man,
without friendships, without hatreds, had but one enemy to whom he was not reconciled and whom he
never forgave: Cardinal de Retz; and the latter, in
writing his immortal Memoirs, has left of his enemy, of
him in whom he saw a fortunate rival, a portrait so
gay, so keen, so amusing, so withering, that the best
historical reasons can scarcely hold their own against
the impression conveyed, and will never succeed in
triumphing over it.

On the other hand, Mazarin has met with various
pieces of good fortune since his death, and it is in our
day especially that his reputation as a great statesman
has found studious, competent appreciators and aven-
gers.   M. Mignet was the first, in the Introduction to
his volume on the Spanish Succession (1835), to do
him signal justice in a grand, full-length, historical portrait that will last.   About the same time (1836)

M. Ravenel published for the Historical Society of
France the "Letters of Mazarin," written during his
retreat out of France, to the queen, the Princess Palatine, and other persons in his confidence, which prove,
at least, that at a time when there were few hearts
truly French among the factious, he was a better
Frenchman than all others in his political views, and
in his wholly reasonable ambition.   Later (1842) M.
Bazin, in the two volumes he devoted to the "History of France under the Ministry of Cardinal Mazarin,"
has taken pains to free the historical account from the
seductive errors cast into it by the pictures of Cardinal
de Retz, even at the risk of quenching a little of its
vivacity and interest.   Last of all comes M. de Laborde,
who has put, as it were, a final touch to the work of
rehabilitation in his *Palais Mazarin,* the palace built
by the cardinal in the rue de Richelieu, where for one
hundred and twenty-five years [dating back from
1850] the Bibliothèque du Roi, now the Bibliothèque
Nationale, has been kept.

It is indeed a fact that Mazarin properly seen, looked
at closely as though we were his contemporaries, possessed those gifts which, as soon as they came into
play, made it difficult to escape his charm.   "He was
insinuating," says Mme. de Motteville; "he knew how
to use his apparent kindness to his own advantage;
he had the art of charming others, and of making himself beloved by those to whom fate subjected him."
It is true that in difficulties where he had the under

CARDINAL MAZARIN
From a portrait by Champaigne

side he used the gifts of flattery and words of honey with which Nature had provided the cautious and readily perfidious race of the Ulysses. We never imagine Mazarin to ourselves as other than old, gouty, moribund under his purple; let us try to see him as he was in the days when he founded and secured his fortunes. He was handsome, magnificent in deportment and of cheerful countenance. Born in 1602, he was only twenty-nine years of age when he gave the measure of his capacity, his boldness, and his luck during the war in Italy. Man of the sword, and the right arm of the Nuncio, the Signore Giulio Mazarini (as he then was) stopped short, before Casale, the Spanish and French armies then on the point of attacking each other. Leaving the Spanish camp and bearing the conditions he had wrung from the Spaniards, he shouted to the French, already advancing: "Halt! halt! peace!" pushing his horse to a gallop and making signs with his hat to stop. The French army, already in movement and on the point of firing, answered back: "No peace! no Mazarin!" But he, redoubling his pacific gestures, came on, passing through, as he came, a few musket-shots. The leaders listened to him and suspended the attack. That wave of the *hat*, by which he stopped and held spellbound two armies, ought to win him, people said, the cardinal's hat.

Richelieu valued him from that day and won him over to the service of France. He seems to have

relished from the first that skilful genius, facile yet
laborious, frank yet insinuating, of a nature other
than his own, of an order in some respects inferior,
but, for that very reason, not unpleasing to him, in
whom he was not sorry to recognise, perhaps on
account of these differences, a successor. The first
time he presented him to the queen [Anne of Austria],
"Madame," he said, "you will like him much; he has
Buckingham's air." If he really permitted himself to
make that speech, he little thought how truly he predicted. As long as Richelieu lived, Mazarin's capacity
was, in a way, buried in the privacy of the cabinet;
he was closely allied with none but Chavigny, who
had the heart and soul of Richelieu, whose son he
was secretly reported to be. On the death of the
great minister and on that of the king there came
a very critical moment for Mazarin: designated by
them for the first place in the Council, he believed
himself rather on the eve of dismissal, and was
already, so it was said, making his preparations to
return to Italy, when his adroitness and his star
carried him, at a stroke, to the summit.

Although there was something of Buckingham
about him, it does not appear that he had any private
relations with the queen before the year 1643. If we
believe La Rochefoucauld, it was during the short
interval that elapsed between the death of Richelieu
and that of Louis XIII, that Mazarin began to open
avenues into the mind and heart of the queen, to

justify himself in her eyes through his friends, and to contrive, perhaps, a few secret conversations of which she herself made mystery to her old servitors. Anne of Austria was about to become queen-regent; but would she be as all-powerful in her own right as she wished, or only through the medium of the Council as the king had intended? Mazarin, who would surely be the soul of that Council, took pains to let the queen understand that it mattered little on what conditions she received the regency provided she had it with the consent of the king; and that afterwards, that point secured, she would not lack for means to free her authority and govern alone. This was letting her feel that henceforth she would have no enemy in him. It is permissible to suppose that in these first approaches Mazarin, still young, only forty years of age, did not neglect to use his personal advantages and put forth those refinements of demonstration of which he was so capable on occasion, and which are sovereign with all women but especially with a queen so much a woman as Anne of Austria.

Brienne has very well narrated the decisive moment when, thanks to the queen, Mazarin tied anew and more tightly than ever the knot of his fortunes. That moment must be long among the first of the regency, or perhaps to the last days of Louis XIII's illness. The Bishop of Beauvais, then the principal minister, was incapable; the queen needed a prime-minister, but whom could she choose? She consulted

two men who had her confidence, President de Bailleul
and the old secretary of State, Brienne. The latter,
who relates the details of the conversation to his son,
spoke after de Bailleul, who gave his opinion first and
began by excluding Mazarin as the creature of Richelieu.
"But I," says old Brienne, "who had more than once
perceived the secret leaning of the queen to his eminence, thought I ought to speak with more reserve."
The fact is, the queen had reached the point where
consultation is held merely to hear advice that is
secretly desired and to prompt it in the direction to
which the heart inclines. The consultation ended, the
queen had made her choice; nothing remained but to
make sure of the cardinal. Calling her head valet-de-
chambre, Beringhen, and telling him what had just
been said: "Go at once," she added, "and repeat it to
the cardinal; pretend to have overheard it by chance.
Spare that poor President de Bailleul, who is a good
servant; praise to the cardinal the good office Brienne
has rendered him; but, above all, discover what the
cardinal's sentiments for me are; and let him know
nothing of my intentions until you know, in the first
place, what gratitude he will show for my kindness."
Beringhen acquitted himself of his errand. He found
the cardinal with Commander de Souvré who had
given him a dinner on that day. The cardinal was
playing cards with Chavigny and some others.
When he saw Beringhen enter the room, he divined a
message, and leaving his cards to be held by Bautur

he passed into the next room. The conversation was long. Beringhen spoke at first with extreme precaution as to the good intentions of the queen. The cardinal, faithful to his habit of dissimulation, showed neither pleasure nor surprise. But when Beringhen, driven at last by the reserve he encountered, said positively that he came from the queen, the effect was that of a magic wand:

" At these words," continued Brienne, " the sly Italian changed his behaviour and language, and passing at once from extreme reticence to extreme effusion of heart: ' Monsieur,' he said to Beringhen, ' I place my career without conditions in the hands of the queen. All the advantages that the king gave me in his declaration I abandon from this moment. I feel troubled in doing so without informing M. de Chavigny; but I venture to hope that her majesty will deign to keep this matter secret, as I will, on my side, religiously.' "

These words were explicit; but Beringhen intimated that he desired some more precise pledge to prove the success of his errand. The cardinal, taking at once a pencil-case, wrote as follows on Beringhen's tablets:

" ' I shall never have any will but that of the queen. I resign, from this moment and with all my heart, the advantages that the king's declaration promised me; I abandon them without reserve, with all my other interests, to the unexampled goodness of her majesty. Written and signed by my own hand.' [Lower down was written]: ' Of her majesty the very humble, very obedient, and very faithful subject, and very grateful creature,
' Jules, Cardinal Mazarini.' "

Mazarin's cleverness consisted in seizing this unique moment ; in divining that, in the instability of things

and alliances at Court, there was for him no plank
safer or more solid on which to launch himself than
the heart of that Spanish princess, romantic and faithful; and that that vessel, reputed so frail by sages,
would, for this once at least, resist all tempests.

From that day forth he was master and might have
taken for his motto: "Whoso has the heart has all."
Chavigny, to whom he owed everything, and with
whom he had been in part allied up to that time, was
sacrificed without regret or shame. Politicians are
not stopped, or, if you choose, were not then stopped
by the trifles that hamper men of honour in the
ordinary walks of life. The first influences of this
mighty rise of Mazarin are admirably depicted by his
enemy, by Retz, who, in an incomparable page,
makes us feel the skill, luck, and hidden prestige, so
to speak, of this insinuating new grandeur. When
Mazarin, to bring to reason the former friends of the
queen who were becoming too importunate and too
important, and claiming her power as a spoil that was
due to them, arrested the Duc de Beaufort, every one
admired and bowed down to him. The moderation
that the cardinal showed on the morrow of that act
of vigour was regarded by all as clemency. The
comparison then made between this power, suddenly
so firm but not terrible, which continued gentle and
even habitually smiling, with that of Cardinal de
Richelieu charmed all minds for a time, and fascinated
imaginations. The cardinal, who had still much to

win, put all his cleverness into seconding his luck.
"In short," says Retz, "he managed so well that he
found himself on the heads of every one when every
one thought him still at their side."

It must not be thought that I am insensible to the
persuasive graces of Mazarin; but where I separate a
little from his ingenious apologisers is in the general
admiration of his personality and character. Why
should we admire so vehemently men who have so
greatly despised other men, and have believed that
the greatest art in governing them was to dupe them?
Is it not enough to recognise their merits and be just
to their memory? Mazarin was certainly a great minister; but I think it was chiefly as a negotiator with
foreign countries, as the man who brought about the
treaty of Munster and concluded the Peace of the
Pyrenees. It is as a fine diplomatic player that he has
his assured place, absolutely beyond attack, in history.
As for the interior of France, its administration and
finances, he seems to have had no views of general
improvement, no thought of the public good; so far
from that, he never ceases to sordidly pursue his own
gain and profit. Though he knew men so well, there
was always a point of French genius that escaped
him; a point on which he was not French, either in
tone, feeling, or intelligence. I forgive him for being
ignorantissime in matters of the old magistracy and of
the parliaments, but he did not feel that inward, po-
tential mainspring of our monarchy, *honour*, and all

that can be drawn from it. He let power debase itself in his hands. He let its noblest prerogative be debased—I mean its favours and benefits; he was liberal in promises, and sometimes in giving; but he gave too visibly to those he feared, and kept back what he promised as soon as he obtained all power. The supreme prosperity of his last years revealed the depths of his heart, and that heart was never either lofty or disinterested. He had not a royal soul: that says all. He mingled petty, almost sordid views with even great projects. No doubt he was fortunate; he succeeded finally in everything; "he died," some one has said, "in the arms of Fortune." Let us respect, to a certain point, that fortune, half-sister of cleverness, but let us not adore it; let us know how to perceive the public contempt that began to glide through it, increasing daily—that contempt which, like a slow fever, undermines all powers and all states. Perhaps a man was needed between Richelieu and Louis XIV to give a certain respite and slacken the tension of spirits; but a single other day of him would have been too much; it was no less necessary for France to have a king who was a king, to raise royalty from its subjection to a minister so absolute and so little royal.

Such is my final and invincible impression after reading all, or nearly all the memoirs and documents on the subject. Mazarin is of the race of ministers such as Robert Walpole, rather than of that of the Richelieus; he is of those (we ourselves have known some) who do not dislike a certain debasement of the spirit of the nation they govern, which, even when they do it true services, cannot rise. What is due to such ministers is justice, not enthusiasm. The son of Robert Walpole, Horace, taking in hand the defence of his father against the enemies who had so insulted him, exclaims:

"Chesterfield, Pulteney, Bolingbroke! those are the *saints* who have vilified my father! . . . those are the *patriots* who have attacked that excellent man known to all parties as incapable of vengeance as any minister ever was, but from whom his experience of the human species wrung on one occasion these memorable words : ' Very few men ought to become prime-ministers, for it is not well that a great number should know how malignant men are.' "

That saying might be applied to Mazarin, except for the words "excellent man," which presuppose a sort of heartiness, which he never had; but it is true to say that Retz Montresor, and many others were singular judges of honour to teach lessons to Mazarin. In his letters to the queen he laughs at them all, at their pretensions and their absurdities, very amusingly.

As for Cardinal de Retz, however, we must come to an understanding; he is too great a writer, too incomparable an author of memoirs, to be left thus without making for him certain reservations, and, in a way, certain conditions. Retz is a man of imagination. Brought up from childhood in the ideas of conspiracy and civil war, he was not sorry to set himself to realise them, then to recount them, like Sallust, and write

them down.   There is true literature in this fact.   He
is a man to undertake, not to succeed, but to give
himself the emotion and pride of enterprise, the pleasure of the game rather than the winnings and the
profit, which never come to him.   He is in his element in the midst of cabals; he feels his affinity and
swims among them, in idea, all through the vivid
description he writes of them.   Such men, gifted
with the genius of the writer, always have, without
fully accounting for it to themselves, an inward reservation, a final resource: that of writing their history
and indemnifying themselves for all they have lost on
the side of actuality.   Those who listened to Retz in
his years of retirement remarked that he loved to recount the adventures of his youth, which he exaggerated and embellished with a few marvels: "The
truth is," says the Abbé de Choisy, "Cardinal de
Retz had a little pea in his head."   That "little pea"
[*petit grain*] is precisely what made the man of imagination, the writer and the painter of genius, the
man of incomplete practicality, who was destined to
miscarry against the common-sense and cold patience
of Mazarin, but was equally certain to pay him off
and take his revenge upon him, pen in hand, before
posterity.

I do not answer, and no judicious reader will answer for the historical truth and accuracy of many of the
tales offered to us in Retz's Memoirs; but what is evident and strikes the eye at once, is something for us

superior to mere accuracy of detail: I mean the moral truth, the fidelity, human and living, of the whole. For example, read that first scene of the Fronde, when, after the imprisonment of Counsellor Broussel, the coadjutor (that is, Retz, bishop's assistant) decides to go to the Palais Royal and represent to the queen the excitement in Paris and the imminent danger of an uprising. He meets on his way the Maréchal de la Meilleraye, a brave soldier, who offers to second him and support his testimony at Court. What a scene of comedy, admirably described, is that at which Retz makes us actually present! The queen, incredulous and angry; the cardinal, who as yet has no fear, smiling maliciously; the sycophants, Bautru and Nogent, cracking jokes; and the others each in his rôle: M. de Longueville, exhibiting sadness, "but in the greatest joy at this beginning of the business"; M. le Duc d'Orléans, playing the eager and ardent in speaking to the queen, "though I never heard him whistle so idly as he did while talking for half an hour in the little grey room with Guerchi"; Villeroy, the maréchal, assuming gaiety in order to pay court to the cardinal, "and owning to me in private, with tears in his eyes, that we were on the brink of a precipice." The scene described by Retz goes on in this way with all sorts of variations until Chancellor Séquier enters the room: "He was so weak by nature that he never until this occasion had spoken a word of truth; but now compliance yielded to fear. He spoke out, and said just that which all he had seen in the streets dictated to him. I noticed that the cardinal seemed much nettled at the liberty taken by a man whom he had never seen take one before." But when, after the chancellor, the lieutenant of the guard came in, paler than an actor in Italian comedy, oh! then it was decisive, and fear, which all had been resisting, came to the surface in every soul. This whole comedy should be read in Retz. The scene is true; it must be, for it is true to human nature, to the nature of kings, ministers, and courtiers in these extremities: it is the scene of Versailles while the Bastille is being taken, or that of the eve of October 5th; it is the scene, so often repeated, of Saint-Cloud, or the Tuileries, on the morning of riots that sweep away dynasties.

These are the aspects that Retz has marvellously caught and comprehended; the characteristics of men, the masking and acting of personages, the general situation, and the instigating influence of events; on all these sides he is superior and beyond attack in the way of thought and moral description, as much as Mazarin himself will ever be in history as the maker of the Peace of the Pyrenees.

When we come to judging great personages, men of action, general family traits will be seen to show out distinctly and are easily identified. For instance, Mirabeau is not well known until we see the source from which he sprang—that original and robust race, already eloquent, of father, uncle, and grandfather. Great as he was, the tribune of '89 only brought to the surface that which his kin had within them, and worked it at will. Napoleon, in the composition of his character, in the combination of primitive elements that were in it and to which his genius gave meaning and a soul, is certainly better known when, before following his whole career, we look around the circle of his brothers and sisters. In the case of Mazarin, although the group of relatives is not in direct line with him, it is by no means useless to look it over in order to define and circumscribe the original nature of the cardinal-minister and make it understood.

The children of his sisters show plainly the strongly constituted race, predestined to action, from which he issued. Nearly all his nieces reveal that race in what it had of unadulterated and *genuine,* as the English say, in the sacred force of blood, as the Greeks would have said, in natural nobleness combined with the terrible instincts of adventurers. These new-comers, whom he risked introducing at the Court of France, where so many malicious taunts and scoffs awaited them, did not shame him, although at times they caused him great embarrassment. The uncle was not obliged to say much to make them take wing; they took it of themselves, they soared, they aimed at thrones and coronets, and lowered their pretensions scarce at all ; they were chips of the old block. Blood never lies. Nearly all of them had beauty, force of character, hardihood, adroitness, and few scruples — although there were among their number (let us not forget it) two virtuous women and one saint.[1]

In bringing them to France their uncle had not ill-speculated for the aggrandisement of the family and for the pleasure of French society. He re-enlivened that fine society (though it did not then stand in much need of it) by this little Roman-Sicilian invasion; with his Olympe, his Marie, his Hortense, he sowed dazzling varieties of splendid existences and furrowed social life with unexpected and fantastic caprices. Among them there was, indeed, one true Christian, an ad-

---

[1] Mazarin's five most noted nieces were the four daughters of his sister, Mme. Mancini, and one daughter of another sister, Mme. Martinozzi. The names of the first four were (1) Olympe Mancini, married to a prince of the blood, the Comte de Soissons, son of the Duc de Savoie and Marie de Bourbon. Being compromised with her sister, the Duchesse de Bouillon, in the trial of Mme. La Voisin, who sold poisons called *Poudres de Succession* (Inheritance Powders), she fled from France, and after leading with her daughters a wandering life, died at Brussels in 1708. She was the mother of the famous Prince Eugène. (2) Marie Mancini, who was Louis XIV's first love: he fell upon his knees to his mother, imploring to be allowed to marry her. Mme. de Motteville gives all the particulars. She subsequently married the Roman Prince Colonna. (3) Hortense Mancini, married to the son of Maréchal de la Meilleraye, who took the name of Mazarin and was made a duke. After the cardinal's death, the Duchesse de Mazarin lived in England, where she became the devoted friend of Saint-Évremond. (4) Mariana Mancini, married to the Duc de Bouillon, was involved with her sister, the Comtesse de Soissons, in the poisoning case, and was exiled from France.

The daughter of the other sister, Anne Martinozzi, married Armand, Prince de Conti, brother of the Great Condé and of Mme. de Longueville; she is the saint mentioned in the text.—Tr.

MARIE MANCINI, PRINCESSE COLONNA
From a portrait by G. Netscher

mirable penitent, who seemed to wish to atone for the others, Anne, Princesse de Conti; but beside her what pagans were all the rest! They had but one word, those terrible nieces, a single cry, with which to deplore the death of that dear uncle, and that heart-cry is in itself a funeral oration: " He has burst!" they said: *Il est crevé!*

Their brilliant minds, as soon as developed, were turned, with instinctive taste, to loving and favouring the most natural and the least conventional geniuses of their day; they became their declared inspirers and patrons. The Duchesse de Mazarin cannot part from her philosopher, Saint-Évremond, nor the Duchesse de Bouillon from La Fontaine, her teller of tales. Their brother, the Duc de Nevers, gives delightful and easy suppers to Chaulieu and La Fare and the grand-prior of Vendôme, all libertines in morals and in mind, who skirted the great century without belonging to it, awaiting the Regency. France was too small for the activity of these nieces of Mazarin; some of them carried to neighbouring Courts and countries their out-breaks and their errors; without, however, forfeiting the great position to which they seemed born and in which they had naturalised themselves as semi-sover-eigns. M. Amédée Renée, in his " Nieces of Mazarin," has charmingly strung for us this chaplet of beauties, violent and volatile, and has pictured, in a series of quotations, extracts, and rapid observations, the exist-ence and character of the Comtesse de Soissons, the

Duchesse de Mazarin, and the Duchesse de Bouillon. He introduces us to the choice company of the Hôtel de Nevers, that mysterious household "which combined the graces of the Mortemarts with the Mancini imagination."

I shall here permit myself, in my quality of critic, to ask M. Renée in his next edition to mark more distinctly the contrast of one of the figures, that of the Princesse de Conti, the eldest of the Martinozzi, to her brilliant sisters and cousins who lived for pleasure, adventure, folly, and orgies of intellect and wit. She was not only a pure-souled woman, that Princesse de Conti; her life, though clothed with a tinge of severity, has nothing veiled about it; it can be studied in the history of Port-Royal, where she has her place as friend and benefactress. She was born with all the qualities that fit a person of her sex for the world; she had the gift of beauty; with it she was serious, gentle, tranquil from childhood, but always full of feeling; firm, intrepid, but nevertheless cautious, and taking care to establish a reputation beyond attack. But this modesty, this exterior propriety made of her, as she said herself, "only a worthy heathen." She was concerned solely to be happy and glorious on earth and to make a lofty marriage. This ambition, great as it was, seemed more than satisfied when she found herself at the age of seventeen married to Armand de Bourbon, Prince de Conti, who was sincerely enamoured of her. Yet, amid the grandeurs and dignities that now environed her, something was still lacking; her heart felt a void within that remained unfilled.

A deep, internal agitation smouldered within her; at eighteen years of age, beneath a calm exterior, the most contradictory thoughts disturbed her. Rather confusedly instructed in the truths and spirit of Christianity, she had seen enough to make her wish to get rid of it wholly, in order not to be hampered by it. She made efforts to extinguish the feeble remains of her languishing faith, hoping in that way to calm her uneasiness: "but God did not permit her to succeed." She did not find relief from such sadness by affecting doubt and an indifference that she did not feel. Secret infirmities warned her in low tones that the hour of eternity might not be as far from her as her youth seemed to promise. Her converted husband lost no occasion for repeating to her "all that charity could make him say on the greatest of subjects to the person in the world to whom it was most important and whom he loved best." She received with the utmost gentleness what he said to her; but all these persuasions at bottom only importuned her and embittered her against piety, which she regarded as her enemy and her rival in the heart of the prince. It was in this condition of a long-standing inward struggle, that she one day found herself suddenly, and without knowing how, turned to God, convinced of the truths of faith, and burning with a desire to rise upward to the divine source. Her heart was changed, and not half-changed; in this she showed the greatness of that heart.

From this moment she walked, without ever turning aside, in the paths of practical piety and charity; there was no question henceforth of aught but the degrees by which she grew to the light. She took a confessor who had been given to the prince, her husband, by the Bishop of Aleth, Pavillon; she guided her whole conduct by the stern principles of the gentlemen of Port-Royal. It became a question which of the two, she or her beautiful sister-in-law, the Duchesse de Longueville, made most progress in the narrow way. Naturally proud, rather inclined to avarice, she controlled her inclinations, cared for the poor and the sick, gave considerable alms with discernment and intelligence, not forgetting justice even in charity. Left a widow at twenty-nine years of age, she redoubled her care and vigilance in ruling her household rightly, and in bringing up in a Christian manner her sons, to whom she had given Lancelot, of Port-Royal, as tutor. Much respected by Louis XIV, she never abandoned to please him those whom he thought too austere. One Sunday in Advent, 1670, when Bourdaloue had preached on "severity of penitence," making a very cutting allusion to the supposed excessive doctrines of Port-Royal, of M. Arnauld, and of his friends, the princess, who was present at the sermon, expressed her displeasure so loudly that the celebrated

HORTENSE DE MANCINI, DUCHESSE DE MAZARIN

From an engraving from her portrait by Sir Peter Lely

Jesuit thought it best to go and give her an explanation. She listened to him, but did not conceal that she was far from edified by that part of his discourse. Such she lived and died. Her sons, those brilliant and dissolute Conti, who answered so ill to her prayers and to the hopes of their early education, raised a monument to her in the Church of Saint-André-des-Arcs, with this epitaph, in which is no word that is not true:

"To the glory of God, and to the eternal memory of Anne-Marie Martinozzi, Princesse de Conti, who, disillusioned of the world at the age of nineteen, sold all her jewels to feed, during the famine of 1662, the poor of Berry, Champagne and Picardie ; practised all the austerities her health would allow ; was left a widow at twenty-nine years of age, and devoted the remainder of her life to bringing up the princes, her sons, as Christian princes, and in maintaining the laws temporal and ecclesiastical on her estates : she reduced herself to a very modest expenditure ; restored property, the acquisition of which seemed doubtful to her, to the amount of eight hundred thousand francs ; distributed all her savings to the poor on her estates and elsewhere, and passed suddenly into Eternity, after sixteen years of perseverance on the 4th of February, 1672, aged thirty-five years."

Here, assuredly, is one of Mazarin's nieces, who, in her black frame, does not resemble any of her famous cousins, and who cannot be too carefully distinguished from them. Let us think for a moment of all there was so reflective, so profound, so enlightened in the Christian sense, in this piety that felt the need of expiating and atoning for others—for her husband, the instigator of civil war and the cause of disaster to so many villages and cottages; for her uncle, the cardinal, the grasping and unscrupulous acquirer of countless possessions. From whichever side we look at her we find ourselves in presence of a rare inspiration, of a noble spirit of sacrifice that fills us with sovereign respect.

What further have I to say of Mazarin that has not been said already ? If I am asked in what manner he loved the queen, and what was the nature of his affection, I answer that there will always be some doubt on that subject; not on the question of love, for love it was, assuredly; true love on her part, and love, more or less simulated so long as he needed her support, on Mazarin's. The letters that we have from him to the queen leave no doubt as to the vivacity of the passionate demonstrations he permitted, or rather, commanded himself to write; but it would appear, if we rely on the testimony of Brienne and his virtuous mother, that this love was restrained to sufficiently platonic terms, that the mind of the queen was especially charmed with the "beauty of the cardinal's mind," and, in short, that it was a love of which she could speak to a confidant in her oratory and on the relics of saints without having to blush too much or to reproach herself.

Such really appears to have been up to a certain day the true state of the queen's feelings. If later Mazarin passed beyond (as is not impossible) and triumphed over the scruples of the queen to complete possession, it was because he saw in that the surest means of government.

The same Brienne who initiates us into these secrets of the cabinet and the oratory has related the last

years and the end of Mazarin in a manner that recalls
the pages of Commines when that faithful historian
relates the end of Louis XI. Mazarin died at fifty-nine
years of age. It was time his end came, for the king
as well as for the queen. In his last years he had
wounded the latter by his harshness and his negligence, after he once felt himself secure from all attack.
According to the testimony of his niece Hortense: "No
one ever had such gentle manners in public or such
rude ones in domestic life." But Louis XIV, who, as
a child, had little liking for Mazarin and felt galled by
him not only as king but as a son (for sons instinctively
dislike the too-tender friends of their mother), had of
late understood and appreciated the extent of his services, though at the same time he was impatient for
the hour to sound when he should reign for himself.
Mazarin, with his sagacious eye, had divined Louis XIV
from childhood, and was more concerned to retard him
as king than to push him; but the moment came
when delay was no longer possible. Death then
served the fortunate Mazarin by removing him in the
height of prosperity and the maturity of human power.
After a consultation of physicians, the celebrated
Guénaud declared to him plainly that he was mortally
ill and had barely more than two months to live; he
then began to think seriously of his end, and he came
to it with a singular mixture of firmness, parade, and
pettiness. He clung to life, holding to it by stronger
ties than those of greater hearts; I mean by the

thousand bonds of the vulgar possessor who clings
to life on account of the property he has amassed:

"One day," relates Brienne, "I was walking through the new
rooms of his palace (I mean the great gallery that runs along the Rue
de Richelieu and leads to his library); I was in the little gallery where
there is a tapestry all in wool representing Scipio and executed from
the designs of Giulio Romano; the cardinal had nothing finer. I heard
him coming by the noise of his slippers, which he dragged along the
ground like a man very feeble and just issuing from a severe illness.
I hid behind the tapestry and heard him say: 'I must leave all that!'
He stopped at every step; he was very feeble and held himself up first
on one side and then on the other; casting his eyes on an object that
met his sight he said again from the depths of his heart: 'I must leave
all that!' Then turning, he added: 'And that! What pains I took
to acquire these things! how can I abandon them without regret? I
shall never see them more where I am going! . . .' I heard those
words very distinctly; they touched me, perhaps more than he was
touched himself. I gave a great sigh which I could not restrain; he
heard it: 'Who is there?' he said, 'who is there? 'It is I, monseigneur, I am waiting the moment to speak to your Eminence.'
'Come here, come here,' he said in a dolorous voice. He was naked
under his camlet dressing-gown, lined with squirrel-skin, and had his
night-cap on his head. He said to me: 'Give me your hand; I am
very weak, I have no strength.' 'Your Eminence should sit down.'
I wished to bring him a chair. 'No,' he said, 'no; I am glad to walk
about, and I have something to do in my library.' I offered him my
arm and he leaned upon it. He would not let me speak to him of
business: 'I am no longer in a state to listen to it,' he said; 'speak to
the king, and do what he tells you; I have other things now in my
head.' Then, returning to his thought, he said: 'See, my friend,
that beautiful picture by Correggio, and that Venus of Titian, and
that incomparable Deluge by Annibale Caracci, for I know you love
pictures, and you understand them very well; ah! my poor friend, I
must quit all that! Farewell, dear pictures I have loved so well and
which have cost me so much!'"

Hearing these words and seeing this scene, so
dramatic, so unexpected, reminding us of the Ode of
Horace: *linquenda tellus et domus,* we are touched

like Brienne; but take notice that there is in this
regret at quitting beautiful things and beautiful pictures, characteristic of Italian passion and of a noble
amateur, still another sentiment: if the first words are
those of a lover of art the last are those of a miser.

Is it as an artist, is it that he loves these pictures for
themselves that their master regrets them? No; it is
because they have cost him dear; he loves them and
clings to them because of the price he paid for them:
there we reach the depths of Mazarin's soul.

Another trait, that we also owe to Brienne, and
which Shakespeare would not have omitted in a
Death of Mazarin, is of great vigour and of awful
truth. One day, Brienne, entering softly into the
cardinal's chamber at the Louvre, found him dozing
in his arm-chair by the fire; his head swayed forward
and back with a sort of mechanical swing, and he
was murmuring, as he slept, unintelligible words.
Brienne, fearing he might fall into the fire, called the
valet-de-chambre, Bernouin, who shook his master
rather roughly: "What is the matter, Bernouin?" he
said, waking up, "what is it? *Guénaud said so!*"
"The devil take Guénaud and his saying!" replied
the valet; "you are always talking of it." "Yes,
Bernouin, yes; *Guénaud said it!* he said but too
true, I must die! I cannot escape! *Guénaud said it
— Guénaud said it!*" Those words he had been
saying mechanically in his sleep, though Brienne at
first did not distinctly hear them.

A complete and anecdotal life of Mazarin would be very curious and interesting to make; nearly all the elements are at hand. M. de Laborde has collected a great number in his Notes to the *Palais Mazarin*. He often quotes from Mazarin's *Carnets* and gives several of the notes written by him, in Italian as well as in French, on subjects that pre-occupied his mind and about which he intended to speak to the queen. We find in these *Carnets* maxims of State, excellent judgments on men, the minor topics of the day; in short, everything, I imagine, except things of grandeur. M. de Laborde succeeds in his apology for Mazarin in the sense that, after reading him, we have obtained a very vivid idea of the mind of the cardinal-minister and of his amiable and potent qualities which is quite equal to what we already thought of him. Nevertheless, I could desire that in another edition he would confine his quotations and notes to signifying no more than they can prove; and that he would never advance anything that impartial and strict criticism cannot justify. I could also desire that he had treated Retz, Saint-Évremond, and all the cardinal's adversaries with less levity; also that he did not despise so heartily what he calls the "silly Memoirs" of La Porte. La Porte was a valet-de-chambre who left Memoirs not by any means those of a man of intellect, but certainly those of an honest man; and no Memoirs of a valet are ever silly for posterity.

IV.

The Duc de La Rochefoucauld.

IV.

François, Duc de La Rochefoucauld.

Author of the Maxims.

A MAN should know how to catch the spirit of
his age and the fruit of his season. There
comes a moment in life when La Rochefoucauld
pleases us, and in which we think him more true than
perhaps he really is. The disappointments of enthusiasm bring disgust. Mme. de Sévigné thought it would
be charming to hang the walls of her cabinet with the
backs of cards; her amiable thoughtlessness saw only
the amusing and piquant side of it. But the fact is
that on a certain day all those beautiful queens of
hearts, those noble and chivalrous knaves of diamonds,
with whom we were playing so confidently, turn
about; we fell asleep trusting in Hector, in Bertha,
in Lancelot; we wake up in Mme. de Sévigné's cabinet
and their backs alone are visible. We feel beneath
our pillow for the book of the night before; it was
Elvire and Lamartine, and lo! in its place we find La
Rochefoucauld. Well, let us open him; he consoles,
for the reason that he is gloomy like ourselves; he
amuses. These thoughts of his which, in days of

youth revolted us as too false, or annoyed us as too true, and in which we saw nothing but book-morality, now appear to us, for the first time, in all the freshness of novelty on the uphill of life, they, too, have their spring-tide; we discover it: "How true that is!" we cry. We cherish the secret insult; we suck the bitterness with pleasure. But this very excess has something reassuring. Enthusiasm for those thoughts is a sign that already we are passing beyond them and beginning a cure.

It is permissible to conjecture that M. de La Roche-foucauld himself softened toward the end, and cor-rected in his heart certain too positive conclusions. During the course of his delicate and lasting intimacy with Mme. de la Fayette it can be said that he often seemed to abjure them, certainly in practice; and his noble friend had some right to congratulate herself on having reformed him, or, at any rate, in having comforted his heart.

The life of M. de La Rochefoucauld, before his great intimacy with Mme. de la Fayette, falls naturally into three divisions, of which the Fronde is only the second: his youth and his first exploits antedate it. Born in 1613 and entering the world at the age of sixteen, he never studied, and merely added to his vivacity of mind a natural good sense, masked, how-ever, by a great imagination. Before the discovery, in 1817, of the true text of his Memoirs, which gives on this early period a mass of particulars withheld by

FRANÇOIS, DUC DE LA ROCHEFOUCAULD

From a steel engraving

the author in the version known until then, no one suspected the degree of romantic chivalry to which the young Prince de Marsillac was carried. Buckingham and his royal adventures seem to have been the object of his emulation, just as Catiline was that of the young de Retz. Such early misleadings bar many a life. All La Rochefoucauld's noble fire was then consumed in his devotion to the unhappy queen (Anne of Austria), to Mlle. d'Hautefort, and Mme. de Chevreuse. In taking this path of devotion he turned, without thinking of it, his back to fortune. He displeased the king, he irritated the cardinal: what matter? the fate of Chalais, of Montmorency, of all those illustrious beheaded-ones seemed only to spur him on. At a certain moment (in 1637, when he was twenty-three or twenty-four years of age) the persecuted queen,

" abandoned by every one," he tells us, " and daring to confide in none but Mlle. d'Hautefort and me, proposed to me to abduct them both and take them to Brussels. Whatever difficulty and danger I saw in the project I can truly say it gave me more joy than I had ever had in my life. I was at an age when one delights to do extraordinary and dazzling things, and I thought nothing could be more so than to carry off the queen from her husband and from Cardinal de Richelieu who was jealous of her, and take Mlle. d'Hautefort from the king who was in love with her."

All these fabulous intrigues ended for him, on the flight of Mme. de Chevreuse, by eight days in the Bastille, and an exile of two or three years at Verteuil (1639–1642). This was getting off on easy terms with Richelieu; and the rather weary exile was agreeably diversified, he owns, by family joys (he had married Mlle. de Vivonne), the pleasures of country life, and, above all, the hopes of the coming reign, when the queen-regent would surely reward his faithful services.

This first part of the Memoirs is essential, it seems to me, to throw light on the Maxims, and to enable us to measure the height from which this chivalrous ambition had fallen before it burrowed into human nature as a moralist; the Maxims were the revenge of the Romance.

From this first period (now better known) it appears that Marsillac, who was in fact over thirty-three years old when his alliance with Mme. de Longueville began, and thirty-five at his entrance into the Fronde, was already at this latter period a disappointed man, irritated, and, to tell the truth, much perverted. This, without excusing him, does explain in part the detestable conduct he then exhibited. We see him tainted from the start. He does not conceal from himself the motives that cast him into the Fronde. "I did not hesitate," he says; "I felt great pleasure that in whatever position the harshness of the queen and the hatred of Cardinal Mazarin had placed me, I still had the means of revenging myself upon them." Ill-rewarded for his early devotion, he was fully resolved not to be caught in that way again.

The Fronde is therefore the second period of La

Rochefoucauld's life; the third comprises the ten or a dozen years that followed the Fronde, during which he recovered as best he could from his bodily wounds, and avenged himself, amused himself, and raised his tone to the moral plane of the Maxims. His intimate friendship with Mme. de la Fayette, which softened and truly consoled him, came later.

We may give to each of the four periods of M. de La Rochefoucauld's life the name of a woman, just as Herodotus gave to each of his books the name of a muse. These four women were Mme. de Chevreuse, Mme. de Longueville, Mme. de Sablé, Mme. de la Fayette; the first two, heroines of intrigue and romance: the third, a moralising and converting friend; the last, reverting, though unconsciously, to the heroine type by a tenderness tempered with reason, blending their tints and illuminating them as if by a last sun.

Mme. de Longueville was the brilliant passion: was she a sincere passion? Mme. de Sévigné writes to her daughter (October 7, 1676): "As for M. de La Rochefoucauld, he went, like a child, to revisit Verteuil, and the places where he had hunted with so much pleasure; I do not say where he had been in love, for I cannot believe that he has ever been what is called *in love.*" He himself (according to Segrais), said he had never found love except in novels. If his Maxim is true, "There is only one sort of love, but a thousand different copies of it," that of M. de La

Rochefoucauld and Mme. de Longueville may very
well be thought merely a flattering copy of the real
thing.

Marsillac, at the moment when he attached himself
to Mme. de Longueville, was anxious, above all, to
advance himself at Court and avenge the neglect in
which he had been left, and he judged her suitable for
his purpose. He has told us how he negotiated for
her, as it were, with Miossens, afterwards Maréchal
d'Albret, who had precedence in her regard:

"I had reason to think that I could make better use of the friendship and confidence of Mme. de Longueville than Miossens; I made
him admit this himself. He knew the position in which I stood at
Court; I told him my views, but added that consideration for him
would always hold me back, and that I would not attempt to take up
an intimacy with Mme. de Longueville, unless he permitted it. I own
that I embittered him against her in order to obtain her, but without
telling him aught that was not true. . . . He gave her up to me
wholly—but he repented it."

Attraction counted for something, no doubt, imagination and desire assisting. M. de La Rochefoucauld loved great passions and thought them necessary
to the making of a man of honour. What more noble
object could there be on which to practise them!
Nevertheless, all this, in its origin at least, was done
in cold blood.

On the side of Mme. de Longueville, there is not
less to reason about and discriminate. We do not
fear to subtilise on sentiment with her, for she herself
was subtile beyond measure. In the matter of devotion we have her secret examinations of conscience at

Port-Royal, in which the refinements of her scruples pass all conception. In love, in gallantry, the same thing—less the scruples. But her life and portrait must not be lightly touched in passing; she deserves a place apart, and she shall have it. Her fate has such contrasts and such harmonies throughout its whole tissue that it would be a profanation to diminish its lights and shades. She is of those, moreover, of whom it is in vain to speak ill; reason loses all rights; it is with her heart as it was with her beauty, which, in spite of many defects, had a radiancy, a languorous habit, in short, a *charm* that attached every one.

Her twenty-fifth year had already passed when her *liaison* with M. de La Rochefoucauld began. Until then she had mingled very little in politics ; though Miossens had tried to initiate her. La Rochefoucauld applied himself to the task, and succeeded in giving her activity rather than skill, to which, indeed, he himself only half attained.

The natural taste of Mme. de Longueville was for that which has been called the style of the Hôtel de Rambouillet. She liked nothing so well as gay and gallant conversations, discussions on sentiments, delicate distinctions that testified to the quality of the mind. She sought, above all things, to show the refinement within her, to detach herself from whatever was common, and to shine in all that was exquisite. When she came to believe herself a political personage she was not displeased to be thought less sincere, imagining that it made her seem the shrewder. Petty considerations of this kind decided her on great occasions. Chimeras, fancies, notions of false glory, and also what we baptise by the name of poesy, were in her; she was always outside of the real. Her step-daughter, the Duchesse de Nemours, who was never, herself, out of it, an Argus of little charity but very clear-sighted, shows her to us in Memoirs so just that we could wish them at times less rigorous. La Rochefoucauld, in his turn, does not say otherwise, and he, well placed as he was to know her, complains of the ease with which she allowed herself to be governed—a weakness he used too much and of which he did not continue the master. "Her fine qualities were less brilliant," he says, "because of a blemish that was never before seen in a princess of her merit, which was, that far from giving the law to those who had a particular adoration for her, she transformed herself so completely into their sentiments that she no longer recognised any of her own." At all times it was M. de La Rochefoucauld, or M. de Nemours, or (at Port-Royal) M. Singlin who governed her. Mme. de Longueville used her own mind less than she did that of others.

In order to guide her in politics M. de La Rochefoucauld was not firm enough in them himself. "There was always a something I know not what in M. de La Rochefoucauld," says Retz. And in a wonderful page, where the old enemy effaces himself and seems to be only the malignant friend, he develops that "I know not what" into the idea of something irresolute, insufficient, incomplete in action amid so many great qualities.   "He was never a warrior, though very soldierly.   He was never of himself a good courtier, though he had full intention to be one.   He was never a man of party, though all his life he was bound to party."   He dismisses him, however, as the most honourable of men in private life.   On one single point I venture to contradict Retz, he denies imagination to La Rochefoucauld who, as I think, had a very great one.   He began by practising romance in the days of Mme. de Chevreuse; under the Fronde he tried history, politics, and failed.   Vengeance and vexation drove him into them more than serious ambition, and the noble remains of romance came back with ill-fortune; private life and its peaceful idleness, in which his days were to end, already called him.   He was hardly embarked on an enterprise before he showed his impatience to be out of it; his inmost thought was not there.   Now, with Mme. de Longueville's disposition to be swayed, let us reflect on what her course would naturally be as soon as this "something I know not what" in M. de La Rochefoucauld became her guiding star; and grouped around that star, like so many moons, were her own caprices.

It would be undertaking too much to follow the pair.   With regard to M. de La Rochefoucauld it would often be too painful and too humiliating for those who admire him to accompany him. The outcome with him is better than the way to it. Let it suffice to say here that during the first Fronde and the siege of Paris (1649) his ascendency over Mme. de Longueville was complete. When, after the arrest of her brothers (the Prince de Condé and the Prince de Conti) she fled by sea to Holland and thence to Sténay, she was weaned from him somewhat. After her return to France and the struggle was renewed we find her still ruled by M. de La Rochefoucauld, who now gives her better advice in proportion as he himself becomes more disinterested. But she finally escapes him altogether (1652) and lends her ear to the amiable Duc de Nemours; who made himself especially pleasing by sacrificing to her claims the Duchesse de Châtillon.

"Persons have great difficulty in breaking apart when they no longer love each other." They had reached that difficult point: M. de Nemours cut through it, and M. de La Rochefoucauld joyfully seized the opportunity to be free by playing the injured party: "When we are weary of loving we are very glad when the other side is faithless to us and so releases us from our fidelity."

He was very glad, but not without some mixture and return of bitter feelings. "Jealousy," he says, "is born with love, but does not always die with it." The punishment of such alliances is that it is equal suffering to bear them or break them. He wanted to

avenge himself, and manœuvred so well that Mme.
de Châtillon recovered M. de Nemours from Mme.
de Longueville, and, flushed with triumph, she also
made the latter lose the heart and confidence of the
Prince de Condé. Between Mme. de Châtillon, M.
le Prince, and M. de Nemours, La Rochefoucauld,
who was the soul of the intrigue, congratulates
himself cruelly. Sight and wound of threefold bitterness to Mme. de Longueville!

Shortly after, M. de Nemours was killed in a duel
with M. de Beaufort, and (whimsicality of heart!)
Mme. de Longueville mourned him as if she still
possessed him. Her ideas of repentance followed
closely on his death.

M. de La Rochefoucauld was soon punished for his
vile action; he received, at the battle of the Faubourg
Saint-Antoine, that musket-shot in the face which
blinded him for some time. For him it was the end
of his active errors. He was nearly forty years old,
gout had already gripped him, and now he was nearly
blind. He retreats into private life and buries himself
in the easy-chair he was never again to leave. As-
siduous friends surround him and Mme. de Sablé pays
him every attention. The accomplished man of honour begins; the moralist declares himself.

M. de La Rochefoucauld makes it felt that he is a
wise man from the moment that he becomes disinterested. Such are men: wisdom on one side, action
on the other. Good sense is at the summit when

they have nothing more to do than to judge those who have none.

The "something, I know not what," of which Retz sought the explanation, reduces itself, so far as I can define it, to this: that La Rochefoucauld's true vocation consisted in being an observer and a writer. This was the end to which all the rest of his life served him. With his divers attempted callings as warrior, statesman, and courtier he was never wholly in any of them: there was always an essential corner of his nature that kept aloof and displaced the equilibrium. His nature, without his then suspecting it, had an *arrière-pensée* in all enterprises, and that hidden thought was an instinct to reflect upon the enterprise when it was over. All adventures were to finish with him in maxims. What would seem to be fragments collected by experience after shipwreck, composed the true core, found at last, of his life.

A slight but very singular sign seems to me to indicate still further in M. de La Rochefoucauld this particular destination of nature. For a man so much in the world he had (Retz tells us) a strange air of shyness and timidity in civil life. He was so embarrassed in public that if he had to speak on official matters before six or seven persons his courage failed him. The dread of a solemn harangue kept him always from entering the French Academy. Nicole was the same, and could never have preached or maintained an argument. A characteristic of the moralist is secrecy of observation, communication with others in a low voice. Montesquieu says of him, somewhere, that if he had had to get his living as a professor he could not have done it. Maxims are things that cannot be taught; half a dozen persons before whom to recite them are too many; the maker of them will be admitted to be right only in a tête-à-tête. Mankind in the mass need a Jean-Jacques or a Lamennais.

The *Réflexions ou Sentences et Maximes Morales* appeared in 1665. Twelve years had elapsed since the adventurous days of M. de La Rochefoucauld, and the musket-shot, his last misfortune. In that interval he had written his Memoirs, which an indiscretion had divulged (1662), and to which he was forced to give a denial that proved nothing. A copy of the Maxims also got about and was printed in Holland. He parried this by giving them to Barbin to publish in Paris. This first edition, without the author's name, although he is plainly indicated, contains a Note to the Reader very worthy of the book, and a discourse, much less worthy, attributed to Segrais, which replies to objections already current by many quotations from classical philosophers, and from Fathers of the Church. The short Note to the Reader makes a far better answer in a single sentence: "Take care; there is nothing more fitted to establish the truth of these *Réflexions* than the heat and subtlety shown in combating them."

Voltaire, judging La Rochefoucauld's Maxims in his

light-hearted and charming way, says that no book
had contributed more to form the taste of the nation:
"People read the little volume eagerly; it accustomed them to think, and to inclose their thoughts in
a lively, precise, and delicate form. This was a merit
no one had had before him in Europe since the re-
nascence of letters." Three hundred and sixteen
thoughts, forming one hundred and fifty pages, had
this glorious result. In 1665, it was nine years since
the appearance of the *Lettres Provinciales;* Pascal's
Pensées were not published until five years later,
while La Bruyère's *Caractères* came twenty years later
still. The great prose monuments, the eloquent
oratorical works which crowned the reign of Louis
XIV, did not issue until after 1669, beginning with the
funeral oration over the Queen of England. In 1665
France was on the very threshold of the great century, on the first landing of the portico, on the eve of
Andromaque; the staircase of Versailles was inaugur-
ating the fêtes: Boileau, accosting Racine, was mount-
ing the steps; La Fontaine, in sight, was forgetting to
mount; Molière was already at the top, and *Tartuffe,*
under its original form, was producing itself clandes-
tinely. At this decisive moment of universal ardour,
M. de La Rochefoucauld, who had little love for lofty
discourse and liked only brilliant talk, said his word:
a great silence fell; he found he had spoken for all
the world, and each word was lasting.

Here was a courteous, insinuating, smiling misanthrope, preceding by very little and delightfully preparing the way for that other *Misanthrope.*

In the history of the French language and literature, La Rochefoucauld comes in date in the first rank after Pascal, and even precedes him as a pure moralist. He has the clearness and conciseness of phrase that Pascal alone, in that century, had before him; which La Bruyère caught; which Nicole could not keep; which was destined to become the sign-manual of the eighteenth century, the perpetually easy triumph of Voltaire.

Though the Maxims may seem at their inception to have been merely a relaxation, a social game, a sort of wager of men of wit playing at proverbs, how completely they detach themselves by their result and assume a character above their occasion! Saint-Évremond, Bussy, who have been compared to La Rochefoucauld for wit, bravery, and loss of favour, are also writers of social quality: at times they charm, and yet they have I know not what that is corrupt; they foretell the Regency. The moralist in La Rochefoucauld is stern, grand, simple, concise; he attains to the noble; he belongs to the pure Louis XIV period.

La Rochefoucauld cannot be too highly praised for one thing: in saying much he does not express too much. His manner, his form is always honourable to the man, even when the matter is little so.

In correctness he belongs to the school of Boileau, but far in advance of the *Art Poétique.* Some of his

Maxims he rewrote thirty times, until he reached the necessary expression; nevertheless, there seems no torturing effort. The original little volume in its primitive arrangement (afterwards broken up) offering its three hundred and sixteen thoughts, so brief, and framed between general considerations of *self-love* in the beginning and reflections on *contempt of death* at the end, expresses to me even better than succeeding editions an harmonious whole in which each separated detail arrests the eye. The modern perfection of style is there: it is aphorism sharpened and polished. If Racine is to be admired after Sophocles, La Rochefoucauld may be read after Job, Solomon, Hippocrates, and Marcus Aurelius.

So many profound, solid or delicate intellects have spoken in turn of the Maxims that it is almost temerity in me to add my word. None have so far better treated of their philosophy than M. Vinet in his *Essais de Philosophie Morale.* He is rather of the opinion of Vauvenargues, who says: "La Bruyère was a great painter and was not, perhaps, a great philosopher. The Duc de La Rochefoucauld was a great philosopher and no painter." Some one else has said, with the same meaning: "In La Bruyère thought often resembles a woman who is better dressed than beautiful; she has less person than style." But, without detracting at all from La Bruyère, we shall find in La Rochefoucauld an angle of observation that is wider, a comprehensive glance

that goes deeper. I even think that he had more system and unity of principle than M. Vinet is willing to
allow, and that in this way he fully justifies the title
of philosopher which that ingenious critic so expressly
grants him. The "often," "sometimes," "nearly
always," "usually," with which he moderates his
grievous conclusions, may be taken for polite precautions. While putting his finger on the mainspring
he pretends to step back a little; it is enough, he
thinks, not to let go. After all, the moral philosophy
of La Rochefoucauld is not much opposed to that of
his century; he profits by the propinquity to dare to
be frank. Pascal, Molière, Nicole, La Bruyère, can
hardly be said, I imagine, to flatter mankind; some
tell the evil and its remedy; others tell the evil only;
there lies the whole difference.

Vauvenargues, who was one of the first to begin
the rehabilitation of the race, has remarked this very
well. "Mankind," he says, "is just now in disgrace
with all those who think; they vie with one another
to load it with vices; but perhaps this only shows
that it is on the point of rising again and compel-
ling the restitution of all its virtues . . . and far
more." Jean-Jacques took upon himself the "far
more"; he pushed it so far, that we might consider
it exhausted. But no; there can be no stopping in so
good a road; the proud stream flows and swells; man
is so rehabilitated in our day that we scarcely dare to
say or write the things that passed for truths in the

seventeenth century. This a characteristic trait of our times. Many a rare mind when talking is not less satirical than La Rochefoucauld; the same men as soon as they write or speak in public put on a tone of sentiment and begin to exalt human nature. They proclaim in the tribune the noble and the grand at which they laugh in the recess of a window, or sacrifice to a flash of wit around a green table. Philosophy practises self-interest, and preaches a pure ideal.

La Rochefoucauld's Maxims do not in any way contradict Christianity, although they do without it. His man is precisely the fallen man, if not as François de Sales and Fénelon understood him, at any rate such as Pascal, Du Guet, and Saint-Cyran consider him. Take from the Jansenist doctrine *redemption* and you have pure La Rochefoucauld. If he seems to forget in man the exiled king that Pascal recalls, and the broken particles of his diadem, what is that but the insatiable pride that he denounces, which, by force or craft, seeks still to be sole sovereign? But he limits himself to satire; it is not enough, says M. Vinet, to be mortifying, he should be useful. La Rochefoucauld's misfortune is to think that men do not correct themselves. "We give advice," he said, "but we cannot inspire behaviour." When it was a question of finding a tutor for the dauphin, he was thought of for a moment; I cannot but think that M. de Montausier, less amiable and more doctoral, was better suited to the place.

La Rochefoucauld's moral reflections seem true, exaggerated, or false, according to the humour and the situation of the reader. They please whoever has had his Fronde and a musket-shot between the eyes. The soured celibate treasures them. The fortunate worthy man, father of a family, attached to life by sacred and prudent ties, cannot accept them without qualifying them, or he thinks them odious. A mother suckling her child, a grandmother whom all revere, a noble, pitying father, devoted and upright hearts not subtilised by analysis, the lifted foreheads of young men, the pure and blushing foreheads of young girls,—these direct recalls to frank, generous, and healthy nature bring back the vivifying hour in which all subtlety of reasoning disappears.

In La Rochefoucauld's own time, and around him, the same objections and the same replies were made. Segrais and Huet thought he had more sagacity than equity; and the latter even remarked, very acutely, that the author had brought certain accusations against mankind for the sole purpose of not losing some witty or ingenious expression he meant to apply to them. However little of an *author* we may pique ourselves in being as we write, we are always one at some point. If Balzac and the "academists" of that school had ideas only through phrases, La Rochefoucauld himself, the strict thinker, sacrifices to the word. His letters to Mme. de Sablé during the time when the Maxims were in making, show him to us full of ardent imagination, but of literary preoccupation as well; there was rivalry between her and himself and M. Esprit and the Abbé de La Victoire. "I know that they dine with you without me," he writes to her, "and that you show them maxims I have not made, about which they will not tell me anything. . . . " And again, from Verteuil, not far from Angoulême, where he was staying: "I do not know if you have noticed that the desire to make phrases is as catching as a cold in the head; we have here some disciples of M. de Balzac who have caught the infection and will do nothing else." The fashion of "maxims " was succeeding that of "portraits." Later, La Bruyère took both and united them.

The postscripts of La Rochefoucauld's letters are filled and seasoned with these "sentences," which he jots down, retouches, and inclines to keep back even when sending them; "for I may regret them," he says, "as soon as the postman has gone." "I am ashamed to send you such works," he writes to a person who has just lost a quarter of his income from the Hôtel-de-Ville. "In earnest, if you find them ridiculous, return them to me without showing them to Mme. de Sablé." But the friend did not fail to show them, as he knew very well. Put thus into circulation before printing, these "thoughts" excited contradiction and criticism. There was one on Mme. de Schomberg, formerly Mlle. d' Hautefort, the object of Louis XIII's chaste love, of whom Marsillac, in the

days of his early chivalry, had been the devoted friend
and servitor: "Oh! who would then have believed it,"
she may have said to him, "Can it be that you have
grown so perverted?"

These "thoughts" were also blamed for obscurity;
Mme. de Schomberg does not think them obscure;
she complains instead of understanding them too well.
Mme. de Sévigné writes to her daughter in sending
her the edition of 1672: "Some of them are divine,
and, to my shame, there are some that I cannot understand." Corbinelli commented on them. Mme. de
Maintenon, to whom they went earlier, writes in
March, 1666, to Mlle. de l'Enclos, "Offer, I beg
you, my congratulations to M. de La Rochefoucauld,
and tell him that the book of Job and the book of
Maxims form my sole reading."

Success, opposition, and praise were not confined
to social interviews and correspondence; the news-
papers took part in them. When I say "news-
papers," I mean the *Journal des Savants,* the only one
then founded, which had been in existence for only a
few months. The matter here becomes piquant and I
shall venture to divulge it all. In turning over, myself, the papers of Mme. de Sablé I came upon the
draft of an article intended for the *Journal des
Savants* and written by that witty lady. Here it is:

"This is a treatise on the emotions of the heart of man, which we
may say was unknown until now even to the heart that felt them. A
seigneur as great in mind as he is by birth is the author. But neither

his mind nor his rank has prevented very different judgments being formed of it.

" Some think it an outrage on men to make so terrible a picture of them, and that the author can have found the original only in himself. They say that it is dangerous to bring such thoughts to the light, and that having been so plainly shown that good actions are only done from bad motives, most persons will believe that it is useless to look for virtue, inasmuch as it is impossible to have any except in idea; that, in short, it is upsetting morality to show that the virtues it teaches us are mere chimeras because they come to none but bad ends.

" Others, on the contrary, find the treatise very useful because it reveals to men the false ideas they have of themselves, and shows them that without religion they are incapable of doing right; it is always well, they say, to know ourselves as we are, even though there may be no other advantage in doing so than that of not being deceived in the knowledge of ourselves.

" However that may be, there is so much wit in this work, and such great penetration in perceiving the true state of man, in considering only his nature, that all persons of good sense will find here an infinity of things of which they might, perhaps, have remained ignorant all their lives if this author had not drawn them from the chaos of the heart of man and set them in the light, where all the world may see them and comprehend them without difficulty."

In sending this draft of her article to M. de La Roche-foucauld, Mme. de Sablé adds the following little note, dated February 18, 1665:

" I send you what I have been able to draw out of my head to put into the *Journal des Savants.* I have put in the side to which you are so sensitive. . . . I did not fear to put it in, because I am certain that you will not allow it to be printed even if the rest pleases you. I assure you, also, that I shall be more obliged to you if you will use it as a thing of your own, by correcting it, or by throwing it into the fire, than if you did it an honour it does not deserve. We great authors are too rich to mind the loss of our productions."

Let us note all this carefully: Mme. de Sablé, now

devout, who, for several years, had had a lodging in the Faubourg Saint-Jacques, rue de la Bourbe, in the buildings of Port-Royal of Paris,—Mme. de Sablé, greatly occupied, even at this time, with the persecutions to which her friends the nuns and the recluses were subjected, is not less concerned in the cares of the world and the interests of literature. These Maxims, known to her in advance, which she had caused to be copied, and had lent, under the rose and with great mystery, to a number of persons, gathering for the author the various opinions of society, she is now to aid before the public in a newspaper; she *works* at their success. On the other side, M. de La Rochefoucauld, who dreads of all things to play the author and allows it to be said of him in the Discourse at the beginning of the book: "He would not feel less vexation in knowing that his Maxims were made public than he felt when the Memoirs attributed to him were published"—M. de La Rochefoucauld, who had meditated so long on man, is now to review his own praise written for a newspaper and take out those parts which displease him! The article was inserted in the *Journal des Savants* of March 9, and if compared with the draft, we shall see that the part to which Mme. de Sablé thinks M. de La Rochefoucauld will be "sensitive" has disappeared; nothing remains of the second paragraph, beginning "Some think it an outrage on men." At the end of the first paragraph, where it is a question of the different judgments formed on the book, the article, as printed, skips suddenly to the third paragraph, with these words: "We may nevertheless say that this treatise is very useful, because," etc. M. de La Rochefoucauld left all as it was, except the least agreeable paragraph. The first literary journal that ever appeared had existed only three months, but already authors were arranging their articles themselves! As journals improved, the Abbé Prevost and Walter Scott wrote theirs at greater length.

The part that Mme de Sablé had in the composition and publication of the Maxims, that rôle of moralising and semi-literary friendship which she filled during those important years to the author, would give us the right to speak of her here more fully, if it were not that we ought above all to study her in connection with Port-Royal: a charming, coquettish, yet solid mind; a rare woman, in spite of some absurdities, to whom Arnauld sent the manuscript of his Discourse on Logic, saying to her: "It is only persons like yourself whom we desire to judge us"; and to whom, almost at the same moment, M. de La Rochefoucauld wrote: "You know that I trust none but you on certain subjects and especially on the recesses of the heart." She forms the true link between La Rochefoucauld and Nicole.

I shall say only one word on her own Maxims, which are printed; they serve to measure the little that belongs to those of her illustrious friend. She

was his counsellor, but nothing else: La Rochefoucauld remains the sole author of his work. In the
eighty-one thoughts of Mme de Sablé that I have
read I could scarcely quote one that stands out in
relief; their base is either Christian morality, or pure
civility and usage of the world; but the form is
especially defective; it is lengthy, long-drawn-out;
nothing comes to a conclusion, nothing fastens on the
mind. The mere comparison makes us better understand the manner in which La Rochefoucauld is a
writer.

Mme. de La Fayette, of whom there is little question until now in the life of M. de La Rochefoucauld,
became his intimate friend immediately after the
publication of the Maxims, and applied herself, in
a way, to correct them in his heart. Their two existences were never, henceforth, separated. I will relate
elsewhere, in speaking of her, the grave comfort given,
the afflictions tenderly consoled, during those last
fifteen years. Fortune as well as friendship seemed
at last to smile on M. de La Rochefoucauld: he had
fame; the favour of his fortunate son raised him at
Court, and even brought him back there; there were
times when he never quitted Versailles, detained by
the king whose childhood he had spared so little.
Family joys and sorrows found him incomparable.
His mother did not die until 1672: "I have seen him
weep," writes Mme. de Sévigné, "with a tenderness
that made me adore him." His great grief, as we

know, was that "hail of fire" at the passage of the Rhine, where he had one son killed and the other wounded. But the young Duc de Longueville, another of the victims, born during the first Fronde, was dearer to him than all else. The youth had made his entry into society about the year 1666, the year of the Maxims: the bitter book, the young hope — two children of the Fronde! In the well-known letter in which Mme. de Sévigné relates the effect of this death on Mme. de Longueville, she adds immediately: "There is a man in the world who is not less moved. I have it in my head that if the two could meet in these first moments, with no one present, all other feelings would give way to sobs and tears, shed, and doubly with all their hearts: this is a vision."

No death, so say all the contemporaries, ever caused so many tears, and such noble tears, as that of this young man. In M. de La Rochefoucauld's room in the hôtel de Liancourt, above a door, hung a portrait of the young prince. One day, shortly after the fatal news, the beautiful Duchesse de Brissac, coming to pay a visit and entering by a door opposite to the portrait, recoiled at the sight; then, after standing a moment motionless, she made a little curtsey to the company and went away without a word. The unexpected sight of the portrait had wakened all her sorrows, and being no longer mistress of herself she could only withdraw.

In his advice and solicitude about the graceful loves of the Princesse de Clèves and the Duc de Nemours La Rochefoucauld doubtless thought of that flower of his youth mown down; finding, perchance through tears, something not quite imaginary in the portrait. But were it not so, the sight of the now aged moralist bending with tenderness over the story of those romantic and charming beings is more fitted to touch us than surprise us. When minds are upright and hearts are sound at their source, after many experiments in taste men revert to the simple; after many aberrations in morality they come back to virginal love, if only to contemplate it.

It is from Mme. de Sévigné that we obtain an account of his fatal illness and his supreme last moments, his sufferings, the anguish of all around him, and his constancy; he looked *fixedly* at death.

He died March 17, 1680, before the end of his sixty-seventh year. Bossuet assisted him in his last moments; from which fact one of his biographers, M. de Bausset, has drawn certain religious deductions very natural in such a case. Another, M. Vinet, seems less convinced: "Persons," he says, "can make what they like of the following passage from Mme. de Sévigné, a witness of his last moments":

"I fear," she writes, "that we must lose M. de La Rochefoucauld; his fever continues; he received Our Lord yesterday; but his state is a thing worthy of admiration. He is well settled as to his conscience; *that is done.* . . . Believe me, my daughter, it was not useless that he made reflections all his life; he approached his last moments in such a way that they have brought nothing new or strange for him."

"It is permissible to conclude from these words," adds M. Vinet, "that he died, as was said later, with *decency.*"

V.

The Duchesse de Longueville.

V.

Anne=Geneviève de Bourbon.

Ducbesse de Longueville.

THE name of Mme. de Longueville, as well as that
of Mme de La Fayette, is bound to that of M. de
La Rochefoucauld by all sorts of attractive relations, conventions, and reverberations more or less
mysterious. Her life, divided into two opposing parts,
one of ambition and gallantry, the other of repentance
and devotion, too often had witnesses who were solely
concerned with one aspect of it. Mme de Sévigné
alone, in a memorable letter, has thrown light upon
her portrait at its most pathetic moment. To me,
who have met her at the very centre and heart of a
subject on which I was writing [the "History of
Port-Royal"] the opportunity has been given to follow her and to have the honour of frequenting her
presence in hours of retreat and through her hidden
experiences. She came before me as the most illustrious penitent and protectress of Port-Royal during
many years. On her, and on her presence in that
monastery, depended solely, towards the end, the

preservation of "the peace of the Church"; her death broke it up. Without pretending to paint a life so varied and so elusive, there was duty and pleasure for me in rightly catching the expression of a countenance to which an immortal enchantment clings, and which, even beneath its doubled veils, came smiling to me from the depths of that austere monastery. I detach it to place it here.

Anne-Geneviève de Bourbon, daughter of a very beautiful mother, Charlotte de Montmorency, whose beauty, so coveted by Henri IV, came near causing a war, was very young when she appeared at Court beside her mother, Mme. la Princesse [de Condé] still loftily brilliant, bringing with her, says Mme. de Motteville: "the first charms of that angelic face, which later had such dazzling lustre, a lustre followed by so many grievous events and salutary sufferings."

Her earliest and tenderest thoughts turned to piety; her end only recovered and realised the mystical dreams of her childhood. She often accompanied Mme. la Princesse to the Carmelite convent in the Faubourg Saint-Jacques; there she spent long hours that later were painted with an ideal halo in her azure imagination, and revived in living colours at last when the whirlwind had gone by. She was thirteen years old (1632) when her uncle Montmorency was immolated at Tours to the vengeance and the policy of Richelieu; the young niece, wounded in her pride as much as in her tenderness by so sharp a blow, would fain have

ANNE-GENEVIÈVE DE BOURBON,
DUCHESSE DE LONGUEVILLE

imitated the august widow, and vowed herself to mourn in conventual perpetuity. Her mother began to fear this marked inclination for the worthy Carmelites; she thought she saw that the blonde, angelic face was not making ready to smile upon the brilliant world which was about to judge it on its first appearance. To this, Mlle. de Bourbon replied, with an instinctive flattery that already belied such fears: "You have such touching graces, Madame, that as I go out only with you and am seen after you, no one finds any in me." The turn of Mme. de Longueville's spirit and mind is early seen in that one saying.

It is told that on the occasion of her first ball, to which she went in obedience to her mother, a great council was held among the Carmelites, at which it was decided, in order to conciliate matters, that before exposing herself to the danger, she should be armed beneath her ball dress with a little cuirass, called a hair-shirt. That done, all was felt to be safe, and Mlle. de Bourbon might think only of making herself beautiful. She had hardly entered the ball-room before a murmur of universal admiration and flattery rose around her; her smile, which her mother had doubted for a moment, responded, and ceased no more; delightful perversion! the prickles of the hair-shirt were blunted, and from that day those good Carmelite sisters were in the wrong.

But she thought of them still, at intervals; in the midst of her greatest dissipations she kept up an intercourse of letters; she wrote to them after each blow, each sorrow; she returned to them in the end and divided her time between their convent and Port-Royal. She was with them in the Faubourg Saint-Jacques when she died; she was there when Mlle. de la Vallière came, and among the agitated spectators of that arrival she was remarked for the abundance of her tears. The life of Mme. de Longueville is full of those harmonious symmetries, those returns upon herself that make her easily poetical, and by which the imagination allows itself, in spite of everything, to be seduced. It was thus (I omitted to say) that she was born in the castle of Vincennes during the imprisonment of her father, the Prince de Condè (1619); in that Vincennes where her brother, the Great Condé, a captive, was one day to cultivate pansies; in that Vincennes of Saint-Louis fated to bear upon its stones in after days the stains of the blood of the last Condé.

She frequented, with her brother, at that time Duc d'Enghien, the hôtel de Rambouillet, then in its first prime; and we have letters to her from M. Godeau, Bishop of Grasse, all full of myrtles and roses. This sort of influence was serious upon her, and her thoughts, even after her repentance, always felt it. At this period, and before politics came into her life, she and her brother and the young cabal (already decided to be a cabal) merely aimed, it is said, to show off the brilliancy of their wits in gay and gallant con-

versations, in discussing and refining till point was
lost on the delicacies and intricacies of the heart.
That was the test, to their minds, of men of honour.
Whatever had an air of solid conversation seemed to
them coarse and vulgar.   With them it was a resolution and a pledge to be *distinguished,* as it was called
sixty years later; *superior,* as we should say to-day:
but then they called it *précieux.*

Mlle. de Bourbon was twenty-three years old when
they married her (1642) to the Duc de Longueville,
then forty-seven, and widowed of a princess of more
virtue than mind who was closely allied with the
Mothers of Port-Royal during the period called that
of the Institution of the Holy Sacrament and of M.
Zamet.   The duke had a daughter, seventeen years
old at the time of his second marriage who, before
she was Duchesse de Nemours, lived for some time
with her young step-mother, noted all her transgres-
sions, and finally, in her Memoirs, spares her the
record of none of them.

The Duc de Longueville was the greatest seigneur
of France, but, coming after the princes of the blood,
he was somewhat beneath Mlle. de Bourbon.   Her
father, M. le Prince, forced her into the marriage; on
which, however, she put a good face.   In the first
days of it a great scandal excited and also flattered
her passionate pride and brought out the vanities of
her heart.

One day, during a "circle" at the Duchesse de

Montbazon's, some one picked up a dropped letter, without address or signature, but in a woman's hand, writing tenderly to some one she did not hate. The letter was read and reread, they all tried to guess the writer, and soon decided that it must be the Duchesse de Longueville, and that the letter had undoubtedly fallen from the pocket of the Comte de Coligny, who had just left the room. It seems that really, whether intentionally or not, they were mistaken. This attack was the first yet brought against the reputation of the young duchess. The malicious tale was told everywhere, without much credence being given to it. At the first rumour that reached the ears of the insulted lady, she, knowing that the story was false (though she may have intended to make it true), thought it best to keep silence. But her mother, Mme. la Princesse, would not allow her to do so, and in the tone of a person proud of having entered the House of Bourbon she exacted formal reparation. Her complaint became a State affair. This was in the first year of the regency [of Anne of Austria]; Mazarin tried his power; it was his first opportunity to disentangle Court intrigues, and to set aside the friends of Mme. de Montbazon, Beaufort, and the "Importants." Mme. de Motteville tells all this to perfection.

The composition of the words of apology was debated and decided in the little cabinet of the Louvre, in presence of the queen, and written down on the tablets of the cardinal, who was playing his own game under cover of this comedy.   The apology was then copied on a little piece of paper which Mme. de Montbazon fastened to her fan.   At a fixed hour she went to Mme. la Princesse and read the paper; but she did so in a haughty tone that seemed to say: "I ridicule it."   Soon after this, Coligny, in consequence of this pretended letter, "called out" the Duc de Guise, who took the part of Mme. de Montbazon. They fought on the Place-Royal; Coligny received a wound, of which he died; it was said at the time that Mme. de Longueville was hidden behind a window to watch the fight.   At any rate, all this uproar about her delighted her; it was the hôtel de Rambouillet in action.   Coligny might have found his reward had he lived.

Was it before or after this event that Mme. de Longueville was attacked by the smallpox?   Probably before; she had it the year of her marriage, and her beauty came out of it with little damage; the eclipse was transient.   "As for Mme. de Longueville," says Retz, "the smallpox took away the first flavour of her beauty but left her nearly all its brilliancy; and that brilliancy, joined to her rank, her wit, and to her langour, which in her was a peculiar charm, made her one of the most charming persons in France."   M. de Grasse thought himself more faithful to his character as bishop in writing to her, as soon as she recovered:

"I praise God for preserving your life.   .   .   .   As for your face, others than I will rejoice with more seemliness that it is not injured;

Mlle. Paulet sent me word of this.   I have such good opinion of your
wisdom that I think you would have been easily consoled if your illness had left its marks.   They are often marks engraven by the divine
Mercy, to show to persons who love their complexion too well that it
is a flower liable to fade before it fully blooms, and consequently does
not deserve to be placed in the rank of things that may be loved."

The courteous bishop dwells so complacently on
these marks of mercy only because Mlle. Paulet has
assured him they do not exist!

Mme. de Motteville goes farther; after the illness
she describes to us this beauty, which consisted more
in certain incomparable tones of the complexion than
in any perfection of feature; those eyes, less large than
soft and brilliant, of an admirable blue, the blue of
turquoise; and the silvery blonde hair, like that of an
angel, adding its profusion to the other charms.   And
with them all a perfect figure, the nameless something that is called "air," elegance in her whole person, and at every point a style supreme.   No one
approaching her ever escaped the desire to please
her; her irresistible charm extended even over women.

The Duc de Longueville, descendant though he was
of Dunois, had little that was chivalrous about him; he
was a great seigneur, magnificent and pacific, without humour, rather clever in negotiations, as much so
as an undecided man can be.   They sent him to complete those of Munster; Mme. de Longueville did not
join him there for two years (1646), by which time the
Prince de Marsillac had made upon her the impression
that he himself had received.

The diplomatic world and the honours of which she was the object left her indifferent and rather reflective; she thought then, as she did on another occasion when she yawned over Chapelain's *Pucelle* which she was asked to admire: "Yes, it is very fine, but it is very wearisome."

"Would it not be better, Madame," writes the careful M. de Grasse, "if you returned to the hôtel de Longueville, where you are even more plenipotential than you are at Munster? Every one wishes for you there this winter. Monseigneur, your brother, has returned, laden with palms; return yourself covered with roses and myrtles, for it seems to me that olive branches are not sufficient for you."

She reappeared in Paris in May, 1647. That year of absence had increased her value; her return put the crown to her success. All desires sought her. Her *ruelle* it is said, became the scene of choice discussions, of the famous duel of the two sonnets, and also of graver preludes. To speak the language of M. de Grasse, myrtles hid blades.

Her brother the victorious, hitherto so united with her in feeling, now, little by little, separated from her; this irritated her. On the other hand, her second brother, the Prince de Conti, became more and more bound to her, and Marsillac seized the tiller of her heart decisively.

To follow the life of Mme. de Longueville at this epoch, through budding rivalries, through intrigues, through the wars of the Fronde, would be to condemn ourselves to winnow the Memoirs of the time (pleasant as that task might be); but especially should we have to register the caprices of an ambitious yet tender soul in which the heart and mind were incessantly duping each other. One might as well attempt to follow step by step the airy foam on each mocking wave: *in vento et rapida scribere oportet aqua.* Let us rather concern ourselves with her character.

La Rochefoucauld, who more than any one was qualified to judge her, has told us his judgment, and I give the passage because it is too essential to her portrait to be omitted here:

"This princess had all the advantages of mind and beauty in so high a degree and with such charm, that it seemed as if Nature had taken pleasure in forming in her person a perfect and complete work; but these fine qualities were less brilliant because of a blemish which was never before seen in a person of her merits; namely, that instead of giving the law to those who had a particular adoration for her, she transferred herself so completely into their sentiments that she no longer recognised her own."

La Rochefoucauld could not at first complain of this defect inasmuch as he led her into it.

It was love that awakened ambition in her soul, but awakened it so quickly that henceforth the two were indistinguishable. Singular contradiction! The more we consider the political career of Mme. de Longueville, the more it blends and is confounded with the caprices of her love; yet if we search closely into that love it seems (and she herself avows it later) it was only the disguise of ambition, the desire to shine anew.

Her character, therefore, lacked stability and a will of her own.   And her mind,—note this well,—brilliant and acute as it was, had nothing that opposed itself directly to this weakness of character.   We may see the right thing, and yet not have the force to do it.   We may have reason in the mind but not in the conduct; between the two the character gives way.   But here the case was different.   Mme. de Longueville's mind was not pre-eminently reasonable; it was delicate, quick, subtile, ingenious, full of recesses; it followed her nature, which was fluctuating; it shone in evasions and in the tangle of cross-purposes before it consumed itself finally in scruples.   There was much of the hôtel de Rambouillet in a mind like hers.

"The minds of most women serve to strengthen their folly rather than their reason."   The author of the Maxims said so, and Mme. de Longueville with all her metamorphoses must have been present to his mind when he said it.   She, the most feminine of women, could offer him the best epitome of womankind.   On the other hand, while he observed, evidently through her, she, in turn, seems to have drawn her conclusions from him.   Mme. de Longueville's final confession, which we shall presently read, will seem to us little else than a Christian translation of the Maxims.

Retz, less involved in this subject than La Rochefoucauld, but who would fain have been as much so, has spoken marvellously of Mme. de Longueville; my own portrait has no other glory than to gather and present these several pictures:

" Mme. de Longueville," he says, " has by nature, a solid foundation of mind, but she has even more subtlety and cleverness. Her capacity, which is hampered by her laziness, has not been carried into those affairs to which her hatred for M. le Prince [her brother, the Great Condé] enticed her, and in which gallantry maintained her. She had a languor of manner, more affecting than the brilliancy of others who were more beautiful; she had the same in her mind, which charmed, because of its surprising and luminous awakenings. She would have had few defects if gallantry had not given her many. As her passion compelled her to make public affairs secondary in her conduct, from being the heroine of a great party she became the adventuress. The Grace of God restored what the world could not give back to her."

As, in the Fronde, we see Mme de Longueville superior in mind to Mme. de Montbazon, for example, or to Mlle. de Chevreuse (which is saying too little), or even to La Grande Mademoiselle, so we find her inferior to her friend the Princess Palatine [Anne de Gonzague], a true genius, firm, possessing the secrets of all parties, and ruling all, advising them with loyalty and coolness; not the adventuress, no! but the statesman of the Fronde: "I do not believe that Queen Elizabeth had greater capacity to guide a State," says Retz, speaking of the Princess Palatine.

Why did not Bossuet do honour to Mme. de Longueville as he did to that other repentant princess, whose funeral oration he pronounced in the church of these very Carmelites in the Faubourg Saint-Jacques? The Prince de Condé, who had asked for his eloquent services in memory of La Palatine, never thought, it

ANNE DE GONZAGUE, PRINCESSE PALATINE

appears, of expressing the same wish, some years earlier, in regard to his sister. Did he consider its accomplishment impossible from those resounding lips? The difficulties, in fact, were great; even in her repentance Mme. de Longueville retained something that seemed rebellious. Bossuet could not say as he did of the Princess Palatine: "Her faith was not less simple than artless. In the famous questions that have troubled, in so many ways, the peace of our times, she openly declared that she took no other part than that of obeying the Church." Port-Royal would have been a more perilous rock to strike than the Fronde; vague allusions might have been allowed in the dim distance to M. de La Rochefoucauld or to M. de Nemours, but never to M. Singlin.

But consider how a few words of the potent orator would have fixed for ever, in its gracious majesty, that figure of dazzling languor, that character of seductive and skilful weakness—weakness that was never more actively effectual than when it was most subjugated! How admirably would he have drawn her upon that background of tempests and civil whirlwinds, on which he first threw and then detached the other princess! We all know that grand page on the Fronde, which cannot be read too often; I refer my readers to it. He would not have written it less grandly for this lacking oration on Mme. de Longueville which is one of my regrets.

In default of that magnificent painting, the chronicle

of Memoirs is here to help us.   In using the key that those of La Rochefoucauld supply, I have already told (in my portrait of the latter) how the influences directing Mme. de Longueville were quite other before the imprisonment of the princes to what they were after it.   During the first period, that is to say, during the siege of Paris (1648), having quarrelled with the Prince de Condé, she followed only the interests and sentiments of M. de La Rochefoucauld; she followed them still after peace was signed (April, 1649), when, she urged and obtained for him patents and privileges at Court, and when, after the arrest of her brothers (January, 1650), she fled, through all sorts of perils in Normandy, by sea to Holland, arriving at last, very proud of herself, at Sténay, where she negotiated with the Spaniards and troubled Turenne.

On her return to France, after the release of the princes, and during the preliminaries of the return to arms, she seemed to follow the same sentiments though with a less decided yielding to them.   We see her in council with the Prince de Condé at Saint Maur, when she seems to wish sometimes for peace, because La Rochefoucauld desired it, and sometimes for rupture, because war would keep her away from her husband, "whom she had never loved," says Retz, "but was now beginning to fear."   And he adds, "this constitution of minds with which M. le Prince had to do would have hampered Sertorius." Strange and sorry omen ! aversion to the husband

struggling against the interests of the lover, while
for the latter not to triumph was to forfeit all. Before long M. de La Rochefoucauld's sentiments ceased
to be Mme. de Longueville's compass; she seemed
to accept without reluctance the homage of M. de
Nemours; losing it not long after through the intrigues of Mme. de Châtillon, who recovered that
homage as her own property and at the same time
found means to obtain that of the Prince de Condé,
then escaping once more from intimate relations with
his sister.

It was M. de La Rochefoucauld whose policy and
vengeance plotted this thrice irritating revenge on
Mme. de Longueville. She had already openly quarrelled with her second brother, the Prince de Conti,
whom, up to that time, she had governed absolutely,
and even subjugated. She lost before long the last
remains of hope to recover M. de Nemours, who
was killed in a duel with the Duc de Beaufort; and
from that moment her anger, her hatred against him
turned to tears, as if he were just torn from her.
About this time peace was finally concluded (October, 1662); the Court and Mazarin triumphed; youth
had fled; doubtless beauty was beginning to follow;
all things failed at once, or were about to fail for
Mme. de Longueville. Being at Bordeaux in a convent of the Benedictines where she had gone to lodge
when peace was evidently approaching, she wrote
to her dear Carmelites in the Faubourg Saint-Jacques,

with whom, even in the midst of her greatest dissipations, she had never quite broken:

"I desire nothing with so much ardour now as to see this war at an end, that I may fling myself among you for the rest of my life. . . . If I have had attachments in this world, of whatever nature you can imagine, they are now broken off and even shattered. This news will not be disagreeable to you. . . . I desire, in order to give me sensibility towards God (which I have not as yet, but without which I shall still do as I have told you if peace comes) that you will do me the favour to write to me often and confirm me in the horror that I have for this age. Send me word what books you advise me to read."

Anterior to this time we have letters from her to the same sisters; every misfortune, as I have said, brought her thoughts involuntarily back to them; she wrote to them when she lost a little daughter, and when her mother, the Princesse de Condé, died. The latter death occurred while the duchess was at Sténay. From there, in answer to a letter of condolence from the convent, she writes a touching request to the Mother-superior for particulars about the death:

"It is in being afflicted that I ought to find comfort," she writes. "The tale will have a sad effect, and that is why I ask you for it; for you see plainly that it is not repose that ought to follow a sorrow like mine, but secret and eternal torture: for which, indeed, I prepare myself, to bear it in the sight of God and in view of those of my crimes that have laid His hand upon me. Perhaps He will find acceptable the humiliation of my heart and the long series of my deep miseries. . . . Adieu, my dear Mother; tears are blinding me; if it were the will of God that they should cause the end of my life they would seem to me more the instruments of my good than the effects of my evil."

M. de Grasse. also, continued to write to her, and

he did so on the occasion of this death with a sort of eloquence. Thus were preserved, even through periods of prodigal delirium, the secret heart-treasures of Mme. de Longueville; her tears, abundant and renewed from time to time, kept them from drying up at their source.

Nevertheless, a new life was about to begin. She was thirty-four years of age. She quitted Bordeaux under an order from the Court and went to Montreuil-Bellay, a domain belonging to her husband in Anjou, and from there to Moulins. In the latter town she stayed with the Filles de Saint Marie, and visited the tomb of her uncle, the Duc de Montmorency, whose tragic death had so moved her at the age, still pure, of thirteen, and was now a solemn lesson to her, coming, vanquished herself, from civil factions. Her aunt, the widow of M. de Montmorency, was superior of the convent. The example of such chaste and pious consistency acted more than all else on her imagination, always so easily stirred, on her soul still adrift, still drenched by the shipwreck. One day, at Moulins, in the midst of some religious reading,

" a curtain was drawn back " [it is she herself who is speaking] " from the eyes of my mind; all the charms of truth, gathered into one object, came before me; Faith, which had remained as it were dead and buried beneath my passions, awoke. I felt like a person who, after a long sleep in which she had dreamed that she was great, fortunate, honoured, and esteemed by all the world, wakens suddenly to find herself loaded with chains, pierced by wounds, weary with languor, and locked in a dark prison."

After ten months' stay at Moulins she was joined
by the Duc de Longueville, who took her, with all
sorts of attentions, to his government of Normandy.
New trials were added daily to the old ones; the
mere announcement of some success of the Prince de
Condé, who had gone over to the Spaniards largely
at the suggestion of his sister, revived her remorse
and prolonged the ambiguity of her relations to the
Court.   She was reconciled during these years to her
brother, the Prince de Conti, and was closely allied with
her sister-in-law, Anne Martinozzi, Princesse de Conti,
niece of Mazarin, who redeemed that suspicious blood
by noble virtues; these three, the brother and sister
and the former's wife, soon became the envy of all
emulators in the path of conversion.

Nevertheless, Mme. de Longueville was still in
need of direction; with her style of character, with
that habit of following adopted sentiments and of
ruling herself only by some chosen will, she, above
all others, needed a firm guide.   She wrote from
Rouen to ask advice of her aunt, Mme. de Montmorency, and from an intimate friend, Mlle. du
Vigean, sub-prioress of the Carmelites of Paris,[1] also
of others.   She questioned the Abbé de Camus, afterwards Bishop of Grenoble and a cardinal, recently

[1] Mlle. du Vigean had been beloved by the then Duc d'Enghien, before the Fronde; he even wished to break his marriage in order to
marry her.   Their love, thwarted by Mme. de Longueville, who
warned M. le Prince, her father, had, on the lady's side, the cloister for
a tomb.

converted himself, who replied: "God will lead you farther than you think, and will ask of you things of which it is not yet time to speak to you. When we examine our conduct by the principles of the Gospel we find fearful voids." But the enlightened physician who could take in hand this vacillating and aching soul did not appear. Then it was that the advice of M. de Bernières, possibly of M. le Nain (head of Mme. de Longueville's council), given very certainly at the instigation of Mme. de Sablé, turned the mind of this anxious inquirer to Port-Royal and its directors.

Under date of April, 1661, we find a letter from Mère Angélique to Mme. de Sablé, telling her that she had seen Mme. de Longueville, and found her mind more solid, more natural, than she had been led to expect: "All that I saw of the princess in that short time seemed to me pure gold." M. Singlin, [director of Port-Royal] already obliged to conceal himself to evade the Bastille, consented to go and see Mme. de Longueville; he was the first to enlighten and regulate her repentance.

I find a letter from Mlle. de Vertus to Mme. de Sablé, which is as follows (I give it because, to my mind, all details relating to persons so lofty, so delicate, and finally so worthy, have a value):

"I received last night a note from the lady" [Madame de Longueville]. "You are entreated to do what you can to induce your friend, M. Singlin, to come here to-morrow. In order that he may have no

uneasiness lest he be seen in the quarter, he can come in a chair and
send away the porters; I will lend him mine to take him back where
he pleases. . . . If he would like to come to dinner they shall put
him in a room where no one whom he knows can see him; and it
would be better, I think, that he should come rather early, that is to
say between ten and eleven at the latest. . . . I am very anxious
that this should be done, for this poor woman has no peace. Have
many prayers offered to God I entreat you. If I could see her in such
good hands I should, I own, be very joyful; it seems to me I should
be like those persons who see their friend provided for and have no
more to do than to rest in that. The truth is, this lady makes strange
troubles for herself which she will not have when her mind is settled.
I am much afraid that your friend will be too harsh. However, we
must pray to God and commend the affair to him."

M. Singlin, once introduced, returned frequently.
He paid his visits disguised as a physician, with the
enormous wig then worn by that profession; he said,
in justification of this disguise, that he was indeed a
physician of souls. He remained for some time hidden at Méru, an estate belonging to the princess. Is
it refining too much to think that these mysteries,
these various concerted precautions in behalf of repentance had for Mme. de Longueville a last charm
of romantic imagination at the entrance of the narrow
way?

We possess her Examination of Conscience, written by herself after her first confession to M. Singlin,
November 24, 1661. It is a document to put beside
that other confession of the Princess Palatine, written
by her on the advice of the Abbé de Rancé, and so
magnificently paraphrased by Bossuet. They should
be read without scorn and with a simple heart; in the

papers themselves there is nothing agreeable or flattering. But considered humanly, so to speak, and
from the single point of view of psychological observation, such papers merit consideration—*respectus*. If
they reveal to us the human heart in its most minute
pettiness, it is because pettiness is the ordinary foundation of it; they follow it, they prove its smallness,
its meanness, through all degrees of its depth. Mme.
de Longueville regarded this new birth as the first
step for her in a truly penitent life:

> " I had long been searching (so it seemed to me) the path that led
> to life; but I always felt I was not in it, without knowing precisely
> what my obstacle was; I felt that there was one between myself and
> God, but I did not know it, and I felt as though I were not in my
> right place. I had a certain anxiety to be there, without knowing
> where it was, nor where I ought to seek it. It seems to me, on the
> contrary, since I have put myself under the guidance of M. Singlin
> that I am in the right place which I was seeking, namely: the true
> entrance to the path of Christian life, on the outskirts of which I have
> hitherto been."

It is to be remarked in this Examination of Mme.
de Longueville, and also in her manuscript letters, of
which I have seen a quantity, that the style is superannuated and much less elegant than we might have
expected; much less vivid and clear, for instance, than
that of the divine letters and Reflections of Mme.
de La Vallière, published in one volume by Mme. de
Genlis. This is chiefly because there is twenty-five
years' difference in the ages of the two illustrious
women: Mme. de La Vallière was the exact contemporary of La Bruyère, almost of Fénelon; Mme. de

Longueville's style was formed before the period of Louis XIV. But go to the depths and end of her long-drawn-out sentences, and delicate refinement will be found. Moreover, Mme. de La Vallière's style has been slightly corrected in the later editions.

Before listening to her general confession and thus engaging himself to direct her conduct, M. Singlin wished to know, from her, whether she felt willing to quit the world in case she was one day able to do so. She answered in all sincerity, "Yes." This acknowledgment and this pledge obtained, he exacted that she should continue to occupy herself with external affairs as long as it was necessary to do so, and without permitting herself to call them "miserable."

Skilful physician and practitioner of the soul that he was, M. Singlin showed her, after his first glance, her capital defect, namely: that pride of which she herself, she says, was quasi-ignorant for so many years. This pride is also what the Duchesse de Nemours, in her Memoirs, denounces in a hundred ways. It is curious to see how the denunciations of the latter, the indications of M. Singlin, and the sincere avowals of Mme. de Longueville fit into one another and agree:

"The things that it" [her pride] "produced," she writes, "were not unknown to me, but I dwelt only on its effects, which I thought great imperfections; but now, from what has been shown to me, I see that I did not go to their source. It was not that I did not recognise that pride was the principle of my errors, but I did not think it as living as it is; I did not attribute to it all the sins that I committed; yet I now see plainly that they *all* drew their origin from it."

She recognises that in the days of her most criminal
errors the pleasures that touched her were those of
the mind, which come of self-love; "the others
naturally did not attract her." These two miserable
emotions, pride and pleasure of the mind, which are
but one, entered into all her actions and were the soul
of her conduct:

"I have always found my pleasure, which I sought so much, in
that which flattered my pride and offered to me what the Devil
offered to our first parents: 'You shall be as gods!' And that
saying, which was an arrow that pierced their hearts, so wounded
mine that the blood still flows from that deep wound and will flow
long, if Jesus Christ by his grace does not stanch its flux. . . ."

The discovery, which she first owed in its full extent to M. Singlin, of this vast stratum in her nature,
on which he made her lay her finger and follow in all
its ramifications, and which now seemed to her to
comprise the whole substance of her soul, alarmed
her and led her to "the very edge of the temptation
to discouragement." She fears henceforth to find
pride in all things; and even this docility, apparently
the only sound spot in her soul, becomes suspicious
to her; she dreads lest she be docile in appearance
only, and merely because by obeying she pleased others
and regained the esteem she had lost. In a word, she
seems to see in this docility her pride "transforming
itself, if I may say so, into an Angel of light, in order
to have something to live upon." Terrified, she stops
short, and can only cry to God, with her face to earth
and after long silence: *Sana me et sanabor.*

But a letter from M. Singlin which she receives and reads after praying, comforts her by proving that this servant of God does not despair of her nor of her trials. I might, if this were the place, multiply extracts and reveal without sparing her, in all their naïve subtilty and old-fashioned negligence of style, these delicacies of conscience in a mind once so elegant and haughty, now so humble and, so to speak, engulfed. She knows herself henceforth; she bares her soul and analyses it. In one place her description falls in with that of Retz and responds to it precisely. We remember how he describes to us her laziness and languor, interrupted suddenly by flashes of light. Here follows her Christian and rigorously moral representation of that apparently charming trait. Once more I ask pardon for the carelessness of its style; poor as it is, when we plunge to the depths of what it says, we are tempted to exclaim with Bossuet (speaking of the dream of the Princess Palatine), ''I take pleasure in repeating these words, in spite of fastidious ears; they eclipse the most magnificent discourses; I would I spoke only such language '':

''On receiving the letter of M. Singlin, which seemed to me very thick and on that account made me hope for many things on the subject which now occupies me, I opened it rapidly, for my nature leads me always to follow whatever fills my mind; just as, on the contrary (I say this to make myself known), it gives me great coldness and negligence for whatever is not my then occupation, which is always very strong and single in me. This is what makes some persons think me vehement and impetuous, because they have seen me in my passions, or merely in my petty inclinations and tendencies; while to

others I seem slow and lazy, even dead, if I may use the word, because they have never seen me moved by what I once was either in
evil or in good.   That is also why I have been defined as if I were
two persons of opposite tempers; so that sometimes I was called sly
and sometimes fickle in humour; which was not so, neither the
one nor the other; but it came from the different situations in which
they saw me.   For I was dead, dead as death, to all that was not in
my head, and all alive to the slightest atom of things that touched
me.   I still have the diminutive of this humour, and I let myself be
ruled by it too much.   So it was this that made me open the letter
so rapidly."

She goes on in this strain, and adds many avowals
of her hasty dislikes, her mobility of temper, her
brusque asperity to others if she did not guard herself
against it.   I find therein an incredible number of
testimonies to that spirit, so acute, so unfettered,
which now has only its own labyrinth to unravel.
She says in closing:

" A thought has come to me about myself, which is that I am very
glad, from self-love, that I have been ordered to write all this; because
I like above everything to occupy myself and occupy others about
myself; for self-love makes us like better to say evil of ourselves than
to say nothing at all.   I expose this thought, and submit it in
exposing it, as I do all the rest."

I have copies of several manuscript letters written
by Mme. de Longueville, all equally full of scruples
and anxieties over some action that she thinks had a
worldly motive, over some forgotten sin, over an ab-
solution received with a clouded conscience.   She
practised repentance and mortification by continual
vigilance and anguish of mind, even more than by
hair-shirts.

By the advice of M. Singlin, Mme. de Longueville
concerned herself especially with restitutions and the
giving of alms in the provinces ravaged, through her
fault, by civil war.   On the death of M. Singlin, she
passed under the direction of M. de Saci.   When the
latter was sent to the Bastille, she had M. Marcel,
rector of Saint-Jacques, and others equally safe.   She
wrote very assiduously to the saintly Bishop of Aleth
(Pavillon) and followed his replies in detail as though
they were oracles.

The Duc de Longueville having died in May, 1663,
she was henceforth free to enter without delay upon
the path of penitence that claimed her wholly.   The
troubles of the Church at this period alone kept her
in the world.   She was very active in behalf of
Port-Royal during those difficult years.   The revision
of the New Testament, called that of Mons, was completed at the conferences held at her house.   After
1666, she kept Arnauld, Nicole, and Lalane hidden
there.   Several anecdotes are told, with an appearance of truth, which must have enlivened the weariness of that retreat.

Arnauld was one day attacked by fever.   The princess sent for Dr. Brayer and asked him to take particular care of a nobleman who had lately come to stay
with her, Arnauld having assumed the secular garments, wig and sword, and other paraphernalia of a
noble.   Brayer went up to see him, and after feeling
his pulse, began to tell him about a new book that

was making a great noise and was attributed to the gentlemen of Port-Royal: "Some," he said, "give it to M. Arnauld, others to M. de Saci; I don't think it is by the latter, for he can't write so well." On which Arnauld, forgetting the rôle of his coat and shaking his ample wig, cried out: "What's that you say, monsieur? my nephew writes better than I do." Brayer came down laughing and said to Mme. de Longueville: "Your nobleman is not very ill; nevertheless, I advise you to keep him from seeing people, and above all, not to let him talk." Such in truth, with his simple ingenuousness, was the great plotter and leader of a party, Antoine Arnauld.

We see (in the "History of Port-Royal" by Racine) that Nicole was more to Mme. de Longueville's taste than Arnauld, as being more polished, more attentive. In their evening meetings, the worthy Arnauld, preparing to go to sleep beside the fire and going headforemost into Christian equality, would gently "untie his garters before her; which made her suffer a little." Nicole had more of the customs of the world, but even he, coming in one day with an absent mind, laid his hat, gloves, cane, and muff on the princess's bed! She accepted all such things as part of her penance.

Mme. de Longueville contributed more than any of the prelates to the Peace of the Church. Those conflicting negotiations, so often broken off and resumed, their secret activities, at the centre of which she was, renewed for her the Fronde, the only Fronde now permissible, and gave her back a few of the same emotions for a good purpose, and in all security of conscience. Learning one morning (about 1663) of one of the ruptures, which was imputed to the Jesuits, she said, with a flash of her old wit: "I was simple enough to believe that the Reverend Fathers were acting sincerely — it is true I have only believed it since last night." Finally, however, serious negotiations began. M. de Gondrin, Archbishop of Sens, concerted everything with her. She wrote to the Pope to justify the accused persons and guarantee their faith; she wrote also to Cardinal Azolini, secretary of State, to interest him in bringing matters to a conclusion. She deserves, with the Princesse de Conti, to be saluted by the title of Mother of the Church.

Peace concluded, she caused to be built at Port-Royal-des-Champs a detached building, or small house, communicating by a gallery with the church. From the year 1672 she divided her time between this retreat and that of her faithful Carmelites in the Faubourg Saint-Jacques; where she already had an apartment. Very sorrowful trials from without pushed her finally into these two havens: first, the death of her sister-in-law, the Princesse de Conti, then the imbecility and misconduct of her eldest son, the Comte de Dunois; but, above all, the death of her cherished son, the Comte de Saint-Paul, then

Duc de Longueville. She never quite left the hôtel
de Longueville until after this last cruel death, so well
known to us through the admirable letter of Mme.
de Sévigné. The young duke was killed immediately
after the passage of the Rhine by flinging himself
with imprudent valour upon a body of the flying
enemy; and with him perished a crowd of young
noblemen. The news had to be told to Mme. de
Longueville. Lest I tell it incompletely I repeat here
the whole of that immortal page:

"Mlle. de Vertus," writes Mme. de Sévigné, June 20, 1672, "had
returned two days earlier to Port-Royal where she usually is; they
sent to fetch her with M. Arnauld to tell this terrible news Mlle.
de Vertus had but to show herself; her sudden return was sign enough
of something fatal. As soon as she entered: 'Ah! mademoiselle, how
is my brother?' [the Great Condé]. Her thoughts dared not go
farther. 'Madame, he is recovering from his wound.' 'Then there
has been a battle! and my son?' They made her no answer.
'Ah! mademoiselle, my son, my dear child! answer me, is he
dead?' 'Madame, I have no words to answer you.' 'Ah! my
dear son! did he die instantly? did he not have a single moment?
Ah! my God! what a sacrifice! And with that she fell upon her
bed, and all that the sharpest sorrow could do, by convulsions, faint-
ings, by deathly silence and by stifled cries, by bitter tears, by appeals
to heaven, by tender plaints and pitiful—all these she underwent.
She sees certain persons, she takes some broth, because God wills it;
she has no rest; her health, already very bad, is visibly failing. For
my part, I wish her death, not comprehending how she can live after
such a loss."

And seven days after the above letter she writes
again:

"I have at last seen Mme. de Longueville; chance brought me near
to her bed; she sent for me to come nearer and spoke to me first; as for

me, I knew not what words to say on such an occasion. She told me that she did not doubt that I felt pity for her; that nothing was lacking to her misfortune; she spoke of Mme. de La Fayette and of M. d'Hacqueville as those who would pity her most; she spoke to me of my son, and of the friendship her son had for him. I will not repeat my answers; they were what they ought to have been, and, in truth, I was so touched that I could not speak amiss. The crowd drove me away. But the circumstance of the peace is a sort of bitterness that wounds me to the heart when I put myself in her place; when I keep in my own I praise God, since it preserves to me my poor Sévigné and all my friends."

It was discovered (compliantly perhaps) that before starting for the war M. de Longueville was secretly converted: he had made a general confession (the gentlemen of Port-Royal had brought it about), he had distributed immense alms, and, in short, that, in spite of his mistresses and a natural son, he was a quasi-saint. This was a sort of final comfort, very permissible under the circumstances; the inconsolable mother was credulous. As soon as the first flood of condolences had abated, Mme. de Longueville went to Port-Royal-des-Champs, where her house was ready, and there she lived in solitude; leaving it from time to time and returning to stay with the Carmelites. In the latter convent she saw the passing, like a funeral procession, of the grandeurs of her time: Mme. de La Vallière taking the veil, and, shortly after, the arrival of Turenne's heart—that heart which she had, alas ! so troubled.

Her austerities, joined to her pangs of mind, hastened her end; a change took place in her during

her last illness, and she had, as it were, a foretaste
of calm.   She died at the Carmelites' on the 15th
of April, 1679, aged fifty-nine years and six months.
Her body was buried in the convent, her entrails at
Saint-Jacques-du-Haut-Pas; her heart was taken to
Port-Royal.   One month after her death, the Archbishop of Paris, M. de Harlay, went to Port-Royal in
person to command the nuns, by order of the king,
to send away their pupils and postulants, and forbid
them to return in future.   The death of the princess
had been awaited to begin the final blockade under
which the celebrated nunnery was fated to succumb.
There was no longer a Palladium in Ilion.

The funeral oration of Mme. de Longueville was
pronounced one year after her death, not by Bossuet,
I regret to say, but by the Bishop of Autun, Roquette,
supposed to be the original of Tartuffe, and of whom
it was said that his sermons were undoubtedly his
own, inasmuch as he bought them.   Mme. de Sévigné, in a letter dated April 12, 1680, praises in a
singular manner, and not without sharp points of
irony, this oration which was never allowed to be
printed.   What was far more eloquent than the
words of the Bishop of Autun on this anniversary
of Mme. de Longueville's death, was the presence of
the Mlles. de La Rochefoucauld in mourning for their
father, of Mme. de La Fayette, whom Mme. de
Sévigné went to see after the ceremony and found
in tears; for Mme. de Longueville and M. de La

Rochefoucauld died in the same year: "There was much to dream of in those two names."

Our worthy historians of Port-Royal have said many commonplaces and much pettiness about Mme. de Longueville; the title of Serene Highness dazzled them. When they speak of her, or of Mlle. de Vertus, or of M. de Pontchâteau they are inexhaustible; in the very legitimate plenitude of their gratitude we must not ask them for discernment of character. We see by a little fragment at the end of Racine's Abridgment, which he did not have time to recast and conceal in his narrative, that if Mme. de Longueville kept, into the last years of her life, the grace, elegance, and what Bossuet calls " the insinuating manners" of those who have retired from the world, she had also kept her touchiness, her dislikes, her readiness to take umbrage; "she was sometimes jealous of Mlle. de Vertus, who was more equable and winning." But why be surprised ? even to the cold shelter of a cloister, even to the funeral slabs on which she pressed her face she brought *herself;* the sphere was purer, but the enemies were the same, and the same inward struggles continued.

The true crown of Mme. de Longueville during those years, that which we must the more revere because she did not perceive it, covering it with both hands,—hiding it, as it were, in a tabernacle, is the crown of humility. That is her Christian glory which inevitable defects ought not to obscure. Many touch-

ing traits are told of it. She had her enemies, persons
who were jealous of her; wounding and even insulting speeches came to her ears; she bore them all,
saying to God: "Strike on!" Once, going in a chair
from the Carmelites' to Saint-Jacques-du-Haut-Pas, she
was approached by an officer who asked her for
some favour—I know not what. She answered that
she could not do it, and the man thereupon flew into
a passion and spoke in the most insolent terms. Her
servants were about to fling themselves upon him.
"Stop!" she cried, "do nothing to him; I have
deserved much more." If I point out beside this
grand chief trait of humility some persistent petti-
nesses it is far less to invalidate a repentance so deep
and so sincere than to expose to their end the obstinate hidden failings and evasions of these elegant
natures.

Lemontey, in a witty notice, but flimsy and sharp,
did not fear to call her a "theatrical and conceited
soul." Who will dare, after having gone with me
so near to her repentance, to call her aught else than
a poor, delicate, anguished being?

Nicole, that spirit also so delicate, who frequented
her presence for many years, has judged her very
well. He had always had a good understanding with
her. She thought him right in the various little quarrels of Port-Royal. He said pleasantly that after her
death he had sunk in public estimation; "I have
even" he said, "lost my abbey; for no one now

calls me M. l'Abbé Nicole, but simply M. Nicole."
In vol. xii of the *Ouvrages de Morale et de Politique*
by the Abbé de Saint-Pierre, we find the following
testimony as to the class of mind and intellectual
capacity of Mme. de Longueville; a place where we
should little have thought of looking for it; its quaint-
ness is none the less piquant.

" I asked M. Nicole one day what was the character of Mme. de
Longueville's mind; he told me she had a very keen and very delicate
mind in knowledge of the character of individuals, but that it was
very small, very weak, very limited on matters of science and reasoning, and on all speculative matters in which there was no question of
sentiment. ' For example,' added he, ' I told her one day that I could
bet and prove that there were in Paris at least two inhabitants who
had the same number of hairs upon their head, though I could not
point out who were those two persons. She said I could not be certain of it until I had counted the hairs of the two persons. Here is
my demonstration,' I said to her: ' I lay it down as a fact that the
best-furnished head does not possess more than 200,000 hairs, and the
most scantily furnished head is that which has only 1 hair. If, now you
suppose that 200,000 heads all have a different number of hairs, they
must each have one of the numbers of hairs which are between 1 and
200,000; for if we suppose that there were 2 among these 200,000 who
had the same number of hairs, I win my bet. But suppose these
200,000 inhabitants all have a different number of hairs, if I bring in a
single other inhabitant who has hairs and has no more than 200,000
of them, it necessarily follows that this number of hairs, whatever it is,
will be found between 1 and 200,000, and, consequently, is equal in
number of hairs to one of the 200,000 heads. Now, as instead of one
inhabitant more than 200,000, there are, in all, nearly 800,000 inhabitants in Paris, you see plainly that there must be many heads
equal in number of hairs, although I have not counted them.' Mme.
de Longueville still could not understand that demonstration could be
made of this equality in number of hairs, and she always maintained
that the only way to prove it was to count them. "

This proves to us that Mme. de Longueville who

had such affinity with Mme. de Sablé in refinements and titillations of the mind was very different from her on one point. Mme. de Sablé liked and could follow dissertations and was a good judge of them; but Arnauld would never have thought of making Mme. de Longueville read his " Logic of Port Royal " to interest her and to obtain from her a competent opinion.

She belonged by nature to those *esprits fins* which Pascal contrasts with the geometric minds: "those delicate, refined minds that are only refined; which, being accustomed to judge of things by a single and rapid glance, are quickly repelled by detailed definitions seemingly sterile, and have no patience to come down to the first principles of speculative things, and things of the imagination, which they have not seen in the world and in its customs."

But, geometry apart, her knowledge of the world and her rapid *coup d'œil,* her subtlety, her elegance, the blood of a princess in all her veins, a soul feminine in its every recess, her vocation, the point of honour to please, which is victory in itself, great passions, great misfortunes, the halo of a saint in dying, the supreme intertwining around her of those consummate names: Condé, La Rochefoucauld, Port-Royal—all this suffices to bestow on Mme. de Longueville a lasting distinction, and to secure to her in French memory a very flattering part that no renown of heroine can surpass; no fame, even that of superior women, can efface.

What more shall I say? If, from the bosom of that world which she has entered, she can smile at the effect, the charm her name produces on those who judge her, she is smiling now.

VI.

Cardinal de Retz.

VI.

Cardinal de Retz.

Instigator of the Fronde.

THE Memoirs of Cardinal de Retz appeared for the first time in 1717, under the regency of Philippe d'Orléans. When it was known that a copy of them was furtively being printed and about to appear, the Regent asked the lieutenant of police, d'Argenson, what effect the book would produce.

" None that need trouble you, monseigneur," replied d'Argenson, who knew the work; " the manner in which Cardinal de Retz speaks of himself, the frankness with which he exhibits his own character, admits his faults, and informs us of the ill-success of his imprudent actions, will encourage no one to imitate him. On the contrary, his misfortunes are a lesson to all mischief-makers and rash minds. I cannot conceive how that man could have left behind him that confession in writing. . . ."

Nevertheless the effect was wholly different from the one foretold by d'Argenson. One might as well have said on the eve of the production of the *Confessions* of Jean-Jacques Rousseau, that they would ruin the authority of philosophy. Errors and wrong-doings may be so well confessed that they instantly become contagious for the human imagination. "This book," said the honest Brossette (the most pacific of men), speaking of the Memoirs of Retz, "makes me a leaguer, a frondeur, and almost seditious by contagion." The Regent knew something of this shortly after the publication; the conspiracy of Cellamare in 1718 was in its way a counterfeit and summary of the Memoirs of Retz. In all the periods of our civil struggles they have been emergent and have roused fresh interest. Benjamin Constant said, during the Directory, that he could no longer read any books but two: Machiavelli and Retz. We are to-day [1837] at a propitious moment to re-read these Memoirs and draw from them a few lessons—if lessons of this kind are ever useful. In speaking of them to-day, I do not seek to make any political application, nor to work out any perspective according to the views of the moment; I prefer to consider them in a more general, more impartial manner; more in themselves only.

Retz belongs to that great and strong generation before Louis XIV, of which were also, more or less, and a few years apart, La Rochefoucauld, Molière, Pascal, a generation which Richelieu had found too young to crush; which revived, or rose on the morrow of his death, and signalised itself in thought and language (when action was denied it) by a free, bold outpour, to which the distinguished men who came through the long régime of Louis XIV were too much unaccustomed. This is so true as to the

CARDINAL DE RETZ
From a portrait by Nanteuil

thought and the language that when the Memoirs of
Retz appeared one of the reasons alleged or stam-
mered against their authenticity by a few fastidious
minds was the language itself of those admirable
Memoirs—that vivid, familiar, superlative, and negligent touch that betrays the hand of a master and
shocks those it does not enrapture.   Our language
under Louis XIV acquired many fine qualities, and
fixed them at the beginning of the eighteenth century
with a seal of conciseness and precision, but it lost
I know not what of breadth and the air of grandeur.

It was precisely that air of grandeur that Retz prized
most, and of which, from the start, he was ambitious
in everything, in his words, his actions, carrying it
into all his projects.   But if he sought for glory he had
in him many qualities of the first order well calculated
to form its basis.   Born in October, 1614, of an illustrious family, destined against his will for the Church,
"with a soul as little ecclesiastic as was ever, perhaps, in the universe," he tried to get out of the profession by duels and affairs of gallantry; but the
obstinacy of his family, and his star, prevented these
first scandals from producing their effect and casting
him back into secular life.   He then chose his course,
and set himself to study with vigour, determined, like
Cæsar, to be second in nothing, not even at the Sorbonne.   He succeeded; he held his own in the final
competitions and in the *Actes* of the great School,
against an abbé protected by Richelieu, and carried

off the victory in a signal manner, not caring whether he provoked the powerful cardinal, who " wanted to be master everywhere and in everything." About this time, a copy of the "Conspiracy of Fiesque," the first secular work of the Abbé de Retz, came into the hands of Richelieu, who saw in it to what point the young man caressed the ideal of a grandiose and seditious conspirator, and he said: "There's a dangerous mind." It is asserted that he said on another occasion to his groom of the chambers, speaking of Retz: "There's a face for the gibbet."

Retz was short, ugly, dark, rather ill-made and near-sighted; qualities little fitted to make a man of gallantry, though they did not hinder his being one, and with success. Sober in eating and drinking, he was extremely licentious ; but being, above all, ambitious, he led everything abreast—his passions, his views, even his schemes, into which there entered, in some degree, regard for the public weal. Possessed by a burning desire to make himself talked of, and to reach the grand, the extraordinary, at a time when he entered the world under the reign of a despotic minister he had no resource except in the idea of conspiracy ; and to that side he turned his first predilections ; just as, in other times, he might have turned them elsewhere. In spite of his turbulence and his impetuosity, Retz was very capable of self-control when the interests of his ambition required it. In Italy, at Rome, during a journey that he made

there in 1638, when twenty-four years of age, he
resolved to give no cause for complaint against him
and to acquire at all risks a good name at the ecclesiastical Court. Retz tells us this, and Tallemant des
Réaux, who accompanied him, expressly confirms it:
" We must praise him for one thing," he says : "neither
in Rome nor in Venice did he see a woman ; or if he
did, it was so secretly that we could discover nothing
of it." At the same time he took pains to relieve the
modesty of the journey by great expense, fine liveries,
a very jaunty equipage ; and one day, to maintain the
point of honour and not yield the ground in a game
of tennis, he came very near drawing swords with his
handful of friends against the whole escort of the
Spanish ambassador.

He was much to the fore in all the conspiracies
against Richelieu, in fact, he staked his head during
the last years of that minister. He details the scheme
of one of these conspiracies, in which it was proposed
that at the first news of a victory by the Comte de
Soissons, Paris should be stirred to insurrection, and
a sudden attack made in combination with the principal prisoners in the Bastille, Maréchal de Vitry,
Cramail, and others. The scheme was novel The
governor of the Bastille was made prisoner by his
own garrison, of which the conspirators had made
sure. They also seized the Arsenal which was close
by. In short, it was " Mallet's Conspiracy," organised
by Retz against Richelieu. It all failed ; but it might

have succeeded. How many great things in history hang by a thread !

Richelieu dead, and Louis XIII having followed him closely, the Regency came ; certainly at first the most easy-going ever seen. Retz obtained, in a trice, the appointment of coadjutor [assistant to a bishop or archbishop, with the right to succeed him] to his uncle, the Archbishop of Paris ; and henceforth, to use his own language, he ceased to "be in the pit, or even in the orchestra playing and joking with the violins" ; he mounted the *stage*. We may observe throughout his Memoirs, where he speaks of himself with so little concealment, that he perpetually uses the expressions and images of the "stage" the "comedy"; he seems to consider everything in the light of a play. and there are moments when, speaking of the principal personages with whom he has to do, he takes account of them and arranges them absolutely as a stage-manager would do with his star-actors. In relating one of the first scenes of the Fronde, in Parliament (January 11, 1649), and telling of the manner in which he managed to take away the command of the troops from the Duc d'Elbeuf to bestow it on the Prince de Conti, he shows us M. de Longueville, then M. de Bouillon, then the Maréchal de la Mothe, entering the hall, one after the other, each, in turn, beginning anew to declare adhesion to the choice of the Prince de Conti, and joining hands in what concerned them :   "We had arranged," he says "to bring these personages on the stage one after the other, because we considered that nothing so touches and stirs the people, and even the Companies, who always stand by the people, as variety in the scene." In all such passages Retz openly shows himself as a dramatic author or a skilful *impresario* who mounts his piece. He was even then of the race of those who in the matter of turmoils and revolutions like the play better than the *dénouement;* great artists in intrigues and influences take delight in them ; whereas, the more ambitious men, the more true, the more practical, look to the object and aspire to results. There are places where, while reading these Memoirs of Retz through the charming scenes so well marshalled under his pen, he seems less at war with Mazarin than in harmony with Molière.

Nevertheless, let us not exaggerate this view to the point of overlooking what there was of real and serious policy in the projects and views of Retz. And let us never forget this: Retz, after all, did not triumph; he failed in the purpose he pursued, which was to drive out Mazarin and himself replace him beside Anne of Austria. We know him to the full as agitator, frondeur, conspirator; but we do not know what he might have been as minister, or what he would have done in that new rôle. It would not have been the first time that a superior nature transformed itself on obtaining power and in using it; and it may even be that such a nature is not wholly

superior unless it has in it that which transforms and
renews it, that which suffices for great situations.
In Retz, as in Mirabeau, we see only the ardent struggle, the vast intrigue, and the plot that is torn in
twain.   The man of the second epoch had, in both
of them, no career in which to develop himself.
Retz, in this comparison, has the disadvantage of
having survived; of being, as it were, present at the
miscarriage of all his hopes,—present as the de-
moralised, lowered, and defeated party, as may well
happen to the strongest natures who let their aim
escape them.   Seeing the battle lost, base diversions
lay hold upon them in their hours of exile.   It is in
his last years only that Retz recovers some dignity in
a retirement nobly borne; that he conveys an idea of
honesty by the complete payment of his vast debts;
and redeems himself to our eyes in the realm of mind
by the composition of his incomparable Memoirs.   But,
in his Memoirs, Retz abandons action and practica-
bilities, and is, more and more, simply a writer, a
painter, a great artist; it is impossible for him henceforth to be anything else; and we arm ourselves easily
against what he was or might have become in other
days, with this last quality, which will for ever make
his fame.

I wished to slip in this observation because I always
wonder at the way that narrow and negative natures
hasten to say to all superior genius: "Thou hast never
done more than this in thy life, up to the present;

fortune has prevented thee from trying thyself in a broader and freer career, consequently, thou couldest not have done more than thou hast done." Such persons have need to receive, from time to time, a few flat contradictions, like that, for instance, given them by Dumouriez in the defiles of the Argonne.

As for Retz, there are, unfortunately, too many reasons to assume that in him the adventurer, the audacious *téméraire,* as Richelieu called him, was the essential part and even the foundation of his nature; and that it would at all times have compromised the statesman, whose ideas he entered into with his mind only. He belongs to those in whom humour rules character; love of his own pleasure, licentiousness, intrigue for intrigue's sake, a taste for disguises and masquerades, a little too much Figaro, if I may so express it, corrupted his serious aims, and destroyed, in practice, designs that his fine and impetuous genius was so capable of conceiving. Many a time, he recognised this himself, he lacked good sense in his purposes; there were times when he blamed himself for not having "a grain of it"; he was liable to be dazzled, to have flights of imagination from which men whose thoughts are to guide and govern empires know how to protect themselves. His contemporaries tell us this, and he himself says it was so. When a La Rochefoucauld paints Retz, and Retz agrees with him by recognising the chief features of the portrait, we can only be silent, poor observers from afar, and bow low.

The second volume of Retz's Memoirs is the one that shows him to most advantage in the elevation of his political thought and in the charm of his pictures. There is no finer and no more truthful painting (I say truthful, for it is redolent of life itself) than that of the opening of the Regency of Anne of Austria and of the establishment, almost imperceptibly and by means of insinuation, of the power of Mazarin. The gentleness and facility of the first four years of the Regency, followed suddenly, and without apparent cause, by smothered discontent and the growl of a tempest, are described and interpreted on these pages in a manner to defy and baffle all future historians. I do not understand why M. Bazin, in reading them, did not instantly recognise and salute Retz as a master, confuting him, of course, in many cases where there was necessity. But any historian who meets at the start, on the subject of which he is treating, with such an observer and painter in a predecessor, and only finds ground to belittle and obliterate what he has left behind him, seems to me to give proof of an aggravating and cavilling spirit which excludes him from the broad road of the vocation. Observe that Retz, while painting, explains; the political and profound reason of things glides into the stroke of his brush.

After those first four years of the Regency, during

which the impulsion given by Richelieu continued to send onward the vessel of State without the necessity arising for any fresh instigation,—after those four years of perfect quiet, of smiles and indulgence, they entered, without at first perceiving it, new waters; a new breeze little by little made itself felt: the gust of reforms, of revolutions. Whence came it? What occasioned it? What were the slender grounds that brought about so violent a shaking up? This is what Retz excels in telling us, and those pages of his Memoirs (which could well be entitled "How Revolutions begin") remind us, by the elevation of their tone and their firmness, both of Bossuet and of Montesquieu.

"It is more than twelve hundred years that France has had kings," says Retz, "but these kings have not always been absolute to the point at which they now are." Then, in a rapid and brilliant summary, he seeks to show that, although the French monarchy was never ruled and limited by written laws, or by charters, like those of England and of Aragon, there had always existed in former times a "wise medium" [*sage milieu*] "placed by our forefathers between the license of kings and the licentiousness of peoples." That wise and golden mean, which in France has always been more a condition of desire, of regret or hope, than a state of actual reality, had a certain shadow and effect of custom in the power attributed to Parliament; and Retz shows all the wise kings — Saint-Louis, Charles V, Louis XII, Henri IV, — seeking to moderate their own power and surround it by the limits of law and justice. To the contrary of this: all that we now call in the language of to-day tendency to centralisation, all the efforts of Louis XI, of Richelieu which were about to be consummated under Louis XIV, all that would render the monarchy sole master, seemed to Retz the road to despotism. We cannot deny that it was pure despotism until oneness in administration was joined and combined, after '89 and after 1814, with a constitutional régime and liberty.

When the work was only half way, and done on one side only, as in the time of Retz on the morrow of Richelieu's death, this invasion without check of the royal and ministerial power was surely despotism if ever there were any; and there is nothing surprising that, in the interval of respite between Richelieu and Louis XIV, the thought occurred to oppose it and build, as it were, a dam with a sort of constitution. That was the first serious thought from which issued the Fronde; a thought which produced itself in the Parliaments only on occasions of special grievance, and was then quickly swept aside in the whirlwind of intrigues and personal ambitions. But Retz expresses it clearly in the beginning, and Parliament confirmed it formally in its Declaration of October 24, 1648 (a true Charter in embryo) which it would be frivolous to misunderstand.

A man of much intelligence, and, what is even better, of sound and judicial mind, M. de Sainte-Aulaire, has made this view the leading idea of his "History of the Fronde." He has sought to disengage, in a way, the constitutional element, too often masked and perverted at the pleasure of factions. It seems sometimes as if M. Bazin had constructed his work on the same period of our history with the sole purpose of counteracting, step by step, the point of view of M. de Sainte-Aulaire. The opinions the two historians express on Retz are diametrically opposite. While M. Bazin leads us to see in him merely the wittiest, most selfish, and boastful of plotters, M. de Sainte-Aulaire seeks in his conduct and through all the tangle of detail a clue that is not solely that of a frivolous and factious ambition:

" Although," says M. de Sainte-Aulaire, " in writing his book Retz did not escape the influences I have just pointed out " [the reigning influences and the changes introduced into opinion by the establishment of Louis XIV's regime] " we find, nevertheless, the proof that he had seen all and comprehended all; that he had measured the dangers to which despotism was about to expose the monarchy, and that he sought to prevent them. My admiration for this great master has increased in copying the pictures drawn by his hand. . . ."

If this favourable judgment has its justification, it is more especially at the beginning of the Memoirs, at the origin of the Fronde.

Richelieu's rule had been so strong and so absolute, the prostration which it caused in the whole body-politic was such, that no less than four or five years were needed for the *reaction* to be felt, for the public organs he had repressed to resume their office and seek to recover strength; and even then they did so, as usually happens, only on occasions of special measures that irritated them personally. Mazarin, a foreigner in France, a skilful negotiator outside of it, but with no idea of our political rights and maxims, followed, with slow steps, the path marked out by Richelieu; but he followed it without suspecting that it was "edged with precipices on all sides." He believed, above all else, in French levity, and saw nothing logical or consistent in it. He did not perceive that the peace of the first four years of the Regency was not real health; instead of husbanding means and preparing by remedies for the morrow, he continued in the old course; which aggravated disturbances and the sufferings of the interior of France: "The ill grew worse and worse," says Retz; "the head awoke; Paris felt itself, and sighed; no notice was taken of its sighs; it fell into frenzy. Let us now come to details." Do you not admire this opening, worthy of Bossuet, or, if you prefer it, of Montesquieu ?

There are, as we know, certain moments when physical diseases of like nature break forth at once in various lands; this is true of moral epidemics as well. The news of the revolution at Naples, that of the revolution in England, sent, as it were, a wind

of sedition to French minds. The vague humours of
public discontent are very quick, in hours of crises,
to be caught by emulation, letting the example of
a neighbour decide them, and taking the particular
form of malady that reigns and circulates. Retz understands and makes us understand all that admirably. Do not suppose that he understands seditions
and riots only; he comprehends and divines revolutions. He describes as an observer gifted with an
exquisite sensitiveness of tact, their period of on-
coming, so brusque sometimes, so unforeseen, and
yet so long in preparation. I know no finer page
of history than that in which he paints the sudden
passage from the discouragement and supineness of
minds, making them believe that present evils can
never end, to the contrary extreme where, far from
considering revolutions as impossible, they think
them, in a moment, simple and easy:

" And this disposition alone," he adds, " is sometimes capable of
making them. . . . Whoever had told us three months before
the *little dawn of troubles,* that a revolution could be born in a
State where the royal family was perfectly united, where the Court
was the slave of the minister to whom the provinces and the capital
were equally submissive, where the armies were victorious, where
the Guilds appeared at all points to be impotent — whoever had told
us that would have been thought insane, I do not say in the minds
of common people, but in those of the Estrées and the Seneterres " —

that is to say, the ablest of those who stood high
at Court.

That which follows takes us, as though we were
present, through all the degrees of that unexpected

awakening, soon to change to terror, consternation, and fury. He is like an inquiring physician writing down all the symptoms of the disease, the very disease he has always desired to study closely: evidently he would rather watch it than cure it.

" There seems a little sentiment," he says, in speaking of the depressed condition of the State, " a gleam, or rather a spark of life; and that sign of life, almost imperceptible in its beginnings, is not given by *Monsieur,* is not given by M. le Prince, is not given by the Nobles of the Kingdom, is not given by the Provinces; it is given by Parliament, which, until our day, had never begun a revolution, and which certainly would have condemned the bloody Decrees it made itself, if any others than itself had made them. It grumbled over the Edict of the Tariff (1647); and no sooner had it merely murmured than everybody waked up. They searched about, groping, as they woke, for the laws; they could not find them; they were alarmed, they shouted, they demanded them; and, in this agitation, the questions to which their excitement gave birth, from obscure as they were and venerable through their obscurity, became problematical; and hence, in the opinion of half the country, odious. The people entered the sanctuary; they raised the veil which should always cover whatever can be said and whatever can be believed about the rights of the people and the rights of kings, which never accord so well together as they do through silence. The hall of the Palais profaned these mysteries. Let us now come to particular facts that will make you see this matter with your eye."

Those are the exordiums that count for much in history. The man who under Louis XIV, at the age of fifty-eight, wrote these things in solitude, in privacy, addressing them by way of pastime to a woman among his friends, had certainly in his mind and in his imagination serious ideas of the essence of societies, and a grandeur of political conception. He had too often changed them and tarnished them in practice; but pen in hand, as often happens to writers of genius, he grasped them again with clearness, brilliancy, and amplitude.

With all historical personages we should fasten first upon their great aspects; I know not if I shall have time to note all the weaknesses, all the infirmities, all the shames even, of Retz and brand them; but I should blame myself if I did not from the start point out in him the manifest signs of superiority and force which capture admiration the more we approach him. I have not yet reached the end of them.

Retz, who to us, because we know his life and his confessions, seems a most scandalous ecclesiastic, did not seem such in his lifetime to those of his cloth, or to his flock. He explains, with a frankness that nothing equals, the means he took to procure respect among the clergy and favour among his people, not only as a man of party but in his quality as archbishop, without in the least retrenching his secret vices and weaknesses. Astonishing as this may seem, we are forced to recognise that respect and consideration remained with him as long as he lived and in spite of all he did to impair it. Learned man, or skilful enough to make himself appear so, careful administrator, always ready to defend the rights and prerogatives of his Order, excellent and eloquent preacher, prodigal in alms for all purposes, he had a dual reputation, and his adventures of every kind, in politics and intrigues, were never able, thanks to the incomplete publicity of those days, to shake his good fame in the Île-Saint-Louis nor yet in the quarter of Saint-Jacques. The Jansenist party, then flourishing, was very favourable to him: "I had much esteem for devout persons," he says, "and in their eyes, that is one of the great points of piety." There was no hypocrisy properly so called in this; for that is a degrading vice; but he profited by the disorder of the times, the dispensations of an extraordinary situation, relying at the same time on prejudices that walled in minds. It may even be believed, as he has very well explained to us, that in peaceful times, his reputation of archbishop would have been more damaged, for he would then have found it difficult to conceal his vices and irregularities, whereas they were lost in the inevitable confusion of civil war.

The fact from which we augur that Retz could never have been any thing than what he was, is the enthusiasm with which he allowed himself to be swept, from the very first days of the troubles, into the rôle of popular leader. He was persuaded "that greater qualities are needed to form a good leader of a party than to make a good emperor of the universe." That title "Leader of a party" was what he had always most honoured in "Plutarch's Lives"; and when he saw that matters were becoming embroiled to the point of allowing him to come naturally into the rôle, he felt a tickling of his feelings, an emotion of vainglory, which seem to indicate that he conceived of nothing nobler or more delightful. He was about to swim in his element.

When Saint-Simon, in his day, describes to us the delights and thrillings he experienced in being able to observe the faces and expressions of the courtiers under the great circumstances that lay bare secret passions and intentions, he does not express himself with a keener sense of delectation than does Retz when he shows us his joy at the thought of seizing the rôle so coveted. We may well conclude that one was in his element as observer, the other as agitator; both artists in their own way, and consoled, after all, by their imaginations when the opportunity came to them to relate their past pleasure and describe it.

In the second volume of the Memoirs there is an admirable conversation between Retz and the Prince de Condé who, returning victorious from Lens, was really the arbiter of the situation. The double rôle of restorer of the public weal and preserver of the royal authority tempted, at first, the lofty and luminous mind of Condé; but Retz, in a wonderful manner, makes us understand how the prince could not hold to it, being too impatient. "Heroes have their defects; that of M. le Prince was that there was not enough persistency in one of the finest minds in the world." Then, going farther, Retz points out to us in what that lack of persistency consisted. On the return of the army, finding Parliament in a struggle with the Court, the glory of "restorer of the public weal" was the first idea of the Prince de Condé, that of "preserver of the royal authority" was the second. But, while seeing both things equally, he did not feel them equally. Balancing between the two ideas, and even seeing them together, he could not weigh them together. He passed from one to the other: thus, that which seemed to him on one day to be the lightest seemed the weightiest on the morrow. The exalted manner in which Retz estimates the Prince de Condé at that moment and his first intentions before they deflected and were embittered in the struggle deserves that we apply the same form of judgment to himself. He says at every turn enough evil of that self to make us believe in his sincerity when he shows himself in another light.

Wishing to convince the Prince de Condé that there was a great and incomparable rôle to play in this crisis between the magistracy and the Court, wishing to temper his impatience and his wrath in regard to Parliament, and to prove to him that, prince of the blood and victor as he was, he could, with a little address, handle and insensibly govern the great Assembly, Retz in a conversation he held with him at the hôtel de Condé (December, 1648) rises to the highest views of statesmanship, to views which outran the times, while at the same moment he keeps in sight that which was practicable then. The Prince, irritated by the opposition he meets at every step in the deliberations and resolutions of the Assembly, was

returning to his instincts, that were very slightly parliamentary, and threatening to bring to reason those
"square caps," as he did the populace, with mailed
hand and force. To which Retz replied, with a pro-
phetic instinct of '89:

> " Is not Parliament the idol of the people? I know that you count
> them for nothing because the Court is armed; but I beg you to let me
> tell you that *they ought to be counted for much each time that they
> count themselves as all. They are now at that point.* They are
> beginning themselves to count your armies for nothing; and the *mis-
> fortune is that their strength consists in their imagination: and it
> may with truth be said that, unlike all other powers, they can, when
> they have arrived at a certain point, do all they think they can do.*"

Cardinal de Retz, we see, knew as much and as far
on the strength of Tiers-État as the Abbé de Sieyès.
Looking back to former ages and to the spirit that then
existed, he defines in singularly happy terms the ancient and vague Constitution of France which he calls
"the mystery of the State." "Each monarchy has its
own" he says, "that of France consists in the religious and sacred silence in which is buried, while
obeying, nearly always blindly, the kings, the right
the people will not believe they have to dispense with
kings, except on occasions when it is not their duty
even to please them." He makes us see how latterly,
on the Court side, they had, with signal clumsiness,
put Parliament under the necessity of defining the
cases in which it might disobey, and those in which
it could not do so. "It was a miracle that Parliament did not at last lift that veil, and did not lift it

formally and by Decree; which would have been far
more dangerous and more fatal in its consequences
than the freedom of the people have taken of late
to look through it."

The conclusion of this memorable speech is an
endeavour to reconcile Condé with the Parliament,
without absolutely separating him from the Court,
and the proposal of a useful, innocent, and needed
rôle, which should make him the protector of the
public and of the sovereign guilds, and would in-
fallibly eliminate Mazarin: in this he reckoned without the queen's heart. However that may have
been, it was a noble dialogue carried on with frankness by the two speakers, about to become adversaries. The parts of the two men, the characters and
language are kept distinct. Condé and Retz parted,
each holding his own opinion but with esteem for the
other; one, for the Court, deciding, after weighing all,
to defend it; the other remaining Coadjutor and,
above all, the defender of Paris.

Many quarrels, treacheries, insulting outrages hap-
pening later lowered the nobleness of this first explanation and soiled its memory; nevertheless, one
takes pleasure, when reading it, in thinking that those
great minds, those impetuous and misguided hearts,
were not originally as evil-intentioned nor as given
over to their selfish and perverse ends as they seemed
to be later, when the passions and cupidities of each
were unchained. One of the greatest evils of civil

war is to corrupt even the best and most generous of those who enter upon them. That was true of the Prince de Condé; that was true of even Retz.

He himself has taken care to point out to us the precise moment, very near to this conversation, when he determined to deliver himself wholly up to his passion and to his hatred of Mazarin (January, 1649): "When I saw," he says, "that the Court would not accept even good except in his way, which was never good, I thought of nothing but of how to do him harm; and it was not until this moment that I made a full and complete resolution to attack Mazarin personally." From that day, all means were good to him to win success   arms, pamphlets, calumnies. Here begins the gala; henceforth, he thinks of nothing but of continuing "master of the ball" as Mazarin himself very aptly said.

It was at this moment that Retz, artist that he is pen in hand, considering that he has issued from the preamble or vestibule of his subject, gives himself free way, and, having up to that time sketched his personages only in profile, he now shows them full face and full length, as if in a gallery. He makes no less than seventeen portraits in a series, all admirable for life, brilliancy, delicacy, and resemblance; even impartiality is there when he paints his enemies. Among these portraits, of which not one is less than a masterpiece, we note, above all, those of the queen, of Gaston, Duc d'Orléans, of the Prince de Condé,

M. de Turenne, M. de La Rochefoucauld, Mme. de Longueville and her brother the Prince de Conti, Mme. de Chevreuse, Mme. de Montbazon, and finally, Mathieu Molé. This gallery, the portraits of which, repeated and reproduced a hundred times, fill all our histories, are the glory of the French brush; and we may say that, before Saint-Simon, nothing else had been written more vivid, more striking, more marvellously lifelike. Even in comparison with Saint-Simon, nothing pales in this gallery of Retz; we admire the difference of manner, something more concise, more clear, freer perhaps in colour, but not less penetrating into the quick of souls: M. le Prince, to whom "nature had given a mind as great as his heart, but whom Fortune did not allow to show the one to its full extent as plainly as he did the other, and who was *never able to fulfil his own merit*"; M. de Turenne, to whom no fine qualities were lacking " but those he had never thought of," and to whom we should deny none, " for who knows? he had in everything, even in his speech, *certain obscurities* which only developed as opportunity offered, and then developed only to his glory"; Mme. de Longueville, whose " languor of manner touched more than the brilliancy of those who were more beautiful. She had the same in her mind, which charmed, *for it had awakenings both luminous and surprising.*" I should like to quote all, to repeat all in these pictures of a touch both strong and captivating.

Coming after the fine and statesmanlike conversation with the Prince de Condé, after the marvellous
scenes of comedy in the first days of the Barricades,
after the grand and lofty considerations that precede
them, these portraits form an introduction to his
subject, and a unique exposition which will last even
if the rest of the pieces fade.

Retz's style is that of our finest language; it is full
of fire, and the spirit of everything circulates through
it. The language itself is of that manner, slightly
anterior to Louis XIV, which unites to grandeur a
supreme air of elegance that makes its grace. The
expression is readily gay, picturesque as it flows,
always true to French genius, yet full of imagination,
and sometimes of magnificence. Speaking of an imprisoned magistrate whose release the insurrection-
ists demanded from the Court, and who was set at
liberty: "They would not lay down their arms," says
Retz, "till their object was secured; even Parliament
did not give a Decree to lay them down, until it
saw Broussel in his place. He returned to it on
the morrow, or rather he was borne to it on the
heads of the people with incredible acclamations."
I do not inquire whether the expression is proportioned to Broussel's importance; but how faithfully
it renders the impression, the enthusiasm of the moment! Retz, as you can well suppose, is not the
dupe of it; and immediately showing us Paris after
its Broussel is restored to it, as "more tranquil than

I ever saw it on a Good Friday" he makes us feel the contrasting absurdity without expressing it.

"The Court felt itself hit in the very pupil of its eye," he says, àpropos of the suppression of intendants, discussed in the collective assembly of the Courts of Parliament; he is full of such lively and perceptive expressions. At other times he expands his images agreeably. He excels in giving to words their full value of meaning, all their quality, and he sometimes makes it better felt in thus developing it. After having said that President Molé was "all of a piece," a good but common expression, he adds: "President de Mesmes, who was at least as well intentioned to the Court as he, but who had more insight, more *jointure,* whispered in his ear. . . ." There is an instance of how a new expression is legitimately created, how it is drawn from some ordinary term. Retz's pen does many such things without taking heed of them, without even thinking of them. He had the gift of speech, and that which pictured itself in his mind made but one bound on to his paper. I ought to add that there are many inequalities in his volumes. The last are languid; the first are strewn, even to affectation (the only instance of it) with political maxims that Chesterfield said were the only just and the only practical ones he had ever seen printed. They would teach experience, if experience were ever learned from books. They at least recall it, and sum it up in a striking manner for those who have seen and lived.

I am astonished that many persons find in these Memoirs of Retz instigations to civil disorders and seditious intrigue. Rightly read, they are more likely to give a disgust for them. But every man reads with his own humour and his own imagination even more than with his judgment. What is well told is seductive, though the thing told may be detestable, and the relator, after the first moment of enthusiasm is past, may not attempt to embellish it.

We will not confine ourselves to the opening of the Memoirs, as so many people do; let us go farther and follow the skilful rebel beyond that honeymoon of the Fronde. What hindrances! what impossibilities! what meannesses! what shame! On the morrow of the Barricades, the queen-regent, the young king, with Mazarin and the Court having fled from Paris (January, 1649), what will the Coadjutor, the tribune of the people, the master of the pavements do? he, having for ally on one side Parliament, that machine so little easy to guide, and on the other those princes of the blood and the nobles of the kingdom (the Bouillons, the Contis, the Longuevilles), who had joined the faction with personal objects only.

Among the numerous pamphlets published at this date, one is rather curious, with an official character, and has for its title: "Contract of Marriage between

Parliament and the City of Paris." It is a species of
Charter under the form of contract and in the style of
a notary.   We read in it the aspiration and the programme of the opening moments of the Fronde: "In
the name of God the Creator," it is declared that "the
wise and illustrious seigneur, the Parliament of Paris,
takes for wife and legitimate spouse the powerful and
good dame, the City of Paris, as likewise the said dame
takes etc., etc., to be, the said seigneur and dame,
joined and united perpetually and indissolubly." The
couple pledge themselves to be henceforth "one and
in common as to all their desires, actions, passions,
and interests whatsoever," for the greatest good of the
State and for the preservation of the king and the
kingdom.   Then follows a list of the principal clauses
agreed upon by the contracting parties:

"That God shall be always served and honoured, feared and loved
as he should be.
"That all atheists, ungodly, licentious and sacrilegious persons shall
be punished in an exemplary manner, and exterminated wholly.
"That vices, crimes, and scandals shall be corrected as much as possible, etc.
"That the good of the State and the preservation of the king and
the kingdom shall be," etc.

I abridge.   But behind these first articles which are
merely for show and blazon, come others far more
essential, for instance: that in view of the tender age
of the young king the Parliament of Paris shall select
for the government of the State illustrious persons,
drawn from the three classes, clergy, nobles, and mag-

istrates, who shall be, after the princes of the blood, the natural councillors and ministers of the Regency. In short, the effect of all the articles is, that Parliament should govern during the minority; that when it demanded the dismissal of any minister or councillor there should be no opposition; that an exemplary reform be introduced into the management of the finances, into the distribution of benefices, into appointments to the various offices, into the levying and collecting of taxes; in short, that "the poor people shall be effectively and really relieved, that order in all things shall be restored, and the reign of justice fully re-established in all the provinces of the kingdom."

The conclusion and the end to which the whole necessarily comes is that Cardinal Mazarin was incompatible with this golden age, this reign of Justice upon the earth, and that "he shall be incessantly prosecuted until he be brought under the arm of the Law to be publicly and exemplarily executed."

The final clause is thus worded :

" For thus have promised and sworn the said seigneur Parliament and the said dame City of Paris on the Holy Gospels and before the church of Notre-Dame, in the month of January in the year one thousand six hundred and forty-nine, and is signed," etc.

It was Retz himself who, in his character of Coadjutor, gave the benediction to this famous marriage which presented itself under such magnificent auspices. But what did he think of it himself?

During the first weeks we can see the idea he had

of the real state of affairs in the shrewd and very serious
conversations he held with the Duc de Bouillon, Turenne's elder brother, and the best head among the
nobles who had joined the faction. Retz, who knows
his Paris better than any one, lays bare to the
Duc de Bouillon all the divisions and the probable
causes of ruin: "The bulk of the people that are
firm," he says, " keeps us from perceiving as yet the
dislocation of parties." But he himself feels this dislocation, *disunion,* to be very near if care is not taken,
and he lays his finger upon it better in his words than
by his açts. Less than six weeks after the breaking
out of the first Fronde, he said, energetically:

" A people are weary some time before they perceive that they are
so.   The hatred against Mazarin sustained and covered that weariness.
We divert their minds by our satires, our verses, our songs; the blare of
trumpets, drums and cymbals, the sight of flags and banners rejoice
the shops in the streets, but, after all, are the taxes paid with the same
punctuality as at first ? "

The taxes — there 's the delicate point to which one
must always return if one wants to organise any kind
of order on the morrow of a revolt; and the first cry
of a revolt is that it is made in behalf of a relief that is
often impossible to grant.

Retz reveals to the Duc de Bouillon his whole
policy under the first Fronde, and we must do him
this justice: if he was seditious, he was only half so.
In concert with the Duc de Beaufort, he made himself master of the populace, he held it in his hand

and it proved but a phantom; he is the idol of the churches as the duke was of the markets. But he will not abuse "this mania of the people," he says, "for M. de Beaufort and for me." He resists firmly the idea of doing without the Parliament, of crushing it by the people, of "purging it" violently, as some advised. Such proceedings of the days of the League horrify him; he leaves such things to the Seize and to sanguinary ambitions. He has no less horror of them than of Cromwell, whose advances he repulsed, just as he objected at all times to a close and complete union with Spain.

It was not that he concealed from himself the hidden intentions of Parliament or the proceedings of its companies; in spite of the fine words that are said on great occasions, "the foundation of the spirit of Parliament is peace, and it never gets far from it except by fits and starts," which are quickly followed by returns. He knows that that Assembly, the slave to rules and formulas, understands no way of making war except by Decrees and by bailiffs; that the loudest thunders of its eloquence end in nothing more than inquests and edicts; that nothing can prevent it from adjourning when midday and five o'clock, the sacramental hours for dinner and supper, strike. In vain may Retz have "the lanterns" (the tribunes of those days) for him; in vain does he have the young heads in Parliament, and the bench of Inquests at his feet; that "holy mob," as he calls it, which knows so well how to shout when the word of command is given, can do nothing in Parliament, where President Molé is not to be led.

What Retz would fain have had, to act upon the mind of that Assembly, to excite it sufficiently without oppressing it, was an army, not in Paris but outside of Paris; an army, a veritable army in the service of the Fronde; he could have cried, like the Abbé Sieyès: "Oh for a sword!" At one moment he thought he had that of M. de Turenne; he might have chosen worse; but it failed him. According to his idea, an army at some distance and a general of renown would act upon Parliament and give him needed energy without threatening it; whereas the action of the populace of Paris is too dangerous, too immediate. Retz, who has it at his disposal, fears to employ it, for such blind forces are apt to strike without warning. " That is the fate and the misfortune of popular powers," he remarks; "they are not believed in till they make themselves felt; and it is very often to the interest and even to the honour of those in whose hands they are to make them less felt than believed in."

The other evils of the civil war that he himself had lighted Retz confesses without reserve. One of the first articles of the Contract of Marriage between Parliament and the City of Paris was, as we have seen, that atheists and licentious persons should be repressed and punished; but one of the actual effects of the Fronde was to let loose licentiousness, a mortal injury to any state of things that seeks to establish and consolidate itself. Speaking of the debauchery of Fontrailles, Matha, and other free-thinkers:

" Their table songs," he says, " did not always spare the good God; I cannot express to you the trouble such follies gave me. President Molé knew very well how to put them in evidence, the people did not really think them good in any way, the clergy were scandalised to the last degree. I could not cover them, I dared not excuse them, and the odium fell, of course, on the Fronde."

Farther on he says: "We had an interest in not stifling the libels and ballads that were made against the cardinal, but we had no less an interest in suppressing those against the queen, and sometimes against religion and the State. No one can imagine the trouble the heated minds of the people gave us in this matter." This was how they kept to the first article of their Contract of Marriage! In short, every page of the Memoirs only confirms this truth: "the greatest misfortune of civil war is that we are responsible for the evil that we do not do."

But, once committed, they are compelled to do it. In more than one case, Retz finds himself compromised and just escapes being discredited with the people and with the hot-heads in Parliament by opposing absurd measures or acts of rapine and vandalism, such as the sale of Cardinal Mazarin's library. He is quickly obliged to repair these good promptings by himself proposing some folly; this is what shows very naturally, he says, "the extravagance of such periods, when all the fools go mad and it is no longer possible for people of sense to speak or act wisely."

After the first Fronde was pacified and before the second broke out, Retz seems to have had, at moments, a sincere intention to reform and become once more an honest man and a faithful subject; but his past reputation weighed upon him, also his acquired habits, and before long he was again involved in the ways of sedition. They distrusted him at Court, and this suspicion provoked him in the end to justify anew that distrust. In all his relations with Queen Anne of Austria there happened to Retz what happened to Mirabeau in his relations with Queen Marie Antoinette. He felt there was no reliance placed upon him; that he was taken solely from a necessity of the occasion. He was a man who would have felt a wholly generous treatment by the queen, or even by Mazarin, and one of his keenest grievances against the latter was that, with plenty of mind, he was absolutely lacking in generosity and soul, and that, supposing others to be like himself, he never believed they would give him advice with good intentions.

Like Mirabeau, Retz could render services to the queen only by maintaining his credit with the multitude; and to maintain that credit he had to do ostensibly certain acts and make certain speeches that savoured of sedition, and seemed the exact opposite of the engagements he had just taken. It was only

too easy to make cause against him at Court and
to present him as a traitor and renegade, at the very
moment when he was merely employing the means
at his command for a secret end that was honourable.

At the time of the multiplied conferences that he
had at night with the queen in the Palais-Royal and
elsewhere, it is to be supposed that in those mysterious oratories where she received him in order to
confer more freely, he tried to interest the woman
in the queen; that he looked often at her beautiful hands, of which Mme. de Motteville tells us, that
at times he replied with a dreamy, abstracted air to
questions of even policy; but the queen's coquetry
was not caught by such wiles; her heart was fixed.
Retz felt he could never displace Mazarin. But he
was not, it would seem, quick enough in feeling it,
and he continued to act outside as if he still had hope
of getting the cardinal finally sent away. A jest
which he allowed to escape him against the queen
and which came to her ears (he called her *Suissesse)*
irritated her as a woman and contributed more, perhaps, to her final vengeance than the political infidel-
ities of the man could have done.

He always denied that he aspired to the ministry,
and the reasons he gave are energetic enough to
strike us, if not to convince us. To one of these
advances, true or false, that were made to him, he
replied that " he was very incapable of the ministry
for all sorts of reasons, and that it was even not for

the queen's dignity to raise to that post a man who
was *still hot and smoking, so to speak, with faction.''*
Elsewhere, he opens himself on this point with a
tone of sincerity even more fitted to convince us; this
was at the close of the second Fronde, in which he
pursued a very different line of conduct from that
he followed in the first; nevertheless that first reputation as an ambitious man with a mailed hand followed him always.

" Is it possible," people said, ascribing to him a yearning for the
ministry, " is it possible that Cardinal de Retz is not content with
being at his age " (he was thirty-seven) " cardinal and archbishop of
Paris ? And how did he get into his mind that the first place in the
king's council is to be conquered by force of arms ? " — " I know,"
he adds, " that even to-day the miserable gazettes which treat of
that period are full of these ridiculous ideas "; and he speaks of those
ideas as being very far from his; " I do not say this by force of
reason only, but I say it from my own inclination, which leads me
with such eagerness to pleasure and to fame. . . ." And he
concludes that the ministry was even less to his taste than within
his reach: " I do not know if I am making my excuses to you,"
he writes, addressing Mme. de Caumartin; " at any rate, I do not
think that I am writing you my eulogy."

This fame, this point of honour, of which Retz
speaks so often, and which he felt after his fashion,
lay in winning a certain popular reputation, the favour
and love of the public; in being faithful to his promises to friends; in seeming never to yield to direct
self-interest. Towards the end, his whole doctrine
of resistance seems to have been little more than a
wager of honour against Mazarin.

The second Fronde (1650–1652) broke out, as we

know, in the name of the princes of Condé, whom
Mazarin had put in prison and was presently obliged
to release. In this second period of the troubles Cardinal de Retz, far from being an agitator and a firebrand,
as too generally believed, was rather a negotiator and
moderator, barely listened to. *Monsieur*, Gaston, Duc
d'Orléans, lieutenant-general of the kingdom, was
seized with a sudden confidence in him, and made
him his intimate counsellor. But when we reflect on
what *Monsieur* was, timid, distrustful, dissimulating,
changing his opinion many times a day, whistling
when he did not know what to say, and employing
his whole mind in hiding his cowardice by inventing
creep-holes, we can readily explain to ourselves the
perplexity and daily embarrassments of Retz. The
weakness of *Monsieur* had various degrees and
"stages," he tells us, and he makes us measure and
count them, one by one. "In him, *fancies* and *will,
will* and *resolution, resolution* and *choice of means,
choice of means* and their *application* were very far
apart. But what was more extraordinary, it happened
quite often that he stopped short in the *middle of the
application.*"

Placed between a prince of this nature and Parliament (that other complicated machine, not less dis-
heartening to influence) ranked in the party by the
Prince de Condé, then his enemy, and whose triumph
he could not desire, Retz consumed himself during two years in parleys, expedients, the perpetual

attempts of an impotent third party to come to birth,
resulting always in miscarriage. What wise maxims
he strews, to no purpose, along the way! What
penetrating glances on the truths of the situation and
the wretchedness of parties! How many times did
he not have occasion to cry out as he quitted the
sessions of Parliament: "Nothing is more *mob* than
these Assemblies! . . . The wisest among them
seem as mad as the populace, and the populace seems
to me more mad than ever." The gaiety of certain
parts of his narrative covers very incompletely his disgust at this anarchic, inconsistent régime, which those
who had plunged into it could not, from a too common optical illusion, perceive.

Retz, whom nothing escapes, is nauseated by it,
again and again. We ask ourselves, in reading him,
how it was that some fine morning, a good sentiment,
a rush of energetic sound sense, of integrity, were it
even no more than a fit of impatience and weariness,
did not decide him to break, once for all, with that
inextricable complication of intrigues, henceforth
without object and without issue. Here it is that the
vices of the man come into line and find their profit.
Retz, while judging the depth of the things he de-
spises, did not dislike the game nor the gambling.
He had brought himself to a disorderly and licentious
manner of living. Every evening, the hôtel de Chevreuse, or some other clandestine amusement, consoled
him for his daily annoyances and for the ruin of the

State. Such, in men of superior minds, is the evil of vices; they quench good aspirations at their source and prevent them from coming to birth. The time came at last when Retz, retiring, toward the end of the troubles, into his cloister of Notre-Dame, withdrawn into the shadow of his cathedral towers, sheltered, as he says, by the hat, hesitated, with all his lights and his worldly generosities, to do a public act that would hasten the issue and put an end to the universal suffering. He brought himself to do it, however, and was one of the chief negotiators for the return of the Court to Paris.

For this he was poorly thanked; his past reputation clung to him, not without cause, and he was treated solely on political grounds; that is to say, having used him in the first moments they imprisoned him in the next.

His imprisonment, his flight, his stay in Rome, his journeys, his career of dissipation in divers regions, his obstinacy to the last in retaining his see of the archbishopric of Paris, supply us with too many aspects of his frailties and the weaker side of his nature. One of his counsellors and servants, Gui Joly, has given us in his Memoirs very shameful details, which may be true as to material facts, but which are false inasmuch as they are solely base, which Retz was not. He had in him certain generous parts that never perished, and of which he gave proof in his old age, after his return to France. His peace made, and his pardon obtained, he had permission, after a rather long stay in his seigneurie in Lorraine, to reappear in Paris and at Fontainebleau (1664). There he once more met all his friends and many of his enemies, with whom he reconciled himself frankly. We now find a Cardinal de Retz quite different (save for beauty of mind) to what he had hitherto appeared. "If he lived like a Catiline in his youth," says Voltaire, "in his old age he. lived like Atticus."

It is Mme. de Sévigné who best enables us to know Cardinal de Retz after his return and makes us like him. She is inexhaustible on that subject. Retz had won her by showing an especial affection for Mme. de Grignan. If he came to Paris without seeing her he was not to be comforted: "You make him wish for the Pope's death," writes Mme. de Sévigné. When the Pope died, Cardinal de Retz did not fail to go to the Conclave to sedulously serve the interests of Louis XIV, and, as he passed through Provence, he was able to see Mme. de Grignan. Though not of advanced age, being still under sixty, he was much worn out in health. Mme. de Sévigné worked with all her might to entertain him:

"We try to amuse our good cardinal," she writes (March 9, 1672). "Corneille read him a play that is to be acted before long; it reminded him of the classics; Molière is to read him *Trissotin* on Saturday, which is a very amusing thing; Despréaux [Boileau] is to give him his *Lutrin* and his *Poétique ;* that is all we can do to serve him."

Incomparable and for ever blessed age, in which the

illustrious shipwrecked in politics had, by way of consolation, in one week a Corneille, a Boileau and a Moliére in the flesh, their works in hand, and Mme. de Sévigné above all to tell of it!

This man who, as I have said, had never been more than half-seditious, and by no means a Catiline, as Voltaire calls him, and who, in his greatest rebellion, had always respected (in all that regarded the royal authority) what he called "the claim of the sanctuary," had now become the most reconciled and the most zealous of the French cardinals for the interests of Louis XIV. In spite of his increasing infirmities, he made three journeys to Rome (in 1667, 1669, and 1676) to support and make effective in the Conclave the intentions of the king.

In 1675, he was seized with an idea which seemed extraordinary, and caused great wonder among his contemporaries: it was to renounce the hat, and strip himself of the dignity of cardinal, to go and live in Lorraine in absolute solitude. The policy of Rome and that of France united to oppose a sort of renunciation which might have become a precedent and, in the future, a political means in the hands of the powers. Retz was forced to resign himself to keep the hat and to remain for his friends the "very good cardinal." He reduced his expenses by a great deal with the laudable object of paying all his debts, on which he staked his honour. This last and brusque idea of a solemn humility which looked like repentance, gave rise to much talk and various opinions:

"I see none, thank God," writes Mme. de Sévigné (July 24, 1675), "but those who view his action in all its beauty, and who love him as we do. His friends do not wish him to nail himself at Saint-Mihiel; they advise him to go to Commercy and sometimes to Saint-Denis. He will keep his equipage for the honour of the purple; and I gaily persuade that his life is not ended."

Every one, on this occasion, wrote to him to compliment him on the grandeur of his action. The exiled Bussy-Rabutin, who judged that action more philosophically, wrote him, nevertheless, a letter full of eulogy. Mme. de Sévigné advised her daughter to write to him on the subject and renew their correspondence by that means: "In writing to him this first letter, do not, believe me, feel too constrained; if some nonsense flows off the tip of your pen he will be as charmed as with things more serious: the solid foundation of religion does not forbid such little *trimmings*."

Better or worse than *trimmings* were the Memoirs in which the cardinal took secret delight, and which, at this date, he had just completed in obedience to Mme. de Caumartin, who asked him for the narrative of his life. It is difficult to admit that the man who wrote them was the least in the world touched by a single religious thought. And yet, as it is supposed that the last parts were written towards this period, 1675–1676, it would be rash to say that thoughts of that kind did not end by germi-

nating in the soul of Cardinal de Retz. Suffice it
that several of his contemporaries, those who approached him closely, seem to have believed in his
final persuasion of Christianity and a future life,
enough, at any rate, to impose upon us respect and
reserve on that vital point.

Towards the end, Retz amused his leisure at Commercy by conversing and discoursing on the philosophy of Descartes, then in its greatest vogue. A
certain Dom Robert Desgabets, prior of the abbey
of Breuil, situated in a faubourg of Commercy, was
a semi-emancipated Carthusian who assumed to
rectify nature. Dom Hennezon, abbé of Saint-Mihiel,
three leagues distant, disapproved of these pretended
rectifications of Dom Desgabets. Hence a regular
philosophical dispute, in which the disputants took
the good cardinal as umpire. M. Cousin has published the very judicious and prudent decision of
Retz. His conclusion on the fundamental question
of this metaphysic was, all points being carefully examined, that " *no one knew anything about it.*" This
great *frondeur* who, in his youth, had tried in vain to
hold the scales between all parties, between *Monsieur,*
the Parliament and the Court, and who, in default
of scales had taken the sword, and taken it even
against the Prince de Condé, came in his old age to
this innocent arbitrament.

The retirement of Cardinal de Retz into Lorraine did
not last long; he returned to his abbey of Saint-Denis.

The scoffers tattled, and tried to see in this return an infraction of his great design. Mme. de Sévigné has amply justified him:

> "You know," she writes to Bussy, who asked nothing better than to be one of the scoffers (June 27, 1678), "you know that he has paid off eleven hundred thousand crowns. He received from no one this example, and no one will follow it. In short, we must trust him in order to maintain our wager. He is much more regular than he was in Lorraine. Those who want to be rid of him can be so as much at Saint-Denis as if he had stayed at Commercy."

He died August 24, 1678, tenderly regretted by Mme. de Sévigné, and praised by her in terms that are the finest of funeral orations, leaving us an idea of the most amiable of men, of easy intercourse, a delightful and perfect friend. Thus ended, with sweetness and dignity, one who never had within him that which was necessary to make him a complete revolutionist; and one who, in his boldest schemes, always stopped half-way on this side of Cromwell or Machiavelli. I mark this as being at once a defect and a claim to eulogy.

An idea has entered my mind within the last few minutes,—I cannot resist expressing it. We are reaching an epoch of desires and prayers; I will offer mine—

May all factious persons, all agitators, all those who have passed their lives in stirring up parliaments and people, end them as sweetly and decently as did Cardinal de Retz; may they range themselves, as he did, under the law of necessity and of their period; play, like him, at whist when growing old, at the philosophy of their time (if there be still a philosophy); continue, or become again, perfectly amiable; converse with the Sévignés, if they meet any; and, in writing their Memoirs, fill them, as he did, with the maxims of experience, rendering them piquant, amusing, instructive, but not so captivating that they instil a desire to imitate and renew their follies.

VII.

Mademoiselle de l' Enclos.

VII.

Mademoiselle de l'Enclos.

" Ninon."

THERE is no better introducer to Ninon than Saint-Évremond, an amiable wise man, a mind of the first quality for good sense, and one that can enter into all the graces. His natural character is one of easy superiority; I cannot define him better than by calling him a sort of softened Montaigne. His mind is distinguished alike for its firmness and its delicacy; his soul is never forced out of itself or its habits. He felt the passions, he let them come to birth; up to a certain point, he nurtured them, but he never blindly gave way to them; even in yielding he did so with discernment and restraint. In his youth he had been, like all the flower of the Court, in Ninon's train, her lover a little, and much her friend; he corresponded with her at times throughout his long exile; the small number of authentic letters that we have by Ninon are addressed to Saint-Évre_mond, and they make us know her on the mental side, the only side on which she deserves to survive.

Saint-Évremond requires a Study on himself alone; to-day all I ask of him is the favour of being introduced into the intimacy of a woman, who, through a long life, renewed her charm so many times, and whose mind continued to perfect itself even to the end.

Saint-Évremond, born in 1613, was three years older than Ninon, who was born in 1616; he died in 1703 at an age of over ninety, and she in 1705 at the same age, less a few months. His life divides itself into two very distinct halves. Until he was forty-eight he led, in France, at Court, with the army, a brilliant and active existence, esteemed by all the great generals, and on the road to some distinguished military fortune. A long letter of his, very witty and very malicious, on the Treaty of the Pyrenees and against Cardinal Mazarin, found among the papers of Mme. Duplessis-Bellière at the time of Fouquet's arrest, irritated Louis XIV, who gave orders to put the writer in the Bastille. Warned in time, Saint-Évremond left France, took refuge in Holland, then in England, where he lived, forty-two years longer, the life of an observer and philosopher; much enjoyed and sought by the highest society, seeing all that was best in foreign lands, and bearing his exile with real pride and apparent indifference. A thing that contributed much to soften it was the arrival in England of the beautiful Duchesse de Mazarin, Hortense Mancini, the niece of the very man who was the original cause of his misfortune. He attached himself to her, and loved

MADEMOISELLE DE L'ENCLOS
From a portrait by Mignard

her for her mind and her solid qualities as much as for
her beauty.   All the nieces of the cardinal had the
singular gift of charm; a magic, as it were.   "The
source of their charm is in the Mazarin blood," said
Ninon.   The Duchesse de Mazarin was an essential
part of Saint-Évremond's life; more essential than
Ninon herself.

The greatest pleasure of Saint-Évremond, that which
he most delighted in from his youth, during the age
of passions, and which grew dearer to him daily as
he aged, was conversation: "Whatever pleasure I
take in reading," he said, "that of conversation will
always be to me the keenest.   Intercourse with
women would be to me the sweetest if the pleasure
we find in their amiability did not involve the pain of
forbidding ourselves to love them."   And he points
out of what sort and in what spirit the ordinary intercourse with women should be in order to please
them:

"The first merit in the eyes of women, is to love them; the second
is to enter into the confidence of their inclinations; the third, to in-
geniously put all they have that is most charming in its best light.   If
nothing leads us into the secret places of the heart, we must at least
win their minds by praises; for, in default of lovers to whom all is
yielded, he will please best who gives them the means of pleasing
themselves most."

The precepts that he lays down for pleasing and interesting women in conversation are the result of the
most consummate experience:

"In conversation, remember, never allow women to become indifferent; their soul is inimicable to such languor; either make yourself loved, or flatter them on what they love, or lead them to find within them something that shall make them love themselves more; for, after all, what they want is love, of whatever nature it may be; their heart is never void of that passion."

If that is the ordinary condition of women, even the most intellectual, their merit is all the greater when they are able to emancipate themselves from the habitual moving springs of their sex, without losing anything of their grace. Saint-Évremond had met with such rare women, and we can readily divine that he thought of them when he wrote:

" Some we find, truly, who gain esteem and tenderness even without love; some are as capable of secresy and strict confidence as the most faithful of our male friends. I have known some who have not less mind and discretion than charm and beauty; but they are exceptions that nature, by design or caprice, takes pleasure in sometimes giving us. . . .   These unusual women seem to have borrowed the merit of men; perhaps they do a species of infidelity to their sex in passing thus from their natural condition into the true advantages of ours."

In an ideal Portrait that he makes of "the Woman who is never found," he finds pleasure in uniting on the head of an Émilie of his own invention all the qualities most difficult to combine and most opposite:

" This is the Portrait," he says, as he ends, " of the Woman who is never found and never will be found, if a portrait can be made of a thing that is not. It is, rather, the idea of a perfected being. I do not look for it among men, because there always lacks in their intercourse a something, I know not what, of gentleness, which we find in that of women. I think it less impossible to find in a woman the sound, strong reason of men, than to find in men the charm and the natural graces of woman."

That sound reason, that sensible mind, joined to sportiveness and charm, he had found in Ninon, and this feature in the Portrait of Émilie was not by any means a purely imaginary idea.

Let us now see what this Ninon, so celebrated, was; and let us look at her on the side that gives her, justly, a place in the history of Letters and of French society. Let us see her—profane* that I am, I was about to say, let us study her—in the species of influence by which she corrected the tone of the hôtel de Rambouillet and the *Précieuses,* and seconded the judicious action of Mme. de La Fayette.

I have sometimes heard it asked why I like to busy myself so much about these amiable and clever women of the past, and take such pains to put them in their true light. Without counting the disinterested pleasure there is in resuscitating for a while in idea that choice company, I shall make answer in the words of Goethe, the great critic of our age:

"It would be," he said, speaking of Mme. de Tencin, "most interesting to follow her history and that of the celebrated women who presided over the different societies of Paris in the eighteenth century: such as Mme. Geoffrin, Mme. du Deffand, Mlle. de Lespinasse, etc.; we should gather details useful to a knowledge of the French character and mind in particular, and of human nature in general; for such details would connect themselves with other times equally honourable to both."

I try, according to my capacity, to carry out, in a way, this programme of Goethe; for if he said that of the eighteenth century, I can say it with even stronger reason of the seventeenth, in which there was, on the part of the celebrated women who influenced it, still more initiative and personal originality. In the matter of polite society and conversation the eighteenth century had only to expand, regulate, and perfect that which the seventeenth had previously founded and established.

Before coming to be, in the end, a personage almost respectable, Ninon had one or two anterior epochs on which I shall merely touch. Mlle. Anne de l'Enclos (for Ninon is only a diminutive), born in Paris, May 15, 1616, of a father who was a nobleman, duellist, intriguer, free-thinker, musician, and man of pleasure, and of a mother strict and severe, was left an orphan at fifteen years of age, and much inclined to enjoy her liberty with a boldness, seasoned with wit and tempered by taste, which was soon to recall the existence of the courtesans of Greece.

There was in France at that period a school of epicureanism and scepticism represented in science by Gassendi and La Mothe Le Vayer; in Letters and in society by Des Yveteaux, Des Barreaux, and many others. Montaigne and Charron were the authors in vogue, and their spirit aided this liberty of opinion. Ninon was among the first of the women to emancipate herself, to profess that there is at bottom one and the same morality for men and women; that in reducing, as was done by society, all the virtues of women to one single virtue, her sex was depreciated, and wrong and injury were done to it by seeming to exclude it totally from the practice of integrity — that male and universal virtue which combines all others; also that integrity is compatible in a woman with the infraction of what society agrees to call the one virtue. "The virtue of women is the finest invention of men"; that singular saying of a witty muse of our day seems stolen from Ninon. We can take in at a glance that whole code of morality, which is much less novel in these days when it has become a rather vulgar commonplace. In the days of Ninon, it was still only an audacity, an exception wholly individual, a daring wager she made it a duty to sustain, all the while giving herself up to inconstancy and variety in her likings. What did she, or rather what did she not do in those days? What did she not permit herself in those wild moments? What caprice did she ever deny herself? The list of her conquests goes everywhere, and however long we make it, it still is left incomplete.

That Ninon, rival and heiress of Marion Delorme, is not to detain us here. I send inquirers to history, to legends, to all that was said, invented, and embroidered upon that topic. "If this mania continues," wrote Voltaire, "we shall soon have as many Histories of Ninon as of Louis XIV." Tallemant des Réaux gives the chronicle in its nudity, and with very circumstantial details. M. Walckenaer, in volumes i and iv of his excellent Memoirs of Mme. de Sévigné, has very well established what may be called the "Chronology of Ninon." The succession of her lovers has been discussed and regulated very much as that of the Assyrian or Egyptian kings. What is certain is, that in the midst of this license, where she allowed the passions to have so large a part, she imposed certain limits upon herself, and governed herself up to a certain point. Her reason gave proof of its solidity in her judgments; her wildest sallies often covered a sound good sense. She reflected at an age and in a way of life where others are scarcely able to think at all; and she, who remained young to old age, through her mind, was matured by that mind in her youth.

Nevertheless, there were moments when very little hindered her capricious and violent existence from running upon the rocks on which her sisterhood are usually shipwrecked and from which the most skilful find no return. The time came, under the Regency of Anne of Austria, when Ninon's laxity, encouraged by that of the times, passed all bounds and was on the point of causing a public scandal. In those days nothing was needed but a pretext, a chance event, for. society and public morality, defied in its principles, its most respectable prejudices, to rise at last and begin reprisals, often brutal but in part deserved. The queen-regent was solicited to take severe action against the sinful woman. It was no small service to Ninon that in this conjuncture the Prince de Condé, once her lover and her friend always, interposed in person to give her at Court and elsewhere public proofs of interest. On one occasion, meeting her in her carriage, he stopped his own, got out, and went, hat in hand, to salute her in presence of the astonished crowd. Such marks of consideration were still all-powerful.

Ninon was said about this time to be on the eve of departure for Cayenne, where a great number of emigrants of all classes were induced to go. It is permissible to suppose that in her case this was only a pretence to quiet the anger of her enemies and give a signal to her friends to assist her. She did not go; she continued the same life, slightly moderating its tone. From the Marais, where she lived at first, she had moved to the Faubourg Saint-Germain, where she spent the period of her greatest license. She now returned to the Marais, and there, surrounded by friends, lived as she pleased; but, warned by the air from without and the reigning influence of Louis XIV, she regulated her life and reduced it, little by little, to the honourable footing on which it ended, so that even the severe Saint-Simon said of her:

" Ninon had illustrious friends of all sorts, and so much intelligence herself that she kept them all, and held them united with one another, or at any rate without clashing. Everything at her house was conducted with a respect and outward decency that many of the highest princesses rarely sustained without failure. She had in this way as friends the choicest and most distinguished persons at Court; so that it became the fashion to be received by her; and people had reason to desire it on account of the intimacies there formed. Never any cards,

or loud laughter, or disputes, or discussions of religion or government;
much wit and graceful talk, news of the past and modern news, social
news of gallantries, etc., but always without opening the door to
malice or evil-speaking; all was delicate, lightsome, restrained, forming conversations she knew well how to sustain by her wit and by
what she knew of events of all periods. The consideration — strange
fact! — which she had acquired, the number and distinction of her
friends and acquaintance, continued to attract society to her when
charms were past and when the proprieties of life forbade her from any
longer mingling body with mind. Her conversation was charming;
Disinterested, faithful, discreet, safe to the last degree; and, frailty
apart, she may be said to have been virtuous and full of integrity.
.   .   .   These things gave her reputation, and a respect that was
altogether singular."

To use a comparison that is not disproportionate,
and to which that term *integrity* so often applied
leads naturally, we may say that Ninon kept, throughout her intrigues and gallantries, something of that
frankness, that uprightness, which the Princess Palatine was able to preserve through the Fronde in the
midst of so many political factions.

Tallemant des Réaux says a remarkable thing about
Ninon, —that " she never had much beauty, but, above
all, she had *charm.*" Somaize in his *Dictionnaire
des Précieuses* says about the same thing: "As for
beauty, though we know she has enough to give
love, we must admit that her mind is more charming
than her face, and that many would escape her chains
if they merely saw her." As soon as she spoke all
were captured and enchanted; it was her mind, her
wit that completed her beauty and gave it its expression and power. The same in music when she

played the lute; she preferred a touching expression to the most scientific execution: "Sensibility," she said, "is the soul of song."

So many Portraits have been written of Ninon that I shall content myself with mentioning one that shows her to us in her youth, in her most favourable and decent light. It is that of Mlle. de Scudéry who, in her novel of *Clélie*, must surely have painted Ninon under the mask of Clarice. The resemblance in many of the essential features makes me believe that the true key of this Portrait, so little known, is the one I indicate:

" The amiable Clarice is, undoubtedly, one of the most charming persons in the world, whose spirit and humour have a very particular character; but before engaging myself to depict them to you, I must tell you something about her beauty. Clarice has a very beautiful figure, of agreeable height, capable of pleasing every one by a certain free and natural air which gives her good grace. She has hair of the finest chestnut ever seen, her face is round, the complexion bright, the mouth agreeable, the lips rosy, a little dimple on her chin becomes her well, the eyes are black and brilliant, full of fire, smiling, and the countenance refined, gay, and very intelligent. . . . As for mind, Clarice undoubtedly has much, and she has even a certain style of it of which few persons are capable ; for with her it is gay, diverting, and accommodates itself to all classes of people, principally to people in society. She speaks readily ; she laughs easily; she makes a great pleasure of a trifle; she likes to make innocent war upon her friends. . . . But, amid all this inclination that she has for joy, we must say that this amiable, sprightly being has the good qualities of melancholy persons who are well brought up ; her heart is feeling and tender; she knows how to weep with afflicted friends ; she knows how to quit her pleasures when friendship requires it ; she is faithful to her friends ; she is capable of secrecy and discretion ; she never makes a quarrel with any one, no matter who ; she is generous and constant in her feelings;

and she is so lovable that she is beloved by all the best persons of
the Court of both sexes, by persons who do not resemble one another
in condition, in temper, in spirit, in interests, but who all agree,
nevertheless, that Clarice is very charming, that she has intellect,
veritable kindness, and many other qualities worthy of being infinitely esteemed."

There is Ninon young; such as she may have
appeared to friendship in the days when she frequented the society of the *Précieuses;* she, who was
so little like them; she who, talking with Queen
Christina, defined them so well in a word: "The
Précieuses" she said, "are the Jansenists of love."
But, with a mind all the more apart from theirs because it was her very own, she knew how to accommodate herself to all, so that she found grace,
at need, and favour even in the eyes of the hôtel de
Rambouillet, and paid Molière in his own coin when
he consulted her about Tartuffe.

Mlle. de Scudéry's Portrait of Ninon may give us,
perhaps, too softened and weakened an idea of her;
she had, on the contrary, great animation, gushes of
wit and piquancy. Joy was the basis of her soul,
and the expression, as it were, of the health of her
mind; it was she who wrote to Saint-Évremond:
"The joy of the spirit shows its strength." They
said of her that at table she "was drunk from the
soup" so gay and merry was she, drunk with bright
humour and sallies, for she herself drank nothing but
water, and drunkards, even though their names were
Chapelle or Vendôme, were never welcomed in her

house. It was one of her maxims that "in life we should make provision for food only, never for pleasures, but take them day by day as they came"; and she used to declare that "wrinkles would be much more in place under heel than on the face." She had a keen sense of the ridiculous, she caught people at a glance and described them in a word. She said of Mme. de Choiseul who dressed her hair absurdly: "She is as like the spring-time of an inn as two drops of water."[1] She said of the poor little Chevalier de Sévigné who, between Ninon and the actress Champmeslé, had engaged himself to more than he could well perform: "He is a pumpkin fricasseed in snow." And her merry exclamation: *"Oh! le bon billet qu'a la Châtre!"* has passed into a proverb. To the Comte de Choiseul, who annoyed her a little and whom she saw one day after a Court promotion, admiring himself with all his orders in a mirror, she said, before the whole company: "Take care, M. le comte, if I catch you at that again I will name to you your comrades"; the promotion of unworthy persons at the same time with him having

---

[1] *Printemps d'hôtellerie.* These jokes are incomprehensible in English. The one that follows is based on the following story: Her lover, the Marquis de la Châtre, being obliged to leave her and go abroad on a mission, insisted that she should give him, in writing, a promise to be faithful to him. Ninon signed the paper, and then forgot it ; but something bringing it to her mind later, she exclaimed: *"Oh! le bon billet qu'a la Châtre!"* and the saying has passed into the Fr nch language, meaning a worthless guarantee.— Larchey's *Dictionnaire d'argot.*

been deplorable. Attacked in her youth by a serious illness, and her life being despaired of, lamentations were made around her; every one declared that he wished to die, and she, teasing them a little even while trying to comfort them, exclaimed: " Bah! I shall leave only dying men behind me." Her gift of repartee was quick, irresistible; it was delicate, sparkling, piquant. She never quoted for the sake of quoting, but only what came into her mind at the moment, applying it with freshness to the circumstance. Imagination was even in her memory; it showed itself in her narratives: " what were called tales from the lips of others, from hers were perfect scenes, to which, for resemblance of characters and witty turns, nothing was lacking."

It was by all these amiable and brilliant qualities, borne upon a strong foundation of solidity and security in friendship, that she won the suffrages of those who knew her; making some forget that she was growing old, and others that she once was young without ever ceasing to be so. La Fare, that fastidious voluptuary, said:

" I never saw Ninon in her beauty ; but at the age of fifty, and even till she was over sixty she had lovers who adored her, and the most honourable men in France for friends. Until she was ninety she was sought by the best society of her time. She died with all her senses, and with the charms of her mind, which was the best and most lovable I have ever known in a woman."

Mme. de Maintenon, very intimate with Ninon in her

youth, but now on a footing at Court and in the highest favour, writes to her (Versailles, November, 1679) recommending her brother: "Continue, Mademoiselle, to give good advice to M. d'Aubigné; he has great need of lessons from Leontium" [friend of Epicurus: a philosophic nickname given to Ninon] "the advice of an amiable friend persuades better than that of a stern sister."

The letters of Ninon, simple, original, and quite in the tone of her conversation, are very few in number; I know of only a dozen that are authentic, and those are addressed to Saint-Évremond. When he left France in 1661 she seems to have owed him one hundred pistoles. Eight years later she still owed them. Saint-Évremond, then in Holland, seems annoyed at the delay: "Her good faith is strong" (he writes to a M. d'Hervart whom he had seen at The Hague and who had since returned to Paris), "but my absence is long, and after eight years nothing is easier than not to remember people when remembrance would cost a hundred pistoles. Perhaps I am wrong to suspect her of that human weakness." He was wrong. Ninon had proved her integrity by returning to Gourville, after many years, the famous strong-box that the latter had left in her care, interference with which she denied to more than one lover, successor to Gourville, who would have been glad enough to be his heir in all things. At the first reminder of her debt Ninon sent word to Saint-Évremond that he could

have fifty pistoles whenever he pleased. Fifty pistoles
instead of one hundred were not the reckoning of
the exiled philosopher; he thought it was treating
him too like a lover,—that is to say, with semi-un-
faithfulness,—and not as a friend. He made some
joke on the subject which was not very well received.
There was, in fact, a misunderstanding, Ninon having
promised to pay the rest of the sum at a certain date.
Before the time expired she paid the whole, and
plumed herself on being more punctual than Marcus
Aurelius, emperor and philosopher, who never paid
his debts in advance: "That spurs courage," she
wrote to Saint-Évremond; "and when you have
thought it all over you will see that you should not
be sarcastic with a blameless banker. . . . I told
you my charms were changed into solid and serious
qualities, and you know it is not permissible to joke
with such a personage."

This was just at the moment when Ninon, ceasing
to be the Ninon of the Fronde, of the Regency, and of
her first gallantries, was becoming Mlle. de l'Enclos
and passing into the "personage" she perfected more
and more and sustained thenceforth to the end of
her life.

Saint-Évremond, proved in the wrong, and a little
ashamed, no doubt, of his unfair jest, hastens to atone
for it, and writes Ninon a letter in which he praises her
as she deserves, and shows her natural self to us at
this moment of transition and metamorphosis. I will

quote a part of this letter, which is very little known and is not to be found in his "Works :"

"In spite of that old dreamer who thought no one happy till after death, I hold you, full of life as you are, to be the happiest creature that ever was. You have been loved by the most honourable men in the world, and you have loved as long as was needed to leave no pleasure untasted, and just so far as was needed to prevent the disgusts of a wearisome passion. Never has happiness been carried farther by your sex. There are few princesses in the world whom you do not cause to feel the hardness of their fate through jealousy of yours; there are few saints in convents who would not willingly change the tranquillity of their minds for the charming troubles of your soul. Of all the tortures, you have felt none but those of love, and you know better than any one that in love no other pleasures are worth 'its pains.' To-day, when the flower of your great youth has passed (the words are rough, but you have written them to me so often, that I only quote them) you retain such good looks on your face and such charms in your mind that, if it were not for the fastidiousness of your choice as to the persons you receive, there would be as great a crowd without selfish interests in your house, as there are Courts where fortunes are made. You mingle virtues with your charms, for at the moment when a lover reveals to you his passion, a friend may confide to you his secrets. Your word is the safest bond on which we can rely. . . ."

Ninon's correspondence with Saint-Évremond through such divers events and wars was not very punctual or well sustained, and the few letters that have been preserved belong to only the last years of their life. They are then decidedly old, very old both of them, and their greatest pleasure is to talk of the past with regret, and to jest of old age very pleasantly. Ninon regrets her friend and wishes he were near her: "I should have liked to pass what remains to me of life with you; if you had thought as I do

you would be here now." At that date, nothing prevented Saint-Évremond from returning to his own
country if he chose. But she says pleasantly that perhaps it is a finer and more meritorious thing to remember the absent after so many years of separation.
"Perhaps this separation of bodies is intended to
embellish my epitaph," she says.

Saint-Évremond gives a letter of introduction to
Ninon to a M. Turretin, a very distinguished Gene-
vese minister and preacher. Ninon at once pro-
cures for the learned Calvinist all the resources at
her command: "He has found here a number of my
friends who think him worthy of the praises you gave
him. If he will profit by the worthy abbés who remain
to us during the absence of the Court, he shall be
treated as a man whom you esteem." These abbés of
distinction were, in fact, very numerous, toward the
last in Ninon's circle. She adds: "I read your letter before him with spectacles; but they are not unbe-
coming to me; I have always had a grave face. If he
loves the merit that they call here *distinguished* perhaps your wish will be accomplished; every day
people try to console me for my losses with that fine
word." Since then the word *distinguished* has been
much abused; we catch it here at its origin, or at
least in its earliest acceptation. To console Ninon for
old age they told her she was a woman of *distinguished merit*. In the seventeenth century the word
had not hitherto been employed so absolutely. Per-

sons were said to be distinguished *for* one quality or
for another; but to *be distinguished* was left for
the eighteenth, and especially the nineteenth century
to bring into general circulation. Everybody nowadays is *distinguished,* just as everybody wears the
ribbon of the Legion of Honour in his buttonhole.

The few letters exchanged between Ninon and
Saint-Évremond give occasion for many remarks both
literary and ethical. They are perfectly sincere, and
human nature is under no disguise, and affects nothing; one might, indeed, wish at moments for a few
efforts to keep its tone higher. In vain does Saint-
Évremond tell Ninon: "Nature will begin to show
by you that it is possible never to grow old," in vain
he tells her: "You are of all countries,—as much
esteemed in London as in Paris; you are of all times,
and when I cite you to do honour to mine the young
men claim you instantly as the honour of theirs; thus
you are mistress of the present as of the past. . . ."
In spite of all these fine words Ninon grows old; she
has her moments of sadness, and her manner of evading them seems saddest of all:

"You used to say in other days," she writes, "that I should die of
reflections; I try to make no more, and to forget on the morrow the
day that I have lived to-day. Every one tells me that I have less reason to complain of time than others. However that may be, had any
one foretold me such a life I would have hung myself. And yet one
clings to a vile body as if it were an agreeable one; one likes to feel
ease and repose; appetite is a thing that I still enjoy. . . ."

That idea of *appetite* often comes up between them,

and mingles rather naïvely with the warm tenderness of friendship. "How I envy those who go to England!" writes Ninon; "what pleasure I should have in dining with you once more! Is it not coarseness to wish for a dinner? The mind has great advantages over the body, and yet the body supplies us with various little tastes that reiterate themselves and soothe the soul under sad reflections."

To hold to life only by the body and to feel that body shrinking and withering day by day is the main idea that pervades the correspondence of these two old persons, and it ends in painfully affecting the reader. We feel more than they did what is lacking to them in the order of higher hopes. They perceive it themselves at the moment when they lose their friends. Ninon sees Charleval die, her old and most faithful friend; Saint-Évremond loses the Duchesse de Mazarin, his sole resource and prop. Ninon tries to comfort him by a letter of feeling and good sense, which she cannot prevent herself from ending with these words: "If one could think like Mme. de Chevreuse, who believes that by dying she will go and converse with all her friends in another world, it would be sweet to think it."

In reading these pages one cannot help desiring some other motive, some other impulse, be it only an illusion, in these two amiable old people. Their grovelling ethics distress us, their horizon lowers at every step. Saint-Évremond does not believe

in a future, and all his hopes, like all his joys, end
for him in the next or the present moment: "I do
not regard reputation," he says. "I look to a more
essential thing; I mean life; eight days of which are
worth far more than eight centuries of fame when
dead. . . . There is no one who thinks more of
youth than I do. . . . Live; life is good when it
has no pain."

But, as there must always be a motive more or less
near and a recompense, in default of posterity and a
future the two friends gave each other praises and
compliments letter after letter.

" Would to God that you thought of me as you say you do!" writes
Ninon, "and I will do without the praise of other nations. Your last
letter is a masterpiece. It has made the subject of every conversation
held in my rooms for a month. You have returned to youth; you do
right to love it. Philosophy goes well with charms of the mind. It
is not enough to be wise, one must also please; and I see that you
will always please so long as you think as you do. Few persons resist age. I believe I have not yet allowed mine to crush me."

It was thus that they gave themselves, through intellect at least and by delicate flattery, their last
pleasures.

It is time to sum up my remarks upon Ninon and
to mark distinctly the only side on which I have
viewed her. Her salon collected a far greater variety
of personages than the hotel de Rambouillet, and it
comprised many sorts. It united with the best of the
great world the best of the good Parisian *bourgeoisie*.
Mme. de La Fayette had attempted for a moment the

same rôle (in which Mme. de Sablé had preceded her),
" to whom," says Gourville, "all the young men were
accustomed to show great attentions, because, having
trained them a little, she gave them a claim to
enter society. But Mme. de La Fayette's health and
her inclination to take her ease kept her from continuing this rôle very long. In a great measure it was
that of Ninon. For it, she had much more gaiety
than Mme. de La Fayette, and more solidity than that
other brilliant woman of the same date, Mme. de La
Sablière. It was therefore in her salon and through
her that young men made their entrance into society.
In her rooms people conversed : cards were not played.
Mothers sought to introduce their children. Mme.
de Sévigné, who had such reason earlier in life to
complain of Ninon in respect to her husband and her
son, saw, without anxiety, her grandson, the Marquis de Grignan, pay her much attention. Fashion
joined in, and, public consideration covering all, the
women ended by seeking Ninon sedulously. " The
women are all running after Mlle. de l'Enclos," said
Mme. de Coulanges, "just as other people used to run
after her formerly." Whereupon Mme. de Sévigné
wrote to M. de Coulanges : "Corbinelli tells me marvels of the good company of *men* he meets in the
house of Mlle. de l'Enclos; so, in her old days, she
gathers them all in, men *and* women, whatever Mme.
de Coulanges may say."

No book shows us better what the salon of Mme.

de l'Enclos really was than the "Dialogue on the
Music of the Ancients" by the Abbé de Châteauneuf;
it gives a conversation at her house, in which we
find her speaking with taste, with judgment and accuracy, excellent musician that she was. Leaving her
salon the interlocutors continue to talk of her and
they recount to one another her various good qualities.
The Abbé Fraquier has also painted her on a very
true page; and the Abbé d'Olivet — (good heavens!
what a collection of abbés àpropos of Ninon!) — in a
Eulogy in Latin on Fraquier, representing the latter
at the moment when he wished to write in French
and to train himself to the best style of our language,
says:

"For this purpose, he put his education into the hands of two
Muses; one was the celebrated La Vergne (Mme. de La Fayette) and
the other was called Leontium (Ninon). Both of them held at that
time the sceptre of intellect and were thought the arbiters of elegance
. . . The latter was so fashioned by nature that she seemed a
Venus in beauty, and a Minerva in mind. But when Fraquier first
knew her, age had long withdrawn what was dangerous in her, assur-
ing him of that only which was profitable and salutary."

"Do you know," said a merry jester to whom
I read the above passage in Latin, "that from the
the way in which your Abbé d'Olivet writes, I conclude that in the seventeenth century Mme. de La
Fayette and Mlle. de l'Enclos, through their function
of oracles of taste to the world, were the two first
vicars of Boileau." It was in terms such as these, or
approaching them, that the later contemporaries of

Ninon spoke of her. Is it necessary to recall the fact that the Abbé de Châteauneuf presented to her one day his godson, François Arouet (Voltaire) then thirteen years old and already a poet? She seems to have foreseen what that child would become, for she bequeathed him 2000 francs in her will to buy books.

From Montaigne and Charron to Saint-Évremond and Ninon, and from Ninon to Voltaire there is but a hand's-breadth, as we see. Thus it is that in the stretch of time certain spirits make a chain.

And now, when one has spoken of Ninon and her charm with justice and without too deeply entering into what was shameful, even debased at a certain period, and baneful during the disorders of her early life, we must never forget that such a career, singular and unique as it was, cannot be run twice; that it came of incomparable luck. aided by a quite peculiar genius for conduct; but that all women who, following her example, should attempt to treat love with license and afterwards turn it into sacred friendship, would run great risk of being left by the wayside, and of withering the one sentiment within them without rendering themselves worthy of the other.

VIII.

Tallemant des Réaux
and
Bussy=Rabutin.

VIII.

Tallemant des Réaux and Bussy=Rabutin.

The Bourgeois Scandal=monger and the Scandal= monger of Quality.

WITHOUT aiming at a parallel, I am tempted to bring together the names of these two writers, and to say something of their class of Memoirs, wholly anecdotical, which, under different forms, succeed still in making themselves read and in pleasing, after the lapse of many years.

The *Histoires amoureuses* of Bussy and the *Historiettes* of Tallemant, though belonging, each of them, to the class of chronicles more or less scandalous, cannot be ranked on the same line, nor ascribed to the same spirit. Bussy is a satirist, Tallemant is merely a teller of tales. In Bussy himself there are various personages who complicate and foil one another, while at the same time they mar the perfect candour of his words. We have the lover and the man *à bonne fortunes,* the wit and the academician, the ambitious soldier and the man who will miss the marshal's bâton: all these conflicting

271

elements may impair his sincerity a little, even in backbiting, and turn his sharp pen one way or another; he is susceptible of envy, or of bitterness; he has his secret leaven, he is affronted, he takes revenge.

Tallemant has nothing of all this; he obeys a single taste, a single humour. Witty after the style of our fathers, inquisitive as no man should be, on the watch for all that is said and done about him, informed to the lowest detail of the incidents and the tittle-tattle of society, he registers everything, though not so much the foul things as the drolleries and gaieties. He writes what he hears for the pleasure of writing it with the salt of his language, which is always good, and joining thereto his judgment, which is natural and shrewd. Such as he was and thus trained he is, in his line, inimitable and incomparable. Whoever had told Bussy, the wit, the brilliant pen of the army and the Court, that he had, in his own day, a rival and a master of pungent and naïve narration in that bourgeois scandal-monger, encountered everywhere in society and out of place nowhere, he would certainly have been much astonished and would not have believed it.

From all that we read, especially from things already classic, we may draw certain serious remarks, or, at any rate, a few notions on the manners and customs of a time that is no more. I open the *Histoire amoureuses des Gaules,* and at once I am struck with what gave the author the idea of writing such a

COMTE DE BUSSY-RABUTIN

From a steel engraving of the period

book. Bussy, forty-two years old, lieutenant-general and commander of the light-horse cavalry, having twenty-six years of good and glorious service behind him, aspiring to the *cordon bleu* and to the office of marshal of France, falls in love with Mme. de Montglat, and during a month's absence sets about writing down, in order to amuse her, the histories of Mesdames so-and-so, which she had asked him to tell her. Mme. de Montglat, a brilliant and graceful beauty, loved music and poetry; she even composed rather prettily herself, and could sing better than any woman in France of her rank; also she spoke and wrote with surprising facility and all the naturalness in the world. She admired intellect; much admired just then, little as they had of it, for society was in process of freeing itself from a brutality and coarseness of manners still prevalent and with which comparison was readily made. Mme. de Montglat had in Bussy a man of intellect all her own, and she wished to employ him as she chose. The result was the ruin of his career.

For us, speaking frankly, the first pages of Bussy's chronicle respond very little to the expectation given by his much-vaunted reputation. There is no art of composition in the book; nothing is connected; all is successive and haphazard. We come upon the name of a man or a woman, quick, a portrait ! The portrait begins with a description that reminds us of a passport: face round, nose well formed, etc. Patience ! the finer traits are coming; they do come. But all this

gives the impression of very elementary art. Something of the same kind appears in regard to the toilet
of the personages about whom Bussy remarks that
they are " clean " or they are " dirty " ; which does not
always tell us whether persons dressed well or not;
it means that they took care, or did not take care of
their person, and we are left to suppose there was
a certain medium of cleanliness which was not the
common and required usage   There was no middle
course between delicacy and neglect. So with the
mind; some had it wholly refined: others, at their
elbow, were still coarse or barbarous. At the beginning of the reign of Louis XIV, and before the fu-
sion of manners and tone was completed, we are
very much struck by these contrasts and this crudity
side by side with refinement. We see the remains
of barbarism still existing in the beautiful morning,
already begun, of civilisation; we might think ourselves, from certain details, in a land of savages, when,
suddenly, we are in the midst of exquisite things.
Bussy's book gives this mingled impression very
plainly.

How did a gentleman on service live in those days ?
The king spent the summers on the frontier, where
the armies fought hard. He then returned, usually,
to Paris, where amusements were in season: cards,
billiards, tennis, hunting, theatres, masquerades, lot-
teries, whatever complete idleness engenders, but
above all love. One might say that such is, more or

less, the history of all periods; but love at that period had its own particular stamp. Speaking of M. de Candale, one of the *beaux* who was most in vogue at that time, Bussy defines him thus:

"His mind was mediocre; but in his first love he fell into the hands of a lady who had infinite intelligence, and as they loved each other very much, she took such pains to form him, and he such pains to please the beauty, that art surpassed nature, and he was really a better appearing man [*plus honnête homme* [1]] than a thousand others who had more mind than he."

Mme. de Châtillon, receiving with marked favour the declaration of M. de Nemours and letting him see she had a good opinion of his merits, drew forth the reply: "Ah, madame, it rests with you to make me seem the best-bred man in France." The Marquis de Sévigné, who left his charming wife for Ninon, was convinced "that a man could not be an *honnête homme* [civil, polished, well-appearing man] unless he were always in love."

That which took place at Court during the winters was not merely the noisy and heedless amusements of young warriors; there was much emulation among those who piqued themselves on being men of good breeding, and many wagers like the following:

"The Duc de Candale," says Bussy, "who was the best-trained man at Court, thought that nothing was wanting to his reputation than to be loved by the handsomest woman in the kingdom. He

---

[1] The term *honnête homme* did not then mean exclusively or chiefly, a man of integrity and honesty — but a man who conformed to good-breeding, good manners, propriety and honour.—TR.

therefore resolved at the army, three months after the campaign, that he would be in love with her (Mme. d'Olonne) as soon as he met her; and he showed by the great passion he then had for her, that they [such passions] are not always strokes of heaven or fate."

Both sexes embarked by fixed intention with some man or some woman, in order to do honour to themselves in society and be talked about, " because women gained for men as much esteem as arms." They owed it to themselves, therefore, to make love in some place of renown. Vanity in love, and as the principle of love, became a sign of the times, and it is still, in a general way, that of French gallantry, into which passion, at the beginning, enters for very little. " To embark " was the consecrated term habitually employed. Thus the Chevalier de Grammont takes a fancy to attach himself to Mme. d'Olonne " about the same time that Marsillac *embarked* with her." Beuvron, formerly in love with the same lady, now keeps aloof from her because " the levity she showed in all things made him fear to *embark* himself with her." The Abbé Fouquet, brother of the Superintendent, intriguer of the first water, man of the sack and rope, whose conduct was the farthest possible from his profession, " *embarked* at first on loving more for fame than for love "; but the taste came to him by degrees, and soon we hear of nothing but his " embarkations." During the time that he tyrannised over Mme. de Châtillon, a friend of the latter, Vineuil, wrote to her as follows, to shame her: " You have become the continual subject of all conversations. Your embarkation is described as the lowest and most abject ever seen in a person of your quality. It is said that your friend exercises a tyrannical empire over you and over all that you approach. . . ."

Thus they embarked; and are said sometimes to "re-embark" with the same person, to repair, if possible, the injury done to their reputation by a first rebuff. In this quantity of embarkations, most of them are made from points of honour, or from "reason," rather than from inclination; from the head far more than from the heart. The heart, however, sometimes ends in taking part in the affair. We look in vain for *charm* in Bussy's narrative; there is neither sweetness nor ardour; but he has the art of keen, delicate, and piquant malice.

In two places Bussy betrays both bad taste and inexperience. He quotes letters, and inserts them in his narrative. These letters apparently seem to him piquant. To understand how they could seem so to him or to others, we must remember that the period was one when the art, the epistolary genius, that was about to shine and sparkle in the correspondence of Bussy's charming cousin, Mme. de Sévigné, was still to be essayed and formed. The letters that he quotes, and perhaps fabricates, were not worth the trouble of invention; they are those of a writing-master. Bussy also loves to quote, on occasion, verses, couplets, madrigals of his own making, and such verses!

Many of the writers of his century and of the next, distinguished for intellect and very agreeable in their prose writings, had a species of infirmity for believing that they added to the charm of a thought by composing, and putting in some place where it was least to be expected, a worthless couplet. They wrote well, they jested with grace, with point, they shot their well-aimed, well-steeled arrows, and then, all of a sudden, without any one's knowing why, a little mania, self-styled poetical, seizes them, they catch up a village violin and make, for a minute or two, a dreadful fiddling that rasps the ears. False taste in wit, in epigram, in cold gallantry, derived from the last troubadours and utterly opposed to true imagination and the genius of poesy! How far the classics were from work like this! In Petronius, whom Bussy imitates and translates now and then (the model of a style he affects too much), there are verses also, mingled with the prose and making a conglomerate composition; but they are the verses of a poet, they sparkle, they are white as Parian marble, they have the cool greenery of Italian groves:

> " Emicuere rosæ violæque et molle cyperon,
>   Albaque de viridi riserunt lilia prato;
>
>   .   .   .   .
>
>   Candidiorque dies secreto favit amori."

The classics were licensed for poesy and for the painting of natural objects. Even at the period when corruption began, they kept the measure of great things and the clear sight that saw all beauty; they had Virgil before their eyes and Homer on the horizon. As for Bussy, he thinks he is a poet when he makes a wretched couplet to a jig tune.

It is not known whether all is Bussy's own in this satirical painting, which he partly disavowed. If the conversation between Mme. Cornuel and Mme. d'Olonne is by him, he has not escaped one of the improprieties and defects of his day: pedanticism and dogmatism in gallantry. It was not worth while to introduce Mme. Cornuel, that person of so much spice and sarcasm, merely to make her profess a code of decent love, and preach a sort of sermon under three heads. The passage is very little worthy of Mme. Cornuel and would come better from the pen of the Chevalier de Méré than from that of Bussy.

But now, all being said, and the wrongs done by betrayal and indiscretion having long passed away, we are, involuntarily, grateful to Bussy (at this distance) for showing us in action all this fine society, nobles, gentlemen, and great ladies; for producing them to us in a state of nature, as it were, in an originality of disorderly living which makes one reflect on the degree of civilisation and decency that belongs to different ages and might serve to bring to reason the enthusiasm of historians and the makers of funeral orations. Bussy's polite diction, his simplicity of phrase, brings out distinctly certain fundamental points. There are, however, charming traits, and delicate, in his narrative; his portrait of Mme. de Sévigné is one of the most lifelike and most carefully worked-up in its malignity; in it he actually surpassed himself and summoned all his treachery against such a model. He makes us think, by this malignant portrait, of those of Hamilton, although he has not the light touch of the latter n)r his almost imperceptible fine irony. However that may be, Bussy has given in the *Histoire amoureuse des Gaules* a dish of his own concoction, a *rabutinade,* which has a particular relish for palates that want something else than the meats of the golden age.

Saint-Évremond judged Bussy well when he said of him:

" What are we to think on the subject of M. de Bussy that everybody has not already thought ? He is a man of quality; he has always had much wit, and in former days I saw him in a position to hope for high fortune, to which have since succeeded many men who were his inferiors.

" He preferred to his advancement in life the pleasure of writing a book and making the public laugh; he has chosen to make a merit of his liberty; he affects to speak frankly and undisguisedly, but he has not always sustained that character to the end.

" After twenty years of exile he returned to a humiliating situation, without office, without employment, without consideration among courtiers, and without any reasonable grounds for hope.

" When one has renounced fortune by one's own fault, and when one has chosen to do what M. de Bussy did deliberately, one ought to pass the rest of one's days in retirement, and support with a sort of dignity the sorry rôle with which one burdened oneself."

I ought to quote all that follows. Saint-Évremond, in speaking thus of a man who had more than one af-

finity with himself in talents as well as in exile, enables
us, nevertheless, to perceive their differences. Both
destroyed their fortunes by an indiscretion, by indulg-
ing a wit more satirical than propriety allowed; their
military careers were broken, and both were driven
into a long exile, to which Bussy could never reconcile himself, while Saint-Évremond bore his to the
end with fortitude, even disdaining at the last to
return to France when he might have done so.
Saint-Évremond at bottom is an epicurean, and he is
that before all. Had circumstances turned otherwise,
he would doubtless have been a very different personage, but he had in him, essentially, the stuff of a
philosopher of indifference and pleasure, of a smiling
and firm observer, who appreciates the real value of
things and detaches himself from them as much as
possible. Provided he spent his afternoons and even-
ings in talking with Mme. de Mazarin he felt he had
not lost his day and was content.

Bussy, on the contrary, was an ambitious man, and
a courtier who had imprudently barred his own fortune, who felt it and suffered from it; his was a vain,
uneasy soul which did not find within itself resources
of consolation. Imagine a soldier of courage and
talent, who has in him, perhaps, the stuff to win ten
battles, to make himself illustrious when he reached
the highest post, but who, by an incurable perversity,
has created for himself all sorts of shackles and impossibilities. Man of war, lieutenant of Turenne, but

complicated with the spirit of a Maurepas, he found
means to give umbrage to his general and to alienate
him by the fear he had of his squibs. A courtier, all
ready, if need were, to crawl before Louis XIV provided he were employed, he found means, at the
opening of the glorious reign, by a scandalous folly to
get himself treated as a libellist and his pen broken,
he, whose sword was eager for action and impatient
of the scabbard. To give himself the pleasure of
writing a book worthy of the Regency and the Directory, and which was wholly of the date when
Fouquet made a collection of his *billets-doux* and
wrote out a list of the great ladies who were his
mistresses, Bussy missed the great century, missed
the war in Flanders, missed that in Franche-Comté,
when the army passed almost before his windows,
all his former companions in arms being with it.
"Ten thousand men have just passed my gates"
(the gates of his château de Bussy), he writes; "there
was not an officer however little out of the common,
who did not come to see me; many of the Court
people slept here." Quick! he writes to the king,
asking to serve in this campaign; and the impassible
king replies: "Let him have patience; not yet, not
this time." And the other time never comes. This
was enough, we must allow, to enrage a gentleman of
good family and lead him to eat his heart out; and
that, in fact, was what Bussy spent the rest of his life
in doing.

In Tallemant we have to deal with a man of another nature, another condition, another temperament. He thinks himself well off where he is; he has found his level at once, he is angry with no one. If he permits himself a grain of malice, he at least puts no rancour into it, nor any secret bitterness. Of the same age as Bussy (Tallemant was born about 1619, and Bussy in 1618), son of a rich financier, nurtured in bourgeois joviality and opulence, he keeps us informed about all the fine passions of his youth; he, too, writes his *histoire amoureuse,* but how different its tone! While still a schoolboy he had read "Amadis" and adored it. When he went from the Place Maubert to the rue Montorgueil to see a certain widow who had favours for him, and, in order to arrive less muddy before her (sedan-chairs and galoshes, a resource some years later, were not yet invented) he hired a horse, people cried out, when they met him, "Where are you going, Sir Knight?" But what sort of knight was he? there was much of Sancho in his chivalry.

At one time he came very near entering, for one of his girl-cousins, into grand sentiments and languishing airs: "A fool of a comrade whom I had in college," he remarks, "who was a bit romantic, managed to spoil me; we took sentiment askew, both of us." This crookedness did not last long. Even when he was melancholy, it was "gentle melancholy which never prevented him from being gay when he wished."

He began again, at the first chance, to jump, and joke, and play tricks and laugh. At eighteen years of age he and two brothers were sent with the Abbé de Gondi (the future Cardinal de Retz) to make a journey into Italy; passing through Lyons, he fell in love with the daughter of a friend with whom they lodged, and he carried away with him the promises, and the bracelets, of his beauty with the intention to be sad; he believes himself a lover after the fashion of Amadis. He, a hero of romance, the deuce!—he does n't support that rôle very long: "This did not prevent me," he says, "from diverting myself much in Italy— so fine a thing is youth."

Tallemant's father would have liked to make him a counsellor at the Parliament of Paris; but the young man did not feel the slightest vocation for the magistracy. To set himself completely at liberty he married his cousin-german, a Rambouillet. Tallemant's mother was a Rambouillet of the financial family of that name which had no connection with the noble Rambouillet d'Angennes but, together with money, had wit and intellect for its patrimony. We know very little of Tallemant's life. He seems to have filled some financial office—controller-provincial of regiments in Lower Brittany, they called it. He bought the estate of Plessis-Rideau in Touraine about the year 1650, and obtained the right to change its name to "des Réaux," which henceforth became his own name. He distinguished his identity in this way from that of his

younger brother, the Abbé Tallemant, the academician; just as Boileau *des Préaux* distinguished himself from his elder brother Gilles Boileau. That Abbé
Tallemant, known to us as the dry translator of the
French of Amyot, did not like our Tallemant and was
envious of him. Between them there may have been
family jars and no doubt antipathies of taste; Tallemant is certain to have sneered at purists. Also he
made verses equal to those of his brother; but those
we have of him are insipid enough, or very flat. We
have an epistle of his in verse to Père Rapier, in which
there is not the least little word to raise a smile.

Born and brought up in the Reformed religion Tallemant was converted in old age; we are not told if this
took place on the revocation of the Edict of Nantes.
He reached his seventy-third year and died in Paris in
his own house, rue Neuve Saint-Augustin, November
10, 1692.

But what need is there for insignificant details as to
the life of this easy-going, happy man? He shows
himself to us in his *Historiettes;* there we see him
naked and undisguised. He finished writing them
in 1657, during the years when Bussy's pen was taking its license. Tallemant took his, but without paying much heed to it. Going everywhere in society, on
good terms with persons of the highest rank, and
specially allied with men of intellect; loving to hear
all, record all, and make good stories out of it; a born
anecdotist, as La Fontaine was a born fabulist, his

friends were constantly saying to him: "Write that down." He did so, and we profit by it. Without Tallemant and his indiscretions, many special studies on the seventeenth century would to-day be well-nigh impossible. Through him we belong to all coteries, all quarters; we know all the masks, even to their stripping off. Are we to pin our faith on what Tallemant tells us? By no means. He tells what he hears; he records current talk; he does not lie, but he gossips with delight and joy of heart. Nevertheless, what he tells is always very worthy of consideration, because he is natural and judicious, veracious and shrewd, without any conceit or any pretension. Of Henri IV, Sully, Richelieu, of all who were older than himself and were beyond his reach in every way, he picked up only the crumbs (yet they fell from good tables); he should in their case be listened to as an echo and collector of rumours; but on the persons he has seen and frequented, whose measure he had himself taken, he counts for as much as any one; he has read physiognomies, and he imparts them to us. He holds the red pencil, brusque, expressive, violent in colour, of our old sketchers lodging near the Halles. He makes a speaking sketch. We must not treat Tallemant lightly, nor contradict him without proof. Burrow into many places and you will find confirmation of what he said as he ran. And it is not only in the *bourgeois* class that he excels; not only when he exhibits and spreads before us Mme. de. Cavoye, Mme. Pilou, or Mme. Cornuel in all the originality and copiousness of their sallies; Tallemant is also the best witness we have to the hôtel Rambouillet and its refined society; he judges it with the French spirit of the good old times, as becomes a friend of Patru and a man who has in him something of La Fontaine in prose, and something of Maucrois in Gallic atticism that has passed through the Place Maubert.   Much has been said of M. de Montausier; but in truth, his portrait was made long ago.   What could give it better than this page of Tallemant?

" M. de Montausier is a man all of a piece; Mme. de Rambouillet said he was crazy by dint of being wise.   Never was there any one who had more need to sacrifice to the Graces.   He shouts, he is rude, he attacks everyone to his face, and when he grumbles at a man he sets before his eyes his past iniquities.   No man ever helped me so much to cure myself of a humour for disputing.   He wanted two citadels built in Paris, one above and one below the river, saying that a king, provided he made good use of them, could not be too absolute — as if that ' provided' were an infallible thing!   Unless he were convinced that a man's life depended on it he would not keep his secret.   His wife helps him mightily in the provinces; without her, the nobles would not visit him.   He rises at eleven o'clock, as he does here, and shuts himself up to read; for he does not like hunting, and has nothing popular about him.   She is just the reverse of him.   He makes wit and intellect too much of a profession for a man of rank, or, at any rate, he does it too seriously.   He goes to the Saturdays very often [Mlle. de Scudéry's day for receiving].   He makes translations; but just see the fine author he has chosen! He turns Persius Flaccus into French verse!   He talks of almost nothing but books, and sees M. Chapelain and M. Conrart more regularly than any one.   He takes fancies, and of pretty bad taste; he likes Claudian better than Virgil.   He wants pepper and spice.   Nevertheless, as we have said elsewhere, he relishes a poem that has neither salt nor sage, 'La Pucelle'; and that is solely because Chapelain wrote it. He has a fine library at Angoulême."

If that is not a masterpiece of truth and likeness, where shall we find one? We have a choice of such pages in Tallemant; open him anywhere; all is gay, clear-cut, smiling, well set-up; never involved or twisted. I much prefer the good Tallemant to Bussy. When Bussy has said a pretty thing he is afraid of losing it. Of the two, it is always the nobleman whose inkstand we see the most.

Tallemant continues without effort the race of tale-tellers and authors of *fabliaux;* a vein of Rabelais runs through him. He uses excellent language, of great precision of meaning, full of idioms, familiar, Parisian in its essence. His style agrees very ill with the true reign of Louis XIV; we cannot imagine Tallemant at Versailles. The scandal-monger of those coming years will have their amplitude and grandeur: that scandal-monger of genius is to be Saint-Simon. The social world that Tallemant shows us is that of the Town, properly so called; of Paris in the days of Mazarin, before and after the Fronde, and under the minority of Louis XIV (corresponding more or less to the period of the first satires of Boileau); the Paris in which was stirring in all directions a rich, bold, and free *bourgeoisie,* the types of which are in Molière, the physician of which is Gui Patin, and, at a future period, Regnard. That is the framework within which Tallemant plays his play. He swims in his element.

After this we need not be surprised if writers profit by Tallemant's pages but do not cite him honourably, or if they often rob him without saying much about it, and even with an air of saying, "Fie"! A Tallemant is not a Tacitus. He writes in a style that is little elevated, that seems easy, and is only moderately honourable. But every man gives what he can.

IX.

The Abbé de Rancé.

IX.

The Abbé de Rancé.

Reformer of La Trappe.

WHO and what was Rancé in the world? A wonderful mind, brilliant, eager for all knowledge and all diversions, seeking ever the honey of the poets; eloquent and winning of speech, generous and magnificent of heart; an ardent soul, impatient, intemperate, exhausted with fatigue yet never in repose; a soul that nothing could fill, grasped in the midst of successes and pleasures by an infinite melancholy, obsessed at times by the idea of death, the image of eternity; rejecting, at a certain moment, that which seemed to it incomplete, and immolating itself finally at the foot of the Cross in a " passionate hatred of life." For it is with life as it is with one beloved—there is no great distance between passionate love and passionate hatred; it is precisely because we have loved too much, dreamed too ideally of this passing life, clasped, in rare and unique moments, too much, that the soul, when it is great, gives itself obstinately to disgust and to relinquishment.

With Rancé the sacrifice was complete, was lasting;
the gleam from on high not only fell, but the lightning
fell with it, and consumed the holocaust: the forehead
of the repentant man beneath the ashes remains for
ever stamped with the sacred stigmata.

Armand-Jean Le Bouthillier de Rancé, born in 1626,
son of a president of the Cour des Comptes, nephew of
a superintendent of finance, nephew also of the Bishop
of Aire and the Archbishop of Touraine, cousin-german of Chavigny, minister of State, was tonsured
while still a child, loaded with benefices, and destined
to receive the ecclesiastical heritage of his uncle of
Tours.   Meantime, he was put to studies both sacred
and profane, and delivered, still a youth, to the whirl
of society.   At twelve years of age (1639) he published an edition of Anacreon, with table-songs
[*scolie*] and comments in Greek of his own making.
Much has been said of the contrast between this pre-
cocious edition and the future destiny of the child.   A
visitor to La Trappe mentioned it one day to the abbé:

" He answered me that he had burned all the copies that remained
except one, and that one he had given to M. Pellisson when the latter
came to La Trappe after his conversion; not, he said, as a good book
but merely as a very clean and well-bound volume: he said, also,
that during the first two years of his retreat, before he became a monk,
he had wished to re-read the poets; but it only served to recall his
old ideas; for there was in such reading a subtle poison hidden beneath the flowers that was very dangerous; so that finally he had to
quit all that."

The most conflicting studies excited the restless curiosity of young Rancé; at one time he gave himself

ARMAND-JEAN LE BOUTHILLIER DE RANCÉ

From a portrait by Rigaud

up to astrology. Theology, however, was not neglected; he did well in it, obtained his degree, and preached eloquently. If not in politics, at least in the variety of his dissipations he seemed to follow closely in the footsteps of Retz, his elder by twelve years, and he, too, in his way, was a *roué* of the first Regency; never stirring, Saint-Simon tells us, from the hôtel de Montbazon, a friend of all the personages of the Fronde, and sharing the great hunting parties of the Duc de Beaufort, the leader of the "Importants." An elegant biographer, the Abbé de Marsollier, pictures him to us at this time with a sort of complacency:

" He was in the flower of his age, being then about twenty-five years old. His figure was above middle height, well set up and well proportioned; his countenance was happy and intellectual; he had a lofty forehead, a large nose, well defined but not aquiline; his eyes were full of fire, his mouth and all the rest of his face had every charm one could wish for in a man. With it all, a certain air of gentleness and of grandeur which predisposed in his favour and made him both beloved and respected."

Compare this portrait of the young man with that of the old man given to us by Saint-Simon forty years later, when the latter tricked him into posing unconsciously for his portrait by Rigaud:

"The resemblance [of the portrait] is absolutely exact," Saint-Simon says: " the gentleness, the serenity, the majesty of his face; the noble fire, keen and piercing, of his eyes (so difficult to render), the delicacy, the intellect and the grandeur expressed in his countenance; that candour, that wisdom, that interior peace of a man who possesses his soul—all was rendered, even to the charm which had not left his attenuated face, worn by penance, age, and suffering."

All the visitors of that day agree in speaking of the "refined and delicate countenance" and the "noble air" of M. de La Trappe which contrasted with the harshness of his life.

With a very delicate constitution people hardly understood how he could suffice for his various exercises; for at that time his activity about incongruous things had the same excessive and indefatigable ardour that afterwards impelled him along a single furrow. Often, after hunting all the morning, he would come twelve or fifteen leagues by post to preach at the Sorbonne at a given hour, as if the effort were a mere nothing. "His speech," says his biographer, M. de Châteaubriand, "had *torrent,* like that of Bourdaloue later, but Rancé's touched more, and he spoke less rapidly." His violence of passion was, at all times, masked by a perfect politeness. He knew Bossuet in early youth and was intimate with him while both were at school, and Bossuet, as we shall see later, claims for himself the happiness and honour of sitting beside Rancé, that man of whom he never spoke without betraying a reverent admiration.

Ardent, active, practical, Rancé was ever going forward, never turning back. When he was in the world, as later, when he was out of it, he did nothing by halves. Hunting, sermons, pleasures, business, intrigues, he was equal to all. Closely in touch with the Coadjutor de Retz, that most stirring of party leaders, tenderly allied with the Duchesse de Mont-

bazon, the most beautiful woman of her day and by
no means a dreamer, Rancé boldly played his part as
a man-of-the-world-abbé, and a man of gallantry.

But this tumultuous life received at times certain
warnings that struck his mind and caused him to
think.   One day, for example, he had gone with his
gun to a barren piece of land behind the church of
Notre-Dame, intending to fire at some bird of passage, when the steel buckle of his game-bag was
struck by a ball fired from the other side of the river;
the buckle deflected the shot, but he keenly realised
the danger, and exclaimed: "What would have become of me alas! had God called me to him at this
moment!"   Thus, at that epoch (more fortunate in
this respect than ours), and even in those dissipated
souls in the height of their license, belief existed;
whatever may have been the surface of the waves or
the swelling of the storm, below was faith: souls
returned in time, and the great souls rose high.
To-day, almost universally, even when the appearance is of honourable and philosophically avowable
belief, the undercurrent is doubt, and our great souls
make no return upon themselves, they think there is
no need of it.   In a word, there was faith even in the
license of those days; in ours, scepticism has glided
into our philosophical beliefs and — why not add?—
into our Christian professions; I speak of those that
are sincere.

Before the moment of his conversion Rancé was

deputy of the second order to the Assembly-general
of the Clergy held in the years 1655-1657. He took a
somewhat active part and one of opposition to the
Court, at any rate in all that concerned the interests
of Cardinal de Retz, his friend, whom Court and
clergy were trying to dispossess. He mingled less in
the other conflicts of that day, and remained aloof
from the Jansenist strife, although he was one of
those who refused to sign the censure of Arnauld at
the Sorbonne. In all these affairs, even the ecclesiastical ones, his conduct was that of a gallant man of
the world who makes it a point of honour to be
faithful to his friends in misfortune.

This was the state of his affairs when the death of
Mme. de Montbazon (1657) struck him the blow of
which so much has been said, which the public
imagination has delighted to adorn with a romantic
legend,—as it did for the history of Abelard and
Heloise,—but about which he himself was more silent
than the grave. It was told that, being in the country
when the death of this most beautiful woman who
preferred him to all others took place, he returned
without being informed of it, and going to her apartment, to which he had secret access, he found his
idol not only dead but headless; for the surgeons
had, so it was said, detached that beautiful head to
put the body into the coffin which was too short for
it. The imagination of the tellers of this tale did not
stop in so romantic a path, and it cost nothing to add

DUCHESSE DE MONTBAZON
From a steel engraving

that the head, that dear head, carried away by Rancé, became in after years the object of his meditations at La Trappe, the sign transformed and present at all hours of his repentant worship.

The facts are (as Saint-Simon being well-informed relates them, and I see no reason to doubt him) that Mme. de Montbazon died of measles after a very few days' illness, that M. de Rancé was beside her, never left her, made her receive the sacraments and was present at her death. Shortly after, he started for his beautiful estate of Véretz in Touraine, where he began to think more and more seriously of his irreparable loss; but retirement only increased his sorrow and a black melancholy took the place of his former joy. His pious biographers are extremely chary of details at this crisis; at most they risk a few veiled statements that "one cause or another, such as the death of certain persons of consideration who were among his best friends, struck him and recalled him to God."

But Rancé was a strong soul, a great soul; he comprehended from the first day that he had lost something he could never recover; that to begin a maimed life on the ruins of the past was unworthy of even a noble human ambition. While he said these things to himself aloud an inward voice spoke to his soul in lower tones, and that voice had for him a name. Happy those for whom that voice preserves its name, distinct and efficacious, calling itself simply the grace of Jesus Christ!

The death of Gaston, Duc d'Orléans, whose chaplain he was, came, soon after, to impress upon him still more strongly the nothingness of man and the one existing truth of Eternity. All the lesser reasons that have been given from time to time, and even down to our day, to lower in its essence the resolution of this repentant man vanish before this one idea of Eternity fully comprehended. Where hidden springs and secondary motives escape us it is right to dwell on the dominant and manifest inspiration. That inspiration rose and resulted from the whole life and the whole soul of Rancé, and we should do wrong to ourselves if we did not perceive it in considering him. "What have you done during these forty years?" was once asked of a Chartreux in the hour of his death: *" Cogitavi dies antiquos, et annos æternos in mente habui,"* he replied,—"I have had in my thoughts the eternal years."

That was Rancé's object, his overmastering occupation from the hour of his awakening, the aim that gave him fortitude and led him, more and more, into the steep and rocky paths of repentance. That idea of Eternity — (let us think upon it!) is such that if a man looks upon it fixedly without having any gleam of immortal hope, there is enough in it to make him rush headlong to the abyss and kill himself in despair! What did Lucretius in his delirium? What did Empedocles on Etna? What might not Pascal have done had he set himself to consider (as he did, but without result) "the short duration of his life absorbed in the Eternity that preceded and followed it "— measuring with terror the two infinities without believing or hoping anything?

Rancé was thirty-one years old at the time of Mme. de Montbazon's death in 1657. Six years elapsed before he took the cowl and began his novitiate in 1663, during which time his purpose widened, strengthened and attained maturity. Living secluded, nearly the whole time on his estate of Véretz, he employed himself in breaking his many ties, in selling his patrimony for the benefit of the poor, in evading the ecclesiastical ambitions of his uncle, the Archbishop of Tours; and, so doing, he passed six years in slowly advancing towards the cloister. "My thoughts," he says in one of his letters, "went at first no farther than to lead an innocent life in the country-house which I had chosen for my retreat; but God made me know that more was needed, and that a gentle, peaceful state, such as I had pictured to myself, did not become a man who had spent his youth amid the ideas, the errors, and the maxims of the world."

He felt at first a great repugnance to the cloister; he kept his prejudices as a man of the world and a man of rank against the frock. The most respected men whom he consulted (Choiseul, Bishop of Comminges, the Bishop of Châlons, and the saintly Pavillon, Bishop of Aleth) did not advise it; on the contrary, they urged him to follow, even in his repentance, "that wise medium course which is always the character of true virtue." But a medium course was precisely that which was most contrary to his nature and most intolerable to his thoughts. The scruple of expiation in view of eternity, the ardent desire for penance were upon him; in vain did moderate reason seek to mitigate them; in great repentant hearts something else cries aloud; conscience seeks its punishment and cannot be consoled so easily. Such souls, once captured, cannot away with a sweet, false happiness in the bosom of which they would feel themselves eternally desolate.

Having decided to become a regular abbé instead of the secular one he already was, it does not appear that Rancé ever looked back. Closing his ears to clamour and even to advice, he entered the monastery of Perseigne, under the strict Cistercian rule, June 13, 1663; and the following year, July 13th, he was consecrated abbé in the church of Saint Martin, at Séez. On the 14th he went to La Trappe, the one poor benefice he had retained for himself; crossing thus the threshold of that high career in which he was henceforth to advance untrammelled, guiding others. He was thirty-eight and a half years old, and God granted him thirty-six years more of life — the time to accomplish many designs.

The poor abbey needed repairs and reformations of every kind. Already, in a stay which he made there the previous year (1662), Rancé had been forced to purge the place of the presence of the monks, six in number,

who had merely the name and titles of religion and
were living in the utmost debauchery. Threatened
by them and at the risk of being stabbed or thrown
into a pond, he held firm, even refusing the assistance offered by M. de Saint-Louis, a cavalry colonel
living in the neighbourhood, an honourable soldier
whose character Saint-Simon has transmitted to us.
The bad monks finally consented to retire on payment of a pension, and six monks from Perseigne
were brought to take their place. Besides this,
materials had to be provided; the buildings, falling
into ruins, needed to be rebuilt, the cattle and night-
birds driven away, the fences set up. At last, thanks
to these first efforts, the Abbey of Notre-Dame of
the Maison-Dieu of La Trappe became a house of
prayer and silence, in that valley made for it, as it
seemed, expressly; encircled by forests and hillsides
and watered by its nine ponds.

The history of the Monastery of La Trappe during
the following years is that of gradual, silent, and
hidden progress; the rumours that came to the outside world told of the least part of its work and often
of the part that was least worth being known. The
austerity of the rule became erelong an irresistible
attraction to some; they came from neighbouring
monasteries as to a hive of more celestial honey.
Rancé might call himself a winner of souls, and sometimes he had to dispute for them with other monasteries that sought to get them back. Such were the

chief events, the quiet contentions, that brought diversion to the early simplicity of the work. About the year 1672 La Trappe had reached its highest perfection, its full monastic fame, and one original monument the more was added, in shadow, to the wondrous splendour which illumined that period of Louis XIV.

If it is permissible, without profaning anything, to grasp the ensemble and place all things at their true value in the picture, I must say that this period of 1672 was, beyond a doubt, the most complete of a marvellous reign. Never did maturity more brilliant, more fruitful, offer more diverse masterpieces, or bring more considerable personages into view. The group of poets had not diminished: Boileau celebrated the passage of the Rhine; Racine in mid-career, was taking breath with *Béjazet;* La Fontaine mingled with new fables certain tales that were decorous. This was the year of the "Femmes Savantes" before the last hours of Molière; Lulli took in hand the Opera; M. de Pomponne was entering as minister on Public affairs, and lending to the noble good sense of the monarch the elegance of an Arnauld's pen. Bossuet, glorious orator through his first Orations, and proved a learned man by his "Exposition of Faith," was devoting himself to the Dauphin's education. Port-Royal, in these sincere years of the "peace of the Church," was flowering and fructifying afresh with the abundance of a late autumn. And afar, in the hidden byways of the

Perche, something angelic, I scarce know what, was operating like an early springtide. "People perceived," says M. de Chateaubriand, "that fragrance was coming from an unknown land and they turned to inhale it."

It was Bossuet who induced Rancé to publish his book on "The Holiness and Duties of Monastic Life." Reading the book in manuscript on his return from the Assembly of 1682, he writes to Rancé: "I own that, coming from the shameful laxities and impurities of casuists, I need to be comforted by these heavenly ideas of the life of hermits and solitaries." Rancé's style, when he is not engaged in a simple discussion which he wants to cut short and finish (as often happens to him), and when he applies it to treatises on doctrine and edification, has compass and beauty: "I know of none," says a contemporary, "more equal, more natural, more polished. The thoughts are full, the images well managed, the words appropriate and choice, the expressions clear, and the periods harmonious."

As the century advanced, the Abbey of La Trappe gained more and more authority in the eyes of the world; also it inherited the influx and concourse of postulants no longer divided among other saintly houses now suspected and inaccessible. Rancé became the sole oracle of the desert; converts and the virtuous of other lands went to him. The Princess Palatine [Anne de Gonzague] consulted him and followed his directions; the King of England, to console himself for the loss of a throne, came to him yearly to talk of God; the Duchesse de Guise, daughter of Gaston d'Orléans, made retreats to La Trappe two or three times a year, lodging in the neighbourhood; the Maréchal de Bellefonds was always within reach, having a house near by. We know of the frequent visits of the Duc de Saint-Simon, who has given us much private information about that austere interior, on which he throws so vivid a light that he makes us enter it. He never mentions that rigorous penitent without tenderness.

Feeling, more and more, the weight of years, Rancé desired to give up his office as head of the monastery and see with his own eyes his successor. Louis XIV consented. Dom Zozime, whom Rancé had designated, was appointed, but died in a few months (1696). His second choice was unfortunate. Dom Gervaise came near ruining everything. Saint-Simon has related the details, long kept secret and truly singular, which led the new abbé to a forced resignation; Saint-Simon was himself too long employed at Court in this affair to allow us to doubt the circumstances he affirms, and which he had no interest, it would seem, in exaggerating. At last, however, Rancé had the satisfaction of seeing the abbey placed in good hands under the management of Dom Jacques de La Cour (1698), and from that moment he thought only of death. He died in the arms of his bishop,

M. de Séez, on the 27th of October, 1700, in the seventy-fourth year of his age.

Shortly after his death, Bossuet laid down certain rules and traced a course for Rancé's biographer such as he himself conceived to be necessary; after doing homage to him living he gave this judgment on him dead:

> "I shall state my feeling on the monastery of La Trappe with much frankness, as a man who has no other view than that God be glorified in the most saintly House there is in the Church, and in the life of the most perfect director of souls ever known in monastic life since Saint-Bernard. If the history of this saintly personage is not written by an able hand and a head as much above all human views as heaven is above earth, all will go ill. In some directions they would want to pay court to the Benedictines, in others to the Jesuits, in others again to Monks in general. . . . All parties wish to draw to themselves the saintly abbé. . . . If he who undertakes so great a work does not feel strong enough to have no need of counsel, the mixture is to be feared, and through it a species of degradation in the work. . . . Simplicity ought to be its sole ornament. I should prefer a simple narrative, such as Dom Le Nain could make, to laboured eloquence. . . ."

It had been proposed to Bossuet to write the life himself; he alone, under the conditions he laid down, was strong enough to do it; but he was unable on account of his multifarious occupations. His chief thought was that every party would seek "to draw the saintly abbé to itself"; whereas, on the contrary, his own conduct in holding himself, as he had done, aloof from all parties should be imitated.

To-day things are changed: we are more prepared to accept, such as he offers himself, that sublime abbé, that monk worthy of Syria, or of the primitive Clairvaux, ardent, impetuous, impatient, man of action and of deeds rather than of discussion or doctrine, but a great intellect all the same; a true monk by *race,* as de Maistre would say; indomitable to all but God himself. We might even be disposed to take him too much in this sense only, and to create a Rancé of a single pattern, which no man ever was, not even he. To picture to ourselves the true Rancé an atom of the world must be introduced, a moral spring must be touched, a secret fibre reached, which the orthodoxy of contemporaries never sought and would not have admitted.

In the "Letters of Rancé" collected and published by M. Gonod, librarian of Clermont-Tonnerre, we have the veritable man himself, speaking in person, simply, gravely, with monotonous sadness or with a smileless joy that resembles sadness and never brightens. We feel, in reading those equable words and in approaching closer to the individual, how little there was, in the very real and practical religion then prevailing, of the poesy which we have since introduced to adapt religion to the taste of to-day and to recover belief by imagination. Even in Rancé's time there were men of the world zealous enough and inquiring enough to go of their own volition and spend twenty-four hours at La Trappe simply as an act of piety. They would be very ready to do so in our day; men would willingly make a pilgrimage that would long be talked-of, and about which they could tell the public the slightest circumstances and "impressions"; but in the mere idea of duration attached to such a life there is something that alarms them, chills and repulses them. Now, that *something* is felt inevitably on every page of the letters of the reformer of La Trappe. Nothing could be less poetic, I assure you, nothing less literary in the modern sense of the word, and I will add, almost as an immediate consequence, nothing more truly humble and sincere.

The letters collected by M. Gonod are of different dates and are addressed, excepting a very small number, to three persons: the Abbé Favier, his former tutor; the Abbé Nicaise, of Dijon, one of the most active correspondents of the seventeenth century, who took the place to Rancé of a gazette or the *Journal des Savants;* and lastly, the Duchesse de Guise, daughter of Gaston d'Orléans one of the souls from without who placed themselves under the guidance of the austere abbé.

Though the letters addressed to the Abbé Favier are, at least in the beginning, of a much earlier date than the conversion and reform of Rancé, we may search them in vain for any trace of his worldly dissipations and his brilliant errors. The young abbé was contented, during those fiery years, to obey his passions without parading them in letters; moreover, they are not the things that a young man is accustomed to relate to a former tutor. The latter had left his pupil on the path of hard study and theological discussion, and he always thought of him under that aspect: "You have too good an opinion of my vocation in the theological way," Rancé writes to him; " provided it has been pleasing to God, that is all that I desire." In vain do we reread and sift the letters of that date; we find kind and respectful feelings for his old tutor, a tone of true modesty when he speaks of himself and his first appearance in the schools or the pulpit, much gravity, much propriety but not the least little ear-tip of the lover of Mme. de Montbazon.

The period of his retreat at Véretz is marked by a softened tone and a few expressions of contentment, if that word is applicable to a nature like that of Rancé. "I live in my house much alone," he writes, "I am seen by very few persons, and all my application is given to my books and to what I imagine to belong to my profession. I feel enough liking for it to believe that I shall not weary of the life I lead. . . . " But after this stage, as it may be called, this first period of repose, Rancé rises, he sets forth in search of a repentance unwearying and almost pitiless; he faces it humanly: "I assure you, Monsieur," he writes to the Abbé Favier (January 24, 1670), "that as soon as a man wills to belong entirely to God and be separated from man, life is good for nothing except to be destroyed; and we ought not to consider ourselves other than *tanquam oves occisionis.*" Beside these stern and

almost savage words we cannot help feeling the constant proofs of affection, always grave, always reserved,
but deepening more and more as the years went on,
which he gave to the worthy old man, his former master; there are days of effusion and tenderness, when
instead of calling him "Monsieur" it escapes him to
say: "My very dear Monsieur."

An historical thought comes out clearly in reading
these letters of Rancé, even in the midst of the reform
which he is undertaking with such heroic energy: it
is, that the time of monks was past, that the world
wanted them no longer, did not understand them, and
would not permit their existence. This appears by
the confession of Rancé himself; he expresses it, in his
own manner, when he says (October 3, 1675): "Inasmuch as you wish to know the news of our affair, I
will tell you that, however just it was, the judgment
has gone entirely against us; and, to speak frankly to
you, my thought is that the Order of the Cistercians is
rejected of God; that having reached the summit of
iniquity it is no longer worthy of the good we have
striven to do to it, and that we ourselves who seek to
procure its re-establishment do not deserve that God
should protect our designs or cause them to succeed."
He returns in many places to this despairing idea; his
judgment on his Order is decisive: "The very ruins,"
he exclaims, "are not repairable!" He had resigned his
abbey of Saint-Symphorien-lez-Beauvais to the Abbé
Favier, who did not know what to do with it, for the

few monks who remained there were living scanda-
lously., "To put reformers there," wrote Rancé, "is
no longer possible; reformers are so decried; and,
partly from the bad conduct of the monks, people will
not allow them to be introduced where they are not
already. It is our sins that have caused this." Thus
the great century, the century of Louis XIV, which we
at a distance imagine to be so devout, had done with
monks, and that, by the confession of the saintliest and
purest monastic reformer of the age.

"We live," he writes to the Abbé Nicaise, "in times
more prudent and wise—I speak of the wisdom of
this world and not of that of Jesus Christ." Since
then, two centuries and over have only increased that
human prudence and wisdom, and the anachronism of
the saintly reformer is not less crying. This is a reflection that cannot be stifled in reading him, and it
leads to many others.

The letters of Rancé to the Abbé Nicaise, without
being of much interest to read, have a very real value
for the literary history of that time. The Abbé Nicaise
was, as everybody knows, the most undefatigable
writer of letters, the newsmonger *par excellence*, and
the officious go-between of the learned men of all
countries. He could not resist the idea of knowing so
celebrated a man as M. de La Trappe, and of keeping
up an intercourse with him. Once in relation with
the recluse he never let him go, and the latter was
compelled to continue a correspondence in which curi-

osity did violence to charity. However, if the Abbé
Nicaise drew his grave and sombre correspondent into
more than one difficulty by the indiscretions he committed, he did him in return a variety of good offices;
if Rancé, for instance, wished to inform the world of
his true sentiments on such or such a point in litiga-
tion, he had only to state them to the abbé.

Nevertheless, that worthy man, always on the watch
with his nose to the wind, puts the patience of the
saint to the proof, and tries again and again to excite
his curiosity. Most of the news on which he comments and the books he extols, wishing to know
Rancé's opinion of them, never reach La Trappe, and
Rancé exhausts himself in saying, gently and quietly:
"We have neither seen nor heard of any of the books
you mention. The republic of letters does not spread
to places where it knows it has none but enemies,
who are incessantly occupied with unlearning and forgetting what curiosity made them know, that they
may give all their application and their study to the
one book of Jesus Christ." Each time that the incor-
rigible Nicaise returns to the charge Rancé reiterates
this profession of forgetfulness: "None of the books
of which you speak to me reach us; we regard them
as lost and flung into a pit whence nothing ought ever
to return." But the good abbé is not discouraged; in
default of the works of others he sends his own, hoping at least to hear what is thought of them. On
one occasion he takes it into his head to compose a

"Dissertation on Syrens, a Discourse on their Face and Form," and straightway sends his manuscript to La Trappe. Oh! this time Rancé cannot restrain a smile; we catch that movement on his countenance (in him so rare) through the simple lines of his answer: "I have cast my eyes over your work on Syrens, but I own to you that I have not dared go farther into the matter. All the fabulous species feel themselves awakened, and I recognise that I am not as dead as I ought to be. That is a thought which has been followed by many reflections — this is how we may profit by everything."

The letters to the Duchesse de Guise are all edifying, noble, sufficiently expansive, but sober nevertheless. This last characteristic is found everywhere in Rancé's correspondence; even when he takes a pen he goes straight to his object, he cuts mere phrases short. Speaking of the death of M. de Nocé, a penitent of rank and one of the hermits living near La Trappe, he writes to Mme. de Guise, who has questioned him: "There were no brilliant circumstances, Madame, in the death of that hermit. His passing was peaceful and tranquil. Struggle he had none, and we only perceived that he had ceased to live because he breathed no longer. God willed that he should say nothing remarkable in order to abridge the Record." *Abridge, shorten* all passing things; that is Rancé's permanent sentiment; he never sees a useless branch without instantly producing his axe or his shears.

Though the mere reading of these letters of Rancé may, if we are not on our guard, seem monotonous, all of them being more or less alike, yet we may draw from them a great quantity of beautiful and noble thoughts. I have already given some, detaching them intentionally, because they are so imbedded on a sombre background that it is almost necessary to present them alone in order to have them noticed. What more lofty thought, for instance, than this, which might serve as the epigram and the motto of the life of the great reformer: "We should do those works and those actions which exist independently of the different passions of men." And what delicacy in this other saying, which reveals a tenderness of soul surviving beneath the hard exterior: "It would be a very sweet thing to be so entirely forgotten that we lived only in the memory of friends." Notice that this profound forgetting on the part of the world, joined to faithful recollection on the part of friends, is the perfect concordance embraced by the hermit's hope.

X.

La Grande Mademoiselle.

X.

Anne—Geneviève de Bourbon.

La Grande Mademoiselle.

ONE of the most original figures, the most singular, and at the same time the most natural of the seventeenth century is certainly La Grande Mademoiselle, daughter of Gaston, Duc d'Orléans, niece of Louis XIII and cousin-german of Louis XIV. In every epoch, a certain type is in fashion, a certain romantic phantom occupies imaginations and floats, as it were, upon the clouds. At the close of the reign of Louis XIII and at the beginning of that of Louis XIV this type, this model, was chiefly formed from the heroes and heroines of Corneille, also from those of Mlle. de Scudéry. La Grande Mademoiselle, a person of imagination, fancy, and high temper, with little judgment, embodied much of this type in herself; to it she added all that belonged to the prejudices of her race and to the superstitions of her royal birth. The result was the most fantastic of compositions, the most vainglorious, the least reasonable, and her whole life showed the effects. Though she held the sword for some time as an amazon, she also produced, pen in hand, a great deal; for not only did she leave interesting and very truthful Memoirs (of which it was said that "they are sufficiently ill-written to assure us they were written by herself"), but we also have, of her making, Portraits, Letters, and short Romances. In short, Mademoiselle was not only a very extraordinary princess, she was an author as well. As such, she belongs to us of right, and it is justice to assign to her the place and date she ought to occupy in the series of literary fashions and varieties.

She was born in the Louvre, May, 1627. Having lost her mother in infancy, she was brought up by an estimable and pious governess but with all the respect due to a granddaughter of Henri IV. Naturally, she grew accustomed to consider herself of different blood from that of other men, even noblemen, and on a par with kings and queens. This idea, which to her was a religion, dictated to her on all occasions speeches of the frankest and most naïve vanity, and imposed upon her sentiments that aimed at grandeur and certainly did not derogate from dignity. Her father, Gaston, Duc d'Orléans, endowed with a thousand fine qualities of the mind and not one of the heart or character, was the soul of all the intrigues against Richelieu, compromising incessantly his followers and friends, whom he

LA GRANDE MADEMOISELLE
From a portrait by Mignard

afterwards abandoned. Mademoiselle from her earliest childhood showed more pride and more honour. Having witnessed at Fontainebleau the ceremony of degrading two knights of the Order (the Duc d'Elbeuf and the Marquis de La Vieuville) she asked the reason; being told it was because they had been of Monsieur's party, she burst into tears and wished to withdraw, declaring that she could not witness that act with decency.

In a period when Richelieu ruled and "tyranny reigned so haughtily over even royal personages" she kept intact within her a worship and lofty idolatry of her race. Her childhood and her first youth were passed in frivolities, in a round of Court, of ceremonial and idle amusements, balls, comedies, collations, with no one to tell her there was anything in life more serious. She went one day on a visit to the convent of Fontevrault, the abbess of which was her aunt, a natural daughter of Henri IV, and began by getting tired of it at once. But the young girls of her suite having discovered a crazy woman locked up in a dungeon, quick! they called Mademoiselle to amuse her with the sight of her antics: "I took my course to the dungeon," she says, "and did not leave it till evening." The next day the abbess, seeing her taste for it, "regaled her with another crazy woman"; "as there was not a third for the next day," she adds amusingly, "it was all so wearisome that I went away, in spite of my aunt's entreaties." This is the tone in which human wretchedness was treated by one who was kind at heart; but no one, I say again, was there to warn and enlighten her. When the Fronde began, the same thing happened. Mademoiselle at first saw nothing in it but a subject of curiosity and amusement: "All these novelties delighted me . . . no matter what importance an affair might have, if it served only to amuse me I thought of nothing else all the evening." Such was Mademoiselle at ten years of age, such at twenty, such at thirty, such nearly all her life, until a tardy passion taught her what it was to suffer.

The first pages of her Memoirs are filled with exterior details only. She went to all the hunting parties of Louis XIII in the days of his amour with Mlle. de Hautefort. Enumerating the young ladies she had in her suite: "We were all dressed in colour," she says, "and mounted on fine ambling horses richly caparisoned; and to guard us from the sun each had a hat trimmed with quantities of feathers." That paints her to us already, proud and of haughty mien, tall of her age and wearing the white plumes from the helmet of her grandsire of Navarre. What matters it that Mademoiselle, at this period, was only ten years old? her mind, in many respects, remained at that age, and never matured. They began even then to talk of marrying her, either to the king, or to the cardinal-Infant, brother of the queen-mother, or to the Comte de Soissons; they amused her with it.

For thirty years more they talked to her of such projects *ad infinitum;* she talked about them herself incessantly, but like a child, unable to resolve upon the step, without perceiving that in the end that eternal indecision would become a jest. She, who called herself MADEMOISELLE *par excellence* could not bring herself to cease to be so, and this lasted until nature, so long set aside, recovered its rights and spoke, once for all, in her heart. But we have not reached that point as yet.

She showed at an early date a taste for things of the mind, wit, spirit, shrewdness, all that serves for conversation. Her father excelled in this; she relates how at Tours, every evening, she loved to listen to Monsieur, who told her his past adventures, "and that very agreeably, like the man in the world who had most grace and natural faculty for talking well." It is rare to find a child so perceptive of that sort of charm. Mademoiselle, in the letters she addressed to Mme. de Motteville in 1660, speaks to her of conversation as being "to your taste and mine, the greatest pleasure in life and almost the only one I care for." It was by that means, even more than by his fine air that Lauzun first insinuated himself into her confidence: "I found in him," she says, "methods of expression that I heard from no one else."

Richelieu dead, Gaston, whom his last intrigues had sent into exile, made peace with the Court; he returned to Paris and went to his daughter's residence:

"He supped with me, where we had twenty-four violins," says Mademoiselle: "he was as gay as if MM. de Cinq Mars and de Thou had not been left by the way. I own I could not see him without thinking of them, and in my joy I felt that his gave me pain." Mademoiselle's good qualities show already; she has humanity in spite of her pride of race, fidelity to friends through their varied fortunes, and dignity. Her father laughs more than once at her pretensions to chivalry and heroism, but in those respects as in others she was worth more than he.

The time that elapsed between the death of Louis XIII and the first Fronde (1643–1648) was a brilliant moment for Mademoiselle. She was sixteen to twenty years of age, and shone at Court in the first rank and in all the pride of hope. There was no alliance that did not seem worthy of her. Not at all gallant in temperament, in no way coquettish, so cold that she was long compared to the virgin Pallas, she saw nothing in marriage but the means to reach a great part and a glorious destiny; and, romantic as she was, she liked almost as well to nurse the idea as to accomplish it. Should she be Queen of France by marrying the young King, Louis XIV, eleven years younger than herself? Should she be Queen of England by marrying the Prince of Wales, then in exile but who could not fail to be restored ? Or should she be an empress by marrying the Emperor of Germany, lately become a widower ? It seemed as if she had only to choose; and no one can show her proud perversity better than she does herself àpropos of a fête given at the Palais-Royal during the winter of 1646, for which the queen-mother was anxious to adorn her:

"They were three whole days arranging my attire; my gown was loaded with diamonds, and scarlet and black and white tassels; I had upon me all the crown-jewels, and those of the Queen of England, who still had some left in those days. No one was ever seen better nor more magnificently adorned than I was that day, and I did not fail to find many persons to tell me, rather apropos, that my fine figure, my good countenance, the whiteness of my skin and the splendour of my blonde hair did not adorn me less than all the riches that shone upon my person. . . ."

They danced in the great theatre, brilliantly lighted. At one end was a throne raised three steps and surmounted by a dais:

"The King (Louis XIV) and the Prince of Wales (afterwards Charles II), would not seat themselves on the throne; I sat there alone, so that I saw at my feet those two princes and all the princesses who were then at Court. I did not feel embarrassed in that position . . . All present did not fail to tell me that I had never seemed less constrained than I did on that throne, and that, as I came of a race to occupy it, when I was in possession of one on which I should sit longer than merely at a ball, I should do so with more ease still. While I was there and the prince was at my feet, my heart looked down upon him as well as my eyes; I had it in mind just then to marry the emperor. . . . I no longer regarded the Prince of Wales as anything but an object of pity."

Such was this romantic princess, who tells everything about herself naturally, sincerely, with a sort of bravura in her sincerity, and a frankness which at times is hearty even in her pride.

The beauty, to which she is the first to do justice, was real at that period of her first youth. Brilliancy, freshness "which, of Lilies, kept their candid innocence," said the poets, fine eyes, blonde hair, a beautiful figure, all this concealed what was wanting in her of delicacy and grace; "she had the air of a great beauty," says Mme. de Motteville. Nevertheless, her teeth, that were not good, and her large, aquiline nose showed the rather common defects of the Bourbon race. Years gave to her features and to her shape more stiffness, without taking from her the quickness and petulance of movement, which never allowed her to have dignity.

When the Fronde broke out, and the good sense inclosed in each head was put to the roughest proof in that brusque civil tempest, Mademoiselle was already known for impetuosities and caprices of temper, which sometimes thwarted and overcame her real feelings to the point of injuring her fortune and even of lessening the consideration paid to her. She could not decide on her choice of a husband and, in her desire for a crown, she allowed opportunities that were under her hand to escape her in order to grasp at distant impossibilities. She was on particularly bad terms with the queen [Anne of Austria] and with Cardinal Mazarin; and for that reason as little disposed to be wise and sensible in the dawning troubles as any one at Court.

The first Fronde, that of 1648, gave her no occasion

to come forward herself; her action was limited to giving way to prejudices that she did not take the pains to conceal: "As I was not much satisfied with the queen, or with Monsieur at that time," she says, "it gave me great pleasure to see them embarrassed." When the queen and the Court left Paris, by Mazarin's advice, and went to Saint-Germain during the night of January 6, 1649, she made it her duty to accompany them, though she was very far from sharing their thoughts and intentions: "I was all excited with joy at seeing they were about to commit a blunder, and in being spectatress of the troubles it would cause them; this avenged me a little for the persecutions I had suffered." The levity, disorder, and bustle of the Court at Saint-Germain are painted to admiration by a person as thoughtless and frivolous as any of them, but who is veracious and tells all. Mademoiselle had great satisfactions to self-love during that sojourn. "The people of Paris," she says, "have always loved me because I was born and brought up there; that has given them a respect for me, and a greater inclination than that they usually feel for persons of my quality." It resulted from this exception in her favour on the part of the Parisians, that they allowed her carriages and horses to leave for Saint-Germain; and while the queen and king lacked everything, she had all she wanted and lacked nothing. All this, however, was but a prelude to the part she was to play in the second Fronde: "I did not then foresee," she says, "that I should find myself concerned in a considerable affair, where I could do my duty and avenge myself at the same time; nevertheless, in doing that sort of vengeance we sometimes avenge ourselves much against ourselves."

That little final touch of repentance does not hinder Mademoiselle from being very proud and very vainglorious of what she did in 1652, when she was able both to obey her father and to give herself up to her instincts for adventure. She was twenty-five years old at this second epoch, the finest age for an amazon. The idea of marriage, which was always flitting in perspective before her eyes, was then suggesting to her a possible union with either the Prince de Condé in case he became a widower (she never shrank from that species of supposition), or with the king if she made herself formidable and necessary. Meanwhile she obeyed, without much consistency, her romantic and grandiose tastes, and, converting her former aversion for the Prince de Condé into sudden friendship, she was fired with a desire to signalise herself for the common cause by some dazzling service.

An occasion presented itself. Her father, Monsieur, was in Paris, which he thought he could not quit without serious inconvenience. He was much needed at Orléans, which belonged to his appanage, and where a rather considerable party wished to open the gates to the royal army, then advancing from Blois. Hence it became of the utmost importance that the city of Orléans should stand firm for the Fronde, otherwise the whole line of the Loire was cut, and the Prince de Condé, coming from Guyenne, would find the enemy master of the position. Mademoiselle offered to go in person to Orléans and hold the town. Her father distrusted her and her judgment: "Such chivalry would be very ridiculous," he said on the day she started, "if the good sense of Mmes. de Fiesque and de Frontenac did not support her." Those were the two ladies who accompanied her and who were called, partly in courtesy and partly in derision, her "field-marshals."

So Mademoiselle started, with joy in her heart on finding herself, at last, on the way to do some extraordinary action and achieve fame. An astrologer predicted it to her on the morning of her departure, and she made no manner of doubt that he was right. As soon as she reached the plains of Beauce, she mounted her horse and put herself at the head of the armies of the Fronde, which were then in that neighbourhood. A council of war was held before her at which it was agreed that nothing should be done except by her order. The difficulty was to enter Orléans; for, pressed hard on either side between the summons of the Keeper of the Seals, Molé, on the part of the king, and that of the Frondeurs, the gentlemen of the Hôtel-de-Ville had a strong desire to remain neutral. Impatient at the parleys, which were much prolonged, Mademoiselle marched up and down before the ramparts, exciting the people behind them by her gestures and words. Then, finding she could rely more on the populace than on the comfortable *bourgeois*, she sprang into a boat which some sailors offered her, crossed the moat and ordered a gate that opened on the quay and was ill-guarded to be battered in. When two planks were down, she passed through the hole, and there she was! followed afar by her ladies, carried in triumph by the people, and mistress of the place in the twinkling of an eye: "for," she says to the governor and sheriffs, who were not a little astonished, "when persons of my quality enter a town they are its mistresses, and with justice: I ought to be so here, as the place belongs to Monsieur—on which, a good deal frightened, they made me their compliment. . . . When I reached my house, I received the harangues of all the public bodies and the honours that were due to me." Not content with being harangued, she improvised a speech before the Hôtel-de-Ville, and acquitted herself no worse than other orators and public speakers in a like crisis.[1]

These first days were the finest. People did not fail, of course, to compare Mademoiselle to the Maid of Orléans. The Queen of England, whose son she

[1] Mademoiselle's insatiable vanity led her in after years to have her portrait painted in military costume, to commemorate this glorious taking of Orléans, and also her really splendid conduct on the day of the battle of Saint-Antoine, when she saved the life of the Prince de Condé and turned the guns of the Bastille on the king's army—an exploit that Louis XIV never, in his heart, forgave. The picture is a small one painted on vellum, and is now in the collection of the " Portraits Nationaux."—Tr.

had refused for a husband, said of her, satirically, that
it was "very right for her to save Orléans like the
Maid, having begun by driving away the English."
The Prince de Condé, hurrying from Agen, incognito
and disguised, arrived at this crisis, fortunately, and
took command of his army near Orléans. Thence he
writes a letter to Mademoiselle to thank her and congratulate her on her prowess: "It is a deed the glory
of which belongs to none but you, and it is of the utmost importance." A report having been rendered to
him of a council of war at which she was present and
gave her opinion, she remarks: "M. le Prince says that
the resolutions taken at the council at which I was
good enough to be present ought to be followed, even
if they were not wise, but in fact they were such that
the King of Sweden (Gustavus Adolphus) could not
have taken better, and that he himself would have done
so even if I had not ordered them." Mademoiselle ac-
cepts and repeats such praises in solemn earnest.
When she returned, shortly after, to Paris, all the people came out to meet her; she was the heroine of the
moment. The Prince de Condé assured her that he
wished for nothing so passionately as to see her queen
of France, and that he would make no terms of peace
in which she was not included. In her credulous exaltation she was, indeed, at the most brilliant moment
of her existence.

Reverses came, and she took part in them valiantly.
Aloof from intrigues, incapable of politics, the affairs

of the Fronde were already in dissolution, and negotiations were begun on all sides before she suspected it.
On the 2nd of July, 1652, when the bloody battle of
the Faubourg Saint-Antoine was fought, where the
Prince de Condé, after prodigies of valour, was about
to be crushed with all his men by Turenne if the gates
of Paris were not opened to his exhausted army, it
was Mademoiselle who, wrenching consent from Monsieur, already half a traitor, flew to the Hôtel-de-Ville
and forced the undecided and unwilling municipals
to open them. To the Maréchal de l' Hôpital, who
resisted as long as he could, she said these noble
words: "Reflect, monsieur, that while you are all
amusing yourselves by disputing over useless things
M. le Prince is in peril within your suburbs. What
sorrow and what shame it will for ever be to Paris
if he perishes for want of succour! You can give
it to him; then give it to him quickly!" It is told,
that as he still hesitated she said to him that if he did
not hasten she would "drag him by the beard and he
should die by no hand but hers." Hastening from
there to the Bastille, armed with full powers, she gathered up as she went the wounded, nearly all men of
mark, whom she recognised with pity. She paints
to us with expressive strokes the moment when, in
one of the intervals of the action, she met the Prince
de Condé:

" He was in a pitiable state ; he had a mass of dust upon his face,
his hair was thick with it ; his collar and his shirt were full of blood,

though he had not been wounded ; his cuirass was dented with blows,
and he held his naked sword in his hand, having lost the scabbard ; he
gave it to my equerry.   He said to me : ' You see a man in despair ;
I have lost all my friends ; Messieurs de Nemours, de La Rochefoucauld,
and Clinchamps are mortally wounded.'   I assured him they were in
better condition than he thought.   .   .   .   That rejoiced him a
little ; he was deeply afflicted.   When he entered he flung himself on a
chair and wept ; he said to me :   ' Pardon the grief in which I am.'
After that, let no one tell me that he loves nothing ; for my part, I
have always known him tender for his friends and for those he loves."

It is to be remarked here that Condé loved and wept
as a soldier for friends whom he might have seen die in
other ways without much regret, perhaps.   On a day
of battle he recovered his good qualities, his humanity,
and his other virtues; he was in his element, and, like
all great hearts at such times, he was kind.

Mademoiselle ordered a few volleys from the cannon
of the Bastille, which manifested plainly the attitude of
the people of Paris and warned the troops of the king
that the hour had not come to enter the city.   Mazarin
said that those cannon-balls, fired by order of Mademoiselle, had " killed her husband," meaning that she
could never henceforth hope to marry the king; but it
is very doubtful if she could ever have married him.
However that may be, she had, on this day of the
Bastille, the satisfaction of having done, not, as at
Orléans, a dashing stroke, but an act of courage and
humanity.   She blushed for her father and for the prolonged indecision from which she had been compelled
to wrench him; she tried to excuse him as well as
she could, and to save him the shame of not having

mounted his horse and done the deeds that she did; but heart and courage were hers, not his.

On a third occasion she again supplied his deficiency. Two days later (July 4th) during the massacre at the Hôtel-de-Ville, by which the Prince de Condé repaid so grievously his welcome by the Parisians, and which Gaston, according to his habit, favoured, to say the least, by his inaction, Mademoiselle offered to go and save those who were being massacred and curb the populace. Starting from the Luxembourg she could not at first enter the Hôtel-de-Ville; she was more fortunate on a second attempt and reached the place very late, much too late, but soon enough, nevertheless, to do some acts of protection and humanity.

The Fronde was at an end and every one was seeking to make his peace. The rumour ran that Gaston had come to terms with the Court by separating his interests from those of the Prince de Condé. President Viole spoke of it to Mademoiselle, who was reduced to replying: "You know him; I will not answer for what he does." When she went to her base father to ask if he had orders to quit the Luxembourg, and, if so, what she was to do herself, he replied that he should not mix himself up in what concerned her; and he disavowed all that she had done in his name:

"Do you not think, Mademoiselle," he said, with the cowardly and contemptuous irony that was common with him, "that the affair of

Saint-Antoine must have injured you at Court? You have been very pleased to play the heroine, and to be told you were that of our party; that you saved it twice. Whatever happens to you, you will console yourself by thinking of the praises people gave you."

She answered proudly and with dignity:

"I do not think I did you ill-service at the Porte Saint-Antoine, any more than at Orléans. Those two irreproachable actions I did by your order; if they were to do over again, I should do them again, because my duty would oblige me to do so. It is better to do as I did than be humiliated for having done nothing. I do not know what being a heroine is. I am of a birth that does nothing that is not great and lofty. People can call that what they choose; as for me, I call it following my inclination and going my way; I was born not to take that of others."

There is, of course, some pomposity and a little swagger in that utterance, we feel it of course; but we cannot fail to recognise also an echo, as it were, of the "Cid," and certain Corneillian accents. Mademoiselle, during the Fronde, was in love with false grandeur, she sought a false glory; but at least she remained disinterested, generous, and put no stain upon her name.

In the years that followed she had to make the king forgive her, and in the long run she succeeded. During the sojourns, more or less enforced, that she made on the estates of her appanage she acquired a taste for literature and its cultivation. She began at that time to write her Memoirs, which have lately been re-edited by M. Chéruel from the autograph manuscript in the Bibliothéque Nationale. The modern editors (M. Petitot and M. Michaud) neglected to consult that manuscript and have continued to print their editions in which the text has been much touched up, and where various mistakes occur in proper names, and some omissions. All such errors have been repaired in M. Chéruel's edition. The Abbé Terrasson said of a Jansenist translation of the Bible that "the scandal of the text was preserved in all its purity." We may equally say that in this good edition of Mademoiselle's Memoirs her style is given in all the purity of its natural incorrectness.

One of her gentlemen and household attendants was the poet Segrais. Through him she knew Huet (the future bishop) who, then young, served her sometimes as reader during her toilet. She liked novels above all else. She composed one or two about this period (1658), also society Portraits, the fashion of which had just been introduced. She had a whole volume of them printed at Caen in 1659, under the supervision of Huet, with a small number of copies; nearly all these Portraits being written by herself. In short, she made literature much as she had made civil war and played the amazon, at a venture, heedlessly, offhand, but not without a certain capacity.

We find her again in 1660, making part of the Court during the Conferences of the Peace of the Pyrenees, and giving herself up once more to her imagination, no longer under the form heroic; now it was the form pastoral. One day, being at Saint-Jean-de-Luz in the chamber of Cardinal Mazarin, and standing at a window with Mme. de Motteville, admiring the beauty of the scenery, Mademoiselle began to imagine a plan of retirement and solitude, and to moralise on the happy life it would offer. Coming away, full of her project, she wrote a long letter to Mme. de Motteville, who replied in turn. This correspondence, which is quite agreeable to read, marks very well a certain moment in French literature. It represents and characterises the Spanish pastoral element that was in vogue from the novels of d'Urfé to those of Mlle. de Scudéry, and to which the good sense of Louis XIV, aided by Boileau, put an end.

Mademoiselle imagined, in a meadow, near a forest, in view of the sea, a society of the two sexes, composed wholly of amiable and perfect beings, delicate and simple, who watched their flocks on sunny days and for their pleasure, and visited the rest of the time, from one hermitage to another, in chair, calèche or coach; who played the lute and the harpsichord, read poesy and new books, united the advantages of civilised life with the easy habits of rural life (not forgetting the virtues of Christian life); and who all, celibates and widowers, polite without gallantry and even without love, lived honourably together, and felt no need to have recourse to the vulgar remedy of marriage. Observe that a convent of Carmelites is at hand in the forest, and the company does not fail to go there for edification at stated times; for one must, even when leading the gentle life, think also of salvation.

Mme. de Motteville, while replying with all sorts of compliments, and calling Mademoiselle in turn the "illustrious princess" and the "beautiful Amelinta," laughs at her slily for the article interdicting matrimony, which was meant to be the great novelty of this Code of the Sheepfold, and she tries to insinuate a little reality, a little common sense into the scheme of this platonic, Christian, and, withal, gallant republic. She points out that as it would be difficult to suppress gallantry and love altogether, it might perhaps be better to "return to the very common error that an old custom has made legitimate, which is called marriage." The pair expatiate on that topic from one to the other, and Mademoiselle gives proof in the discussion of a romantic spirit rather elegant and distinguished, even elevated now and then. But, on the whole, here, as in the Fronde, it is the sentiment of reality, it is common sense, a sense of the fitness of things, that is always lacking in her.

I shall not follow her through her various compositions and literary rhapsodies (Portraits, Romances of Society, and what not), but come at once to the great event of her life which completes her picture. Mademoiselle was forty-two years of age; she had missed so many and such great marriages that there seemed nothing else for her but to continue in the free and independent position of the richest princess of France, when she began to notice M. de Lauzun, a favourite of the king, and younger than herself by several years. Still cold

and pure, never having loved until then, she now, for
the first time, felt love with an extreme youth-
fulness, or, as one might say, childlikeness of heart;
she describes it to us with the naïveté of a shep-
herdess.

She perceived one day that this little man, captain
of the guards, a Gascon with haughty mien and satirical, witty air, had a nameless something about him
that she had never yet remarked in any one. The first
time he went on duty as captain of the guards, and
"took his baton," as they say " he did his functions
with a grand and easy air, full of attentions without
eagerness. When I made him my compliment," she
relates, " he replied that he was very sensible of the
honour I did him in taking part in the kindness that the
king had for him." That simple speech enchanted
her: " I began from that time to regard him as an *extraordinary* man, very agreeable in conversation, and
I sought very willingly for occasions to speak to him."
She began to be vaguely annoyed when she did not
see him. " That winter," she says (1669), " without
quasi knowing why, I could not endure Paris nor to
leave Saint Germain." Every day that she succeeded
in conversing with him in the embrasure of a window
(a thing not so easy to do because of etiquette and her
rank) she found more and more intellect and accom-
plishments in him. When she held him thus, she forgot herself for hours. She took pleasure in discovering
all sorts of distinctions about him, an elevation of

soul above the common, and "a million singularities" that charmed her.

After dreaming thus for some time, she ended by fixing her mind resolutely; and as she was very honourable and very lacking in foresight, and as, moreover, the idea of love without marriage never entered her head, she thought that the shortest way would be to make the grandeur of the gentleman and wed him. The difficulty was to make him understand this, for the respect behind which Lauzun intrenched himself left her no access to him. It has been remarked that "in friendship as in love princesses are condemned to take all the first steps, and that the respect which surrounds them often obliges the proudest and most virtuous to make advances that other women would not dare to permit themselves." Mademoiselle was compelled to take all these steps. Lauzun's strategy consisted in adding to and raising higher these barriers of respect, already so high, in still further intrenching himself behind them, and getting out of sight. It was all low bows, assurances of submission without end, but he turned a deaf ear to every tender word; and not only did he persistently follow this course , but Baraille, officer of his company and his confidential man, did the same: " Every time I met him (Baraille)," says Mademoiselle, "I bowed to him, to give him a desire to approach me; he always pretended to think I was bowing to some other person, and while he made me profound

bows on one side he was going away on the other;
at which I was in despair." These were Lauzun's tac-
tics and order of the day. If Mademoiselle had not
had any idea of marriage in her head he would have
led her and constrained her to it by his conduct; so
careful was he not to lend himself to any overture
that was simply tender and wooing. The man of
bonnes fortunes became for the nonce a man of
principle; he played the virtuous and the chaste to
get himself married.

Poor Mademoiselle, as much of a novice as a school
girl, and without a confidant, did not know what
to invent to reveal to this conceited coxcomb what
he knew very well already. She sent for the Works
of Corneille and re-read them, looking for images of
her own fate in order to take lessons; she counted
on the secret sympathy of souls: Lauzun would see
nothing. She pretended to consult him on the various marriages proposed to her, hoping that he would
declare himself and give her the opportunity to make
her own confession. But Lauzun was strictly, cruelly
respectful, respectful to excess. Always homage,
never presumption. She had made him, as if in spite
of himself, her counsellor, her confidant; she wished to
marry, she told him,—to marry in France, to make
the fortune of some one who deserved it; to live
with that honourable man and friend in perfect esteem, with sweetness and tranquillity; it was only
a question of finding some one worthy of that choice.

Lauzun discussed the matter with her at length; he weighed the advantages and the disadvantages of such a step, taking very good care not to seem to divine that he himself was in question. There were days, however, when he seemed to be beginning to understand; but he always escaped in time "by respectful manners full of witty sense," which only inflamed the innocent princess more and more.

She loved like Dido, like Medea, like Ariadne, but twenty years too late. She did things that would have been quite charming in a very young girl. During a journey into Flanders where M. de Lauzun commanded as general, on a day when it poured with rain he came often to the side of the king's carriage, bareheaded and hat in hand. Mademoiselle at last could not contain herself and said to the king: "Make him put on his hat !" At Saint-Germain, where the Court then was, being, for the hundredth time, on the point of naming to Lauzun the man she had chosen to render happy, about whom she consulted him perpetually, without having the courage to articulate the name, she said to him: "If I had an inkstand and paper I would write it down for you"; then pointing to a mirror beside her, she added: "I have a mind to breathe upon it and write the name in big letters that you might read it plain."

One thing is remarkable, and it is, as it were, a stamp of the times; namely that the idea of the king, the official worship and idolatry vowed to him, forms

a third in the whole affair. It is in the king's name
and as if under his invocation that they love each
other and dare, in the end, acknowledge it: "The
king has always been and is my first passion, M. de
Lauzun the second," writes Mademoiselle; and Lauzun, on his side, says he would not flatter himself
to have pleased Mademoiselle definitely and have
touched her heart, except by reason of the respect
and "true tenderness" that he felt for the person
of the king. As soon as the marriage is decided we
find him stipulating that he is not to leave the king
for a single instant, that he is to continue to do all
the duties of his office, first at the *lever* and last at the
coucher; and quite resolved not to give up sleeping
in the Louvre. The first use he intends to make of
Mademoiselle's enormous wealth is to put his company of the guards into new uniforms to "pay court
to the king." In her letter to the king, asking permission to marry Lauzun, Mademoiselle is careful
to clang very loud that chain of servitude, which, to
her eyes, is more honourable than all else and in
which she claims her share: "I say this to Your
Majesty," she writes, "to prove to you that the more
we have of grandeur the more worthy we are to be
your servants [*domestiques*]." There was one thing
for which Lauzun cared more than to be the husband
of Mademoiselle, Duc de Montpensier, and the greatest noble of the kingdom, and that was to stand well
with his master. I note expressly the reigning form

of grovelling in those days: let us not flatter ourselves that we escape it in ours.

The rest is well known. Louis XIV consented, at
first, to the marriage. They were very unwise not
to profit by the permission within twenty-four hours,
and give him no time for reflection. The marriage,
consented to the evening before, was announced on
Monday, December 15, 1670, and held good till the
following Thursday. The king then withdrew his
permission abruptly. Mademoiselle was thrown into
a state we can well suppose, but without daring, as
yet, to blaspheme against the king. Lauzun received
the blow like an accomplished courtier and as if he
had said: "The king gave, and the king has taken
away, I can only thank and bless him." He seemed
for a moment, on the point of increasing in favour.
Nevertheless, for reasons that have always remained
obscure, he was arrested a year later (November 25,
1671) and imprisoned in the castle of Pignerol. His
captivity lasted no less than ten years.

Mademoiselle, during those years, had no thought
that was not of him; she did everything she could to
obtain his deliverance, and she bought it at the price
of enormous sacrifices of property, the gift of which
Mme. de Montespan drew out of her in behalf of her
son, the Duc du Maine, the king's bastard. She
passed through all they put upon her in order to see
once more the man she loved. She was ill-rewarded.

When Lauzun left prison he was no longer the

honourable man, the gallant man, the polished man who had so charmed her; the courtier alone survived, the rabid courtier, who had no peace because he did not recover footing and a patching up of favour with the master; in other respects, hard, openly selfish, covetous, daring to reproach Mademoiselle for the sacrifices of property she had made to deliver him! Imprisonment had only brought out defects of character and of heart which he had known how to hide in his splendid years. Besides which, marriage (for it seems that a secret marriage really took place at this time) relieved him henceforth from the necessity of restraining himself.

Mademoiselle came late to a knowledge of life, but she ended by knowing it and by passing, too, through all stages of trial; she had the slow suffering that wears out love in the heart, the contempt and indignation that break it, and she came at last to the indifference that has no cure and no consolation other than God. It is a sad day that, on which we discover that the one person we have delighted to adorn with all perfections and crown with all gifts is so worthless a thing. Mademoiselle had several years to meditate on that bitter discovery. She died in March, 1693, at sixty-six years of age.

Her obsequies, celebrated with great magnificence, were disturbed by a singular accident. The urn that contained her embalmed entrails, which were badly embalmed, exploded in the middle of the ceremony with a loud noise and sent all present flying. It was written above that a little absurdity should mingle in all that concerned Mademoiselle, even her funeral.

What was lacking in her life, in her character, and in her mind was grace, reasonableness, fitness (*justesse*), those qualities, in short, which were to mark the best epoch of Louis XIV. With her ten years more than the king, Mademoiselle was always a little behind the age and an echo of the old Court. She belonged, by her turn of imagination, to the literature of the last years of Louis XIII and the Regency, to the literature of the hôtel Rambouillet, a literature that did not come under the reform of Boileau nor that of Mme. de La Fayette. There was always a sort of pell-mell in her admirations; she valued Corneille highly; she had Tartuffe played before her, but she received the Abbé Cotin: "I like verses, no matter what kind they are," she said. But, above all, she loved grandeur, she loved glory; she often mistook it, but at all times she had emotions of pride, honour, and goodness that were worthy of her race. The days on which she is at her best she is conscious of the neighbourhood of Corneille. Her conduct on the day of Saint-Antoine ought to be reckoned in her favour. Her Memoirs, also, have most durable claims; they are truthful and faithful Memoirs, in which she tells everything about herself and about others, naïvely, and openly, and according to what comes into her mind. Persons of good sense who read them and who enjoy, as a lost singularity, such amazing confessions and her princely fashion of seeing things, can supply without effort the reflections and the morality that she herself does not put into them.

XI.

The Comtesse de La Fayette.

XI.

Marie Madeleine de La Vergne.

Comtesse de La Fayette.

IN the time of Mme. de Sévigné, beside her, and in
her most cherished intimacy was a woman whose
history was closely interwoven with that of her
amiable friend. It is she whom Boileau described
as "the woman of most mind in France and the
best writer." She wrote, however, very little, at
her leisure, for amusement, and with a sort of negligence that had nothing of the professional about it;
above all, she hated to write letters, so that we have
but a very small number of hers, and those very
short; it is in the letters of Mme. de Sévigné rather
than in her own that we shall know her. But she
had in her day a rôle apart, serious and elegant, solid
and charming; a rôle that was, in fact, considerable
and, in its class, on a level with the highest. To
tenderness of soul and a romantic imagination she
added a natural precision and, as her witty friend said
of her, "a divine reason" that never failed her; she
had them in her writings as well as in her life; they
belong to the models that ought to be studied in that

century, where they present, one with another, so balanced a mixture.

A recent attempt has been made, in rehabilitating the hôtel Rambouillet, to show its perfected and triumphant heiress in the person of Mme. de Maintenon; a saying of Ségrais decides the matter far more in favour of Mme. de La Fayette; showing the direct affiliation, from which all the *précieux* has disappeared. After a rather prolonged portrait of Mme. de Rambouillet, he adds incontinently: "Mme. de La Fayette had learned a good deal from her, but Mme. de La Fayette's mind was more solid." This perfected heiress of Mme. de Rambouillet, this friend for ever of Mme. de Sévigné, and of Mme. de Maintenon for many years, has her rank and her assured date in our literature, inasmuch as it was she who reformed the novel, and applied a part of the "divine reason" that was in her to treating gently and fixing within its due limits a school of tenderness, the excesses of which had been great, but which she had only to touch to make it find grace once more in minds of serious mould who seemed disposed to abolish it.

For, this secondary class of literature where elegance and a certain interest sufficed, but where no genius (if any there be) is out of place; a class that the *Art Poétique* does not mention, which Prevost, Le Sage, and Jean-Jacques have consecrated, and which, in the days of Mme. de La Fayette, was confined, at least in its higher reaches, to the affecting

MARIE MADELEINE DE LA VERGNE,
COMTESSE DE LA FAYETTE

parts of Berenice or Iphigenia—for this class Mme.
de La Fayette has done what her illustrious contemporaries strove with rivalry to do in the graver and
more respected walks of literature. *L'Astrée,* by im-
planting, so to speak, the novel in France, had served
as stock to those interminable grafts, *Cyrus, Cleo-
patre, Polyxandre,* and *Clélie.* Boileau, with his
satire, cut them short, as he did that long line of
epic poems, *Moïse Sauvée, Saint-Louis, La Pucelle.*
Mme. de La Fayette, without apparent satire, and
seeming merely to come after and under cover of
her predecessors (from whom Ségrais and Huet have
very ill-distinguished her, enveloping them all in the
same praises), dealt them a heavier blow than any one
by her *Princess de Clèves.* And she knew very well
what she was doing, and what she meant to do.
She was accustomed to say that a sentence cut out of
a work was worth a gold louis, and a word left out,
twenty sous; that saying has great value in her
mouth when we reflect on the novels in ten volumes from which it was so necessary to escape.
Proportion, sobriety, decency, simple methods, and
heart, substituted for great catastrophes and grand
phrases, those were the features of the reform, or, to
speak less ambitiously, the retouching she gave to
the novel; in that, she belonged to the purer period
of Louis XIV.

The long and inviolable friendship of Mme. de
La Fayette with M. de La Rochefoucauld makes her

own life resemble a novel, a virtuous novel, but a novel all the same; more out of rule than the life of Mme. de Sévigné, who loved no one but her daughter, less schemed and calculated than that of Mme. de Maintenon, whose sole aim was the sacrament with the king. We like to see a tender heart allying itself with a bitter and disillusioned mind to soften it; a tardy passion, but faithful, between two serious souls, where the one that feels corrects the misanthropy of the other; where delicacy, tenderness, reciprocal consolation and sweetness reign rather than illusions and fire: Mme. de Clèves, in short, ill and a little sad beside M. de Nemours, grown old and a maker of maxims. Such was the life of Mme. de La Fayette and the exact relation between her person and her novel. The lack of illusion that we remark in her, the melancholy reason that formed the basis of her life, passed a little into the ideal of her novel and also, it seems to me, into all those other novels that, in a way, emanated from her and which are her posterity: *Eugène de Rothelin, Mademoiselle de Clermont, Édouard.* Whatever tenderness there may be in those charming creations, reason is there too, the breath of human experience blows from a corner and cools passion. Beside the loving soul that is ready to yield there is something that warns and restrains. M. de La Rochefoucauld with his maxims is ever there.

If Mme. de La Fayette reformed the novel in France, the chivalrous and sentimental novel, and gave to it the particular tone that conciliates to a certain point the ideal with the actual and the observed, it may also be said that she was the first to give an example altogether illustrious of those attachments, lasting, decent, legitimate, and sacred in their constancy of every day, every minute, through years till death, that came of the manners and morals of the old society and were well-nigh extinguished with it. The *Princesse de Clèves* and her attachment to M. de La Rochefoucauld are the two almost equal titles of Mme. de La Fayette to serious and touching fame; they are two points that mark the literature and the society of Louis XIV.

I should have left the pleasure of recomposing this existence, so simple in events, to the imagination of the readers of Mme. de Sévigné if a little unpublished document, but a very private one, had not invited me to make a frame in which to set it.

The father of Mme. de La Fayette, a general and the governor of Havre, had, it is said, some merit, and he took great pains with the education of his daughter. Her mother (*née* de Péna) came from Provence, and counted a certain troubadour-laureate among her ancestors. Mlle. Marie-Madeleine Pioche de La Vergne had, at an early age, more reading and study than many persons of the preceding generation, even intellectual ones, ever had in their youth. Mme. de Choisy, for example, had amazing natural wit in conversation or in letters, but she could not spell correctly.

Mme. de Sévigné and Mme. de La Fayette, the latter younger by six or seven years than her friend, added to an excellent foundation a perfect culture. We have for direct testimony as to their education the raptures of Ménage, who ordinarily, as we know, fell in love with his beautiful pupils. He celebrated, under every form of Latin verse, the beauty, the grace, the elegance in speaking well and writing well of Mme. de La Fayette or rather Mlle. de La Vergne, Laverna, as he called her. Later, he presented to her his friend, the learned Huet, who became to her a literary counsellor. Ségraiṣ, who, with Mme. de Sévigné, suffices to make Mme. de La Fayette known to us, says:

" Three months after Mme. de La Fayette began to learn Latin she knew more of it than M. Ménage and Père Rapin, her masters. One day, in making her translate, they had a dispute themselves about the meaning of a passage, and neither would give way to the sentiment of the other. Mme. de La Fayette said to them: ' Neither of you understands it,' and she gave them the right explanation of the passage; they agreed then that she was right. It was a poet she explained, for she did not like prose, and had never read Chéron; but she took great pleasure in poesy, reading Virgil and Horace specially; and as she had a poetic mind and knew all that belonged to that art, she entered without difficulty into the meaning of those authors."

A little farther on he refers again to the merits of M. Ménage: "Where shall we find such poets as M. Ménage, who can make good Latin verses, good Greek verses, and good Italian verses? He was a great personage, whatever jealous people chose to say. Yet he did not know all the delicacies of poesy; but Mme. de La Fayette knew them well." The woman who preferred poets to all other writers and felt their truth, was she who proved herself "true" *par excellence* as M. de La Rochefoucauld told her, using that expression, which has lasted until now, for the first time: "Poetic spirit, true spirit!—her merit, like her charm, is in that alliance."

She lost her father when fifteen years of age. Her mother, a good woman, Retz tells us, but rather foolish and very bustling, remarried, soon after, with the Chevalier Renaud de Sévigné, much mixed up in the intrigues of the Fronde, and who was one of the most active in rescuing the cardinal from the castle of Nantes. We read in the cardinal's Memoirs, àpropos of that imprisonment at Nantes (1653), and the amusing visits he received there:

"Mme. de La Vergne, who had married for her second husband M. le Chevalier de Sévigné, and who lived in Anjou with her husband, came to see me and brought her daughter, Mlle. de La Vergne, now Mme. de La Fayette. She was very pretty and very amiable, and had much the air of Mme. de Lesdiguières. She pleased me much, and the truth is, I did not please her at all, either because she had no inclination for me, or because the distrust that her mother and step-father had sedulously put into her, even in Paris, on account of my various amours and inconstancies, had put her on her guard against me. I consoled myself for her cruelty with the ease that was natural to me. . . ."

Mlle. de La Vergne, then twenty years old, needed nothing more than her own good sense to take small account of this idle and trivial caprice of the daring prisoner, so quickly consoled.

Married in 1655 to the Comte de La Fayette, what was probably the most interesting fact about the marriage and the most in accordance with imagination, was that she thus became the sister-in-law of Mère Angélique de La Fayette, superior of the convent of Chaillot, formerly maid of honour to Anne of Austria, whose perfect love with Louis XIII made so chaste and simple a romance, resembling those described in the *Princesse de Clèves*. Her husband, after giving her the name that she was to make illustrious, effaces himself and disappears, so to speak, from her life; we hear nothing more by which to distinguish him. She had two sons by him, whom she deeply loved; one, a soldier, whose advancement in life occupied her greatly, and who died shortly after her, and another, the Abbé de La Fayette, provided with good abbeys, of whom we chiefly know that he carelessly lent his mother's manuscripts and lost them.

Mme. de La Fayette was introduced while young to the hôtel Rambouillet and learned a great deal from the marquise. M. Roederer, who is anxious that none of Molière's mockery shall touch the hôtel Rambouillet, depopulates it and brings it to a close much sooner than is accurate. Mme. de La Fayette went there before her marriage and profited by its intercourse, as did Mme. de Sévigné. M. Auger, in the notice, correct and interesting but dry in tone, that he gives to Mme. de La Fayette, says: "Introduced early to the society of the hôtel Rambouillet the natural correctness and solidity of her mind might not, perhaps, have resisted the contagion of bad taste of which that house was the centre, if her reading of the Latin poets had not given her a preservative."

The preservative ought to have acted on Ménage first of all. The above is most unjust to the hôtel Rambouillet, and M. Roederer is completely right in protesting against that manner of speaking ; but he, himself, is assuredly misled when he makes that hotel the cradle of good taste and shows us Mlle. de Scudéry as being more tolerated there than extolled and admired. He forgets that Voiture, as long as he lived, ruled the roast in that company, and we know very well, in the matter of taste, as well as of intellect, what Voiture was. As for Mlle. de Scudéry, it is enough to read Ségrais, Huet, and others to see what was thought at the hôtel Rambouillet of that incomparable spinster, of her *Illustre Bassa* and *Grand Cyrus*, and of her verses "so natural, so tender," disparaged by Boileau but to which, nevertheless, "he could never attain himself." What Ségrais and Huet admired in such terms as these was not likely to be judged more severely in a company of which they were the final oracles.

Mme. de La Fayette, whose mind was solid and acute, came out of that intercourse, as did Mme. de Sévigné, by

simply taking its best. In age she belonged wholly
to the young Court; even with less solidity of mind
she would not have failed to possess its appropriate
elegancies. From the first days of her marriage she
had occasion to see frequently at the Carmelite convent of Chaillot the young Princess of England with
her mother, Queen Henrietta, who, being in exile,
had retired there. When the young princess became Madame [Henrietta Anne, Duchesse d'Orléans]
and the most lively ornament of the Court, Mme. de La
Fayette, though ten years her elder, was still admitted
to their old familiarity, had her private *entrées,* and might
have passed for Madame's favourite. In the charming sketch she has drawn of the brilliant years of the
princess, speaking of herself in the third person, she
judges herself thus:

" Mlle. de La Trémouille and Mme. de La Fayette were of this
number " (the number of those who frequently saw Madame). " The
first pleased her by her goodness and by a certain ingenuousness in
telling all that was in her heart, which had something of the simplicity of early youth ; the other was agreeable to her by her happiness, for, although she thought she had merit, it was a sort of merit
so serious in appearance that it seemed hardly likely to please a
princess as young as Madame. "

So, at thirty years of age, Mme. de La Fayette was
at the centre or the politeness, good-breeding, and
gallantry of the flourishing years of Louis XIV; she
was present at all Madame's parties at Fontainebleau;
a spectator rather than an actor; having no share,
she tells us, in Madame's confidence on certain affairs;

but after those affairs had taken place and were a
little noised abroad she heard them from her lips and
wrote them down to please her. "You write so
well," Madame said to her: "write, and I will supply
you with good memoirs."—"It was rather difficult
work," says Mme. de La Fayette, "to turn the truth
of certain matters in a way to make it known and
yet not let it be offensive or disagreeable to the
princess."

One of these "certain matters," among others,
which set Mme. de La Fayette's delicacy on edge
and excited Madame's laughter at the pains the amiable writer was giving herself, must have been, I fancy,
the following:

"She [Madame] became intimate with the Comtesse de Soissons
. . . and thought only of pleasing the king as a sister-in-law. I
think that she pleased him in another way; I think also that she
thought he pleased her as a brother-in-law, though, perhaps, he
pleased her much more; in short, as they were both infinitely charming and both were born with dispositions to gallantry, and as they
saw each other daily in the midst of pleasures and diversions, it
appeared to the eyes of every one that they felt for each other that
attraction that usually precedes great passions."

Madame died in the arms of Mme. de La Fayette,
who did not leave her in her last moments. The
narrative she has left of this death equals the finest
that we have of the most affecting deaths; it has
expressions, as it were by the way, that light up the
whole scene:

"I went up to her. She told me she was vexed; but the ill-
humour of which she spoke would have made the good-humour of

other women, so much natural sweetness had she, and so little was she capable of bitterness or anger. . . . After dinner she lay down upon the floor . . . she made me sit beside her, so that her head was partly on me. . . . During her sleep she changed so considerably that I felt much surprised, and I thought it must be that her mind contributed greatly to embellish her face. . . . I was wrong, however, in making that reflection, for I had seen her asleep many times, and never did I see her less lovely."

And, farther on:

" Monsieur was beside her bed; she kissed him, and said gently, with an air capable of wooing the most barbarous heart: 'Alas! Monsieur, you ceased to love me long ago; but that is unjust; I have never wronged you.' Monsieur seemed much touched, and all who were in the room were so affected that nothing was heard but the noise of persons weeping. . . . When the king had left the room, I was beside her bed and she said to me: 'Madame de La Fayette, my nose is already sunken,' I answered her only by tears. . . . She failed steadily."

On the 30th of June, 1673, Mme. de Lafayette wrote to Mme. de Sévigné: "It is three years to-day since I saw Madame die; I received yesterday many of her letters; I am all full of her."

For the space of ten years in the midst of that brilliant and gallant society, was Mme. de La Fayette, still young, with nobility and charm of face, if not beauty,—was she only an attentive observer, without active interest of heart other than her attachment to Madame? was she without any single and secret choice of her own? Towards the year 1665, as I conjecture and will explain farther on, she had chosen out of the vortex M. de La Rochefoucauld, then about fifty-two years of age, to be her friend for life.

Mme. de La Fayette wrote while still young from taste, but always with sobriety. It was the day of "Portraits." She wrote one of Mme. de Sévigné, (1659), supposed to be written by a stranger: "It is better than myself," said the latter, finding the Portrait, in 1675, among the old papers of Mme. de La Trémouille: "but those who loved me sixteen years ago might find some resemblance." It is under these youthful features, for ever fixed by her friend, that Mme. de Sévigné still appears to us immortal. When Madame, inviting Mme. de La Fayette to set to work, said to her: "You write well," she had doubtless read the *Princesse de Montpensier*, the first short novel of our author, printed in 1662. For elegance, and vivacity of narration, it detaches itself from all the other novels and historiettes of its day, and shows a spirit of correctness, accuracy, and reform. Mme. de La Fayette's imagination in composing turned willingly back to the polished and brilliant epoch of the Valois, to the reigns of Charles IX or Henri II, which she idealised a little, and embellished in the same direction as that in which the graceful and discreet tales of Queen Marguerite shows them to us. The *Princesse de Montpensier,* The *Princesse de Clèves*, and *La Comtesse de Tende* do not belong to those reigns, whose vices and crimes have, perhaps, too much eclipsed to our eyes their intellectual culture. Madame's Court, for wit, for intrigues, for vices also, was not without affinity to

that of the Valois; and the history Mme. de La
Fayette has made of it recalls more than once the
Memoirs of Queen Marguerite, so charming in her day,
but who is not to be believed at all times. The
perfidious Vardes and the haughty de Guiche are
figures that have their counterparts at the Court
of Henri II; and at Madame's Court the Chevalier
de Lorraine was not wanting. Mme. de La Fayette
held in that society a rôle of authority, as it were
exercising on its tone a sort of wise criticism. Two
months before the unhappy death of Madame, Mme.
de Montmorency wrote to M. de Bussy, by way of
a joke (May 1, 1670):

" Mme. de La Fayette, Madame's favourite, has had her skull
broken by a chimney cornice that did not respect a head so brilliant with the glory given by the favours of a great princess. Before this mishap I read a letter from her, which has been given to
the public, in ridicule of what are called words à la mode, the use
of which is worthless. I send it to you."

Here follows the letter, which is composed in a bur-
lesque jargon by which she meant to correct the
absurdities of the great world; it purports to be
from a jealous lover to his mistress. Boileau, in his
line, could not have done better. In fact she is, by
one degree softened, a species of Boileau to the
manners of the Court.

Mme. de La Fayette never knew, I think, those
passions that rend the soul with violence; she
gave her heart voluntarily. When she made choice
of M. de La Rochefoucauld and allied herself with

him she was, as I have said, thirty-two or thirty-three years old; he was fifty-two. She had seen him and known him no doubt for a long time, but it is of their particular intimacy that I now speak. We shall see by the following letter, hitherto unpublished, which is one of the most confidential ever written, that about the time of the publication of the Maxims and of the Comte de Saint-Paul's first entrance into society, there was talk of the liaison of Mme. de La Fayette and M. de La Rochefoucauld as of something quite recently established. Mme. de La Fayette writes the letter to Mme. de Sablé, an old friend of M. de La Rochefoucauld, the same who had so much share in the making of the Maxims, and who, for some time past, was wholly given up to Port-Royal, more, it would seem, from intention to reform and in fear of death than from any complete conversion. Here is the letter:

"Monday evening; I could not reply to your note yesterday, because I had company; and I think I may not reply to it to-day, because it is too kind. I am ashamed of the praises you give me; on the other hand, I like you to have a good opinion of me, and I wish not to say anything to contradict what you think. Therefore, I will only answer by telling you that M. le Comte de Saint-Paul has just left me, that we talked of you for one hour, as you know well I should talk.

"We also talked of a man that I always take the liberty of putting on a par with you for charm of mind. I do not know whether that comparison will offend you; but if it would offend you on the lips of others, on mine it is great praise, if all *they say is true*. I saw plainly that the Comte de Saint-Paul had heard talk of those sayings, and I entered slightly into the matter with him. But I fear he may take too seriously what I said to him. I conjure you, the first time you see him, speak to him yourself about those rumours. It can come about easily, for I gave him the Maxims, of which he will speak to you no doubt. But I beg you to speak to him in the right way to put into his head that the whole thing is merely a jest. I am not certain enough of what you think yourself to be sure that you will say the right thing; and I believe I must begin by convincing my ambassadress. Nevertheless, I must rely on your skill; it is above all ordinary maxims. But do convince him. I do hate like death that young men of his age should think I have gallantries. They think those who are older than themselves a hundred years old, and they are quite astonished that there should still be any question of them; besides which, he will believe more readily what is told him about M. de La Rochefoucauld than about others. In short, I do not want him to think anything, unless it is that he is one of my friends; and I beg you also not to forget to get it out of his head, if it is in it, that I forgot your message. It is not generous to remind you of one service by asking another.

(On the margin.) "I must not forget to tell you that I found a terribly clever mind in the Comte de Saint-Paul."

To add to the interest of this letter, the reader must kindly remember the exact situation: M. de Saint-Paul, son of Mme. de Longueville and, probably, of M. de La Rochefoucauld, coming to see Mme. de La Lafayette, who is thought to be the object of a last tender passion, and who wants to have him undeceived —or deceived—on that score. The "terribly clever mind" of the young prince went straight, I imagine, to the heart of Mme. de Longueville, to whom the postscript at least, and the rest of the letter probably, was certain to be quickly shown. There is a charming sentence in the letter that all belated lovers should meditate upon: "I do hate like death that young men of his age should think I have gallantries." It is the counterpart of the following thought in the *Princesse de Clèves:*

"Mme. de Clèves, who was at that age when it is not believable that a woman can be loved if she is more than twenty-five years of age, regarded with extreme astonishment the king's attachment to the Duchesse de Valentinois." That idea, as we see, was familiar to Mme. de La Fayette. She feared above all to seem to inspire, or feel, the passion that at that age others affect. Her delicate reasonableness became a chastity.

I hold the more to the conclusion that the intimate and declared relations between M. de La Rochefoucauld and herself did not begin until this period, because it seems to me that the influence of this affectionate friend upon him was directly contrary to the Maxims; that she would have made him correct and cut out some of them if she had influenced him before as she did after their publication; and that La Rochefoucauld, the misanthrope, who said he had never found love except in novels and that as for himself he had never felt it, is not the man of whom she said later: "M. de La Rochefoucauld gave me a mind, but I have reformed his heart."

In a little note written by her to Mme. de Sablé, (unpublished), who had herself already composed Maxims, she says:

"You will cause me the greatest vexation in the world if you do not show me your Maxims. Mme. Du Plessis has given me an extreme desire to see them; and it is just because they are virtuous and reasonable that I have that desire; they will convince me that all persons of good sense are not so sure of the general corruption as M. de La Rochefoucauld is."

It is this idea of general corruption that she set herself to combat in La Rochefoucauld, and which she rectified. The desire to enlighten and soften that noble spirit was, no doubt, an allurement of reason and beneficence leading her to the borders of the closer relation.

The former Knight of the Fronde, now become bitter and gouty, was not in other respects what might have been expected from his book. He had studied little, Segrais tells us, but his marvellous perception and his knowledge of the world stood him in place of study. Young, he had plunged into all the vices of his time, and had come out of them with more health of mind than of body, if one can call anything healthy that was so soured. This did not interfere in any way with the sweetness of his intercourse and his infinite charm. He was good-breeding itself, perfect, unfailing; he gained more and more each day by being better known; but he was a man for private intercourse and conversation; a wider audience did not suit him; if he had been obliged to speak before five or six persons rather solemnly strength would have failed him; the harangue that must be made before the French Academy deterred him from seeking to enter it. One evening in June, 1672, when word was brought to him of the death of the young Duc de Longueville (Comte de Saint-Paul) that of the Chevalier de Marsillac, his grandson, and of the wound of the Prince de Marsillac, his son,

when all this hailstorm fell upon him, he was wonderful, says Mme. de Sévigné "in his sorrow and his
firmness.   .   .   .   I saw his heart uncovered," she
adds, "at that cruel moment; he is in the front rank
of all that I have ever seen of courage, merit, tenderness, and reason." Not long after this she said of
him that he was patriarchal, and felt almost as
strongly as she did the parental feeling. There is
the real La Rochefoucauld as Mme. de La Fayette
reformed him.

It was not until after the death of Madame, and
after Madame de La Fayette's health had begun to
fail, that the *liaison*, such as Mme. de Sévigné shows
it to us, was completely established. The letters of
that incomparable friend, which continue uninterrupt-
edly precisely from that period, permit us to follow
all its circumstances, even to the happy monotony of
its tender and rooted habit:

"Their ill health," she writes, "made them necessary to each
other, and . . . and gave them leisure to taste their good qualities,
which is not the case in other *liaisons*. . . . At Court, people
have no leisure to love; that vortex, so violent for others, was peaceful for them, and gave great space to the pleasure of an intercourse
so delightful. I believe that no passion can exceed in strength such
an intimacy. . . ."

I shall not quote all that could be extracted from, I
might say, every letter of Mme. de Sévigné, for there
are few in which Mme. de La Fayette is not mentioned, and many were written or closed in her house,
with the compliments of M. de La Rochefoucauld

"now present." On the good days, the days of toler-
able health and of dinners *en lavardinage ou bavardi-*
nage, all is graceful enjoyment, roulades of mischievous
gaiety on that goose of a Mme. de Marans, on the
manœuvring of Mme. de Brissac and M. le Duc.
Some days are more serious but not less delightful,
when, at Saint-Maur for instance, in the house that
the Prince de Condé had lent to Gourville, and which
Mme. de La Fayette willingly enjoyed, the *Poétique*
of Boileau was read to a choice company who declared it a masterpiece. Another time, in default of
Boileau and his *Poétique* they took to Lulli, and at
certain parts of the opera of "Cadmus" they wept:
"I am not alone in being unable to bear them," writes
Mme. de Sévigné, "Mme. de La Fayette is much agitated." That agitated soul was sensitiveness itself.

There were also days when Mme. de La Fayette
went to pay little visits at Court; and the king took
her in his calèche with other ladies to show her the
beauties of Versailles, as any private individual might
have done; and such a trip, such success furnished
Mme. de La Fayette on her return, wise as she was,
with a topic for very long conversations and even,
though she did not like to write them, for letters less
short than usual; Mme. de Grignan at a distance is a
little jealous; so she is again, àpropos of an inkstand
in mahogany that Mme. de Montespan presents to
Mme. de La Fayette. But Mme. de Sévigné smooths
such matters over by compliments and sweet mes-

sages, which she arranges and exchanges constantly
between her daughter and her best friend.   Even
when Mme. de La Fayette no longer went to Versailles and no longer embraced the king's knees,
weeping with gratitude, even when M. de La Rochefoucauld was dead, she maintained her influence and
the consideration shown to her. "Never did a woman without leaving her own place," says Mme. de
Sévigné, "manage so many good affairs."   Louis
XIV liked her always as the favourite of Madame, a
witness of her touching death, and of the beautiful
years with which she was associated in his memory.

But Versailles, and Boileau's *Poétique,* the operas
of Lulli, and the gaieties on Mme. de Marans are often
interrupted by the wretched health which with its
tertian fever never allowed itself to be forgotten and
became, little by little, their principal occupation. In
her fine and vast garden of the rue de Vaugirard, so
verdant, so balmy; in Gourville's house at Saint-Maur,
where she made herself frankly at home as a friend;
at Fleury-sous-Mendon, where she went to breathe
the air of the woods, we can follow her, ill and
melancholy; we see that long and serious face grow
thinner, consuming its own vitality. Her life, for
twenty years, was converted into a little fever, more
or less slow; and the bulletins read thus:

" Mme. de La Fayette goes tomorrow to the small house at Mendon
where she has been already.   She will spend a fortnight there, to be,
as it were, suspended betwixt earth and heaven; she will not think,

speak, answer, or listen; she is weary of saying good evening and
good morning; she has fever every day and repose would cure her;
repose therefore she must have. I shall go and see her sometimes.
M. de La Rochefoucauld is in that chair that you know. He is un-
utterably sad; one understands very well what is the matter with
him."

What was, no doubt, the matter with M. de La
Rochefoucauld, besides the gout and his ordinary
ailments, was missing Mme. de La Fayette.

The sadness that such a state naturally nurtured
did not prevent the return of smiles and pleasures
at slight intervals. Among the various nicknames
that society bestowed, — Mme. Scarron being " Thaw "
Colbert "North," M. de Pomponne, " Rain,"—Mme.
de La Fayette was called " Mist "; the mist rose
sometimes and then there were charming horizons.
A gentle, resigned, melancholy reason, attracting yet
detached, reposeful in tone, strewn with striking and
true sayings easily remembered, such was the habitual
course of her conversation and of her thought. " It
is enough to be," she said of herself, accepting her
inactive existence. That saying, which describes
her fully, is from the woman who said also, àpropos
of Montaigne, that it would be a pleasure to have
a neighbour like him.

An extreme sensitiveness, often full of tears, appeared at moments and suddenly athwart this steady
reason, like a spring gushing from a tract of level
land. We have seen her "agitated " by the emotion
of music. When Mme. de Sévigné leaves Paris for

Les Rochers or for Provence she must not bid her
farewell or let the visit appear to be the last; Mme.
de La Fayette's tenderness could not support the departure of such a friend.   One day, when they were
talking before her, M. le Duc [de Bourbon] being present, of the campaign that was to open in another
month, the sudden idea of the dangers M. le Duc was
about to run brought tears to her eyes.   These ef-
fusions of feeling had the greater charm and the more
value as coming from so judicious a woman and so
calm a mind.

Her attention, in the retirement of her feeble life,
was none the less given to essential things; without
stirring from her place she watched over all.   If she
reformed the heart of M. de La Rochefoucauld she
also improved his business affairs.   She was well
informed as to lawsuits; she prevented him from
losing the finest part of his property by supplying him
with the means of proving that it was entailed.   We
can conceive from that why she wrote few letters and
those only necessary ones.   This was her one stormy
point with Mme. de Sévigné.   The few letters that
she did write to her friend are nearly all to say that
she can say only two words, and would say more
only she has a headache.   Even M. de La Fayette
makes his appearance one day in person, arriving
from I know not where, as an excuse for not writing.
The pretty letter should be read: "There! there! my
dearest, why are you screaming like an eagle?" etc.,

to understand fully Mme. de La Fayette's way of life, and to catch the difference in tone between her and Mme. de Sévigné.   Here we find those words so often quoted: " You are in Provence, *ma belle;* your hours are free, your head still more so; the taste for writing to everybody still lasts with you; with me it has gone by; if I had a lover who wanted a letter from me every morning, I should break with him."

Mme. de La Fayette was very "true" and very frank; " her word was to be believed."   " She would not have given the slightest freedom to any one if she had not been convinced that he deserved it; and this made some persons say that she was stiff; she was only upright."   Mme. de Maintenon, with whom Mme. de La Fayette had close relations, was also marvellously upright in mind, but her character was less frank; as judicious but less true; and this difference must have contributed to the cooling of their friendship.   In 1672, when Mme. Scarron was secretly bringing up Louis XIV's bastards in the Faubourg Saint-Germain near to Mme. de La Fayette's house, the latter was still intimate with her; she heard from her, as did Mme. de Coulanges, and she must have visited her.   But Mme. Scarron's confidence being withdrawn by degrees, there resulted the usual words reported and conjectures made that cause trouble between friends: " The idea of entering a convent never came into my mind," writes Mme. de Maintenon to the Abbé Testu; " pray reassure Mme.

de La Fayette." Giving her brother a lecture on econ-
omy, she writes in 1678: "If I had fifty thousand
francs a year, I would not keep up the style of a
great lady, nor have a bed trimmed with gold lace
like Mme. de La Fayette, nor a valet-de-chambre like
Mme. de Coulanges; is the pleasure they get out of
it worth the ridicule they incur?" I know not if
Mme. de La Fayette's gold-lace bed did lend itself to
ridicule, but lying in it, as too often happened, she
was, by all odds, more simple than her friend in that
"dead leaf" mantle she affected to wear to the very
end.

All friendship finally ceased between them, Mme.
de Maintenon declares it: "I am not able to preserve
Mme. de La Fayette's friendship; she puts its contin-
uation at too high a price. I have at least shown her
that I am as sincere as herself. It is the Duke who
brought about our quarrel. We had others formerly
about trifles." In Mme. de La Fayette's Memoirs,
àpropos of the "Comedy of Esther," we find:

"She (Mme. de Maintenon) ordered the poet to make a comedy but to
choose a pious subject: for, as things are now, outside of piety there is
no salvation at Court, nor in the other world. . . . The comedy
represents, in some sort, the fall of Mme. de Montespan, and the rise
of Mme. de Maintenon; all the difference being that Esther is a little
younger and less affected in the matter of piety."

In quoting these words of two illustrious women, I
certainly take no pleasure in bringing out the bitterness
that spoiled a long affection. In truth, Mme. de

Maintenon and Mme. de La Fayette were powers too considerable, and the claims of each were too high, not to produce in the end a coolness between them. Mme. de Maintenon, coming last to grandeur, must have changed by degrees to Mme. de La Fayette, who remained what she ever was; it was, perhaps, this uniformity of conduct that Mme. de Maintenon would fain have changed a little when her own fortunes changed.

In July, 1677, one year before the appearance of the *Princesse de Clèves,* we see that Mme. de La Fayette's health was at its worst, although she was to live fifteen years longer, dying by degrees without a respite, being of "those who drag their miserable existence to the last drop of oil." Nevertheless, it was in the following winter that M. de La Rochefoucauld and she busied themselves finally with the charming novel which was published by Barbin, March 16, 1678. Segrais tells us, in one place, that he has not taken the trouble to reply to criticisms made on the book; and in another place he says that Mme. de La Fayette disdained to reply to them, so that a doubt might be raised, if we chose, about the degree of his co-operation. But, as to that, I shall not discuss it; the novel is too superior to all that he ever wrote to admit of hesitation. No one, moreover, mistook the author; confidential readings had spread the news and the book was received by society as the work of Mme. de La Fayette alone.

As soon as the *Princesse* thus heralded appeared, she became the subject of all conversations and correspondences. Bussy and Mme. de Sévigné wrote to each other; everywhere persons were on the *qui-vive* to discuss her; they met in the great alley of the Tuileries and questioned one another. Fontenelle read the novel four times over. Boursault turned it into a tragedy, as nowadays we should make it into vaudevilles. Valincourt wrote, quite incognito, a little volume of criticism which was attributed to Père Bonhours, and an Abbé de Charnes replied by another little volume that was attributed to Barbier d'Ancourt, a noted critic and adversary of the witty Jesuit. The *Princesse de Clèves* has survived the vogue she well deserved and still remains among us as the first in date of interesting novels.

It is touching to think of the peculiar situation in which were born these beings so charming, so pure, these noble, spotless personages, their sentiments so fresh, so perfected, so tender; to think, too, how Mme. de La Fayette put into them all that her loving and poetic soul held in reserve of early dreams long cherished; how M. de La Rochefoucauld took pleasure, doubtless, in finding in M. de Nemours that flower of chivalry that he himself had misused, an embellished reflection, as it were of his own romantic youth. Thus the two friends, grown aged, went back in imagination to the first beauty of their youth when they did not know, but might have loved each

other.   The ready blush of Mme. de Clèves, which at
first is almost her only language, marks well the
thought of the writer, which is to paint love in all
it has of freshest, purest, most adorable, most troub-
lous, most undecided, most irresistible, — most *itself,*
in short.   At every moment we are made to see
"that joy which first youth joined to beauty gives,
that sort of trouble and embarrassment in every action
that love produces in the innocence of early youth,"
in short, all the emotions that are farthest from her
and from her friend in their tardy union.

In the tenor of her life, she was, above all, sensible;
she had a judgment greater even than her wit, so they
told her, and that praise flattered her more than all
the rest.   But here, in her novel, poesy, inward sensibility, recovered their rights, though reason was not
wanting either.   Nowhere have the contradictions
and the delicate duplicities of love been so naturally
expressed as in the *Princesse de Clèves.*   We love
even its colour, a little faded; the moderation of its
paintings that touch so lightly; the manner, everywhere restrained, that gives so much to dream of;
a few willows beside a brook where the lover passes;
and all description of the beauty of the princess:
"her hair loosely knotted"; "eyes enlarged by tears
a little"; and, at the last, "a life that was short
enough," a final impression, itself moderated.   The
language is equally delightful, exquisitely choice, with
negligences and irregularities that have their grace,

and which Valincourt notes in detail as being denounced by a grammarian, though with some shame at putting too direct a blame on the author.

As she advanced in the composition of the *Princesse de Clèves* the thoughts of Mme. de La Fayette, after this first flight backward toward youth and its joys, return to gravity. The idea of duty increases and bears her along. The austerity of the end shows us that "sight so far and yet so near of death which makes the things of this world and of these present eyes seem so different from those we see in health." She herself had felt this from the summer of 1677, when, as Mme. de Sévigné indicates, she turned her soul toward the end. Her disillusion as to all things is shown in the fear she gives to Mme. de Clèves that marriage will be the grave of the prince's love, and open the door to jealousies; these fears turn the princess's mind against a marriage with her lover as much as the scruple of duty. In completing their ideal romance, it is clear that the two friends, M. de La Rochefoucauld and she, came to doubt what there would have been of imaginary bliss for their dear personages, and so turned to their own gentle and real relation as the most consoling and the safest.

They did not enjoy it long. On the night of March 16, 1680, two years to a day after the publication of the *Princesse de Clèves* M. de La Rochefoucauld died:

" I have had my head so full of this misfortune, and of the affliction of our poor friend," writes Mme. de Sévigné, " that I must tell you of it all. . . . M. de Marsillac is in a state of affliction that cannot be described; and yet, my daughter, he will return to the king and Court; all the family will return to their place in the world, but where will Mme. de La Fayette find another such friend, such society, such gentleness, pleasantness, confidence, and consideration for her and for her son? She is infirm, she is always in her chamber, she never goes into the streets. M. de La Rochefoucauld was sedentary also; this made them necessary to each other, and nothing could be compared to the confidence and charm of their friendship. Think of it, my daughter, and you will see it was impossible to have met with a greater loss and one that time can less console. I have not quitted my poor friend through all these days; she did not go into the crowd around that family, so that she needed some one to have pity on her. Mme. de Coulanges has done well also; and together we shall continue it for some time longer. . . ."

And in all her following letters she says again: "Poor Mme. de La Fayette does not know what to do with herself. . . . Every one will be consoled, except her. . . . That poor woman cannot draw the threads together so as to fill the place." Mme. de La Fayette did not seek to fill it; she knew that nothing could repair such ruins. Even the tender friendship of Mme. de Sévigné did not suffice,—she felt this but too well; too many shared it. If we need to be convinced of the insufficency of such friendships, even the best and the dearest, we have only to read Mme. de La Fayette's letter to Mme. de Sévigné, dated October 8, 1689, so perfect, so imperious, so, from its very tenderness, without ceremony, and then read Mme. de Sévigné's comments upon it in writing to her daughter, and we shall comprehend that too much must not be asked of friendships that are not single and unshared, inasmuch as the most delicate of women judged thus.   After love, after absolute friendship without reservation, without change, a friendship *entire,* in which the other is *the same* as ourselves, there is nothing but death or God.

Mme. de La Fayette lived thirteen years longer; the slender details of her exterior life during those desert years will be found in Mme. de Sévigné's letters. A lively beginning of intimacy with young Mme. de Schomberg awakened some jealousy in other and older friends; but it does not appear that this effort of a soul to recover its hold on something lasted long. Perhaps it was from the same restless need that she built, during the first months after her loss, an addition on the garden side to her house, already too vast, alas! in proportion to her diminishing existence. Also, to fill the hours, Mme. de La Fayette spent her time on various writings, some of which went astray and were lost. The *Comtesse de Tende* dates from that period. The severest criticisms of Bussy and society in general on the *Princesse de Clèves* turned on the extraordinary confession that the heroine makes to her husband: Mme. de La Fayette, by inventing another analogous situation which led to a still more extraordinary confession, thought that she thereby justified the first. She succeeded in the *Comtesse de Tende,* though with less development than was needed to give the *Princesse de Clèves* a sister comparable to herself. We feel that the writer had her object and rushed upon it.

Mme. de La Fayette had, as I said, more than one affinity with Boileau in uprightness of mind and irrefutable criticism, and she was, in her way, an oracle of good sense in her society. Her sayings *à la Boileau* that have been preserved are numerous; I have quoted several, but others should be added, for instance: "Whoso puts himself above others, no matter what his mind may be, puts himself beneath himself." Boileau, conversing one day with d'Olivet said :

"Do you know why the classics have so few admirers ? It is because at least three fourths of those who have translated them are fools. Mme. de La Fayette, the woman who had the most mind in France and wrote the best, compared a foolish translator to a footman whom his mistress sends to give her compliment to some one. What she gave him in terms polite, he offers in a vulgar way, he maims it; the more delicacy there was in the compliment the less well the footman acquits himself. And there, in a word, is the most perfect image of a bad translator."

Boileau seems, in this remark, to certify himself to the resemblance, the harmony between them that I have indicated. M. Roederer is a thousand times right when, speaking of the relations of Molière to the social word of Mmes. de Sévigné and de La Fayette, he shows that *Les Femmes Savantes* did not relate to them in any way. As for La Fontaine, it is certain that at one time he was on terms of much familiarity with Mme. de La Fayette; we have some very affectionate verses that he addressed to her on sending her a little billiard table. This must have been about the time that he dedicated a fable to the author of the Maxims, and another to Mme. de Sévigné.

After the death of M. de La Rochefoucauld Mme. de La Fayette's thoughts turned more and more to religion; we have a precious testimony to this in a long and beautiful letter to Du Guet, written by her. She had chosen him as her director. Without being actually connected with Port-Royal, she inclined that way, and the hyprocrisy of the Court drove her more and more into it. Her mother, as we have seen, gave her for step-father the Chevalier Renaud de Sévigné, uncle of Mme. de Sévigné, and one of the benefactors of Port-Royal-des-Champs, the cloisters of which he had rebuilt. He did not die till 1676. Mme. de La Fayette knew Du Guet, who was beginning to take a great spiritual part in the direction of consciences, and had, in connection with the decadence of Port-Royal, very just and well-informed views on that subject, in which there was nothing contentious or narrow. Here are a few of the stern words this priest of the mind addressed to the repentant woman who had asked for them:

"I have thought, madame, that you ought to employ usefully the early moments of the day when you cease to sleep, and begin to dream or muse. I know that such are not connected thoughts, and that often you have striven not to have them; but it is difficult to keep from yielding to our nature when we are willing it should be our master; and we return to it without difficulty, having had so much in quitting it. It is important, therefore, that you be fed on food more solid than thoughts that have no aim, the most innocent of which are useless; and I believe you cannot better employ such tranquil moments than in rendering account to yourself of a life already very long, of which nothing now remains to you but reputation, the vanity of which you know better than any one.

"Until now the clouds with which you have tried to cover religion have hidden you from yourself. As it is in relation to religion that we ought to examine and know ourselves, by affecting to ignore it you have merely ignored yourself. It is time to leave everything in its place, and to put yourself in yours. Truth will judge you; you are in the world solely to follow it, not to judge of it. In vain do we defend ourselves against it, in vain do we dissimulate; the veil is torn from our eyes as life and its cupidities vanish, and we become convinced that we must lead a new life just as we are not permitted to live longer. We must therefore begin by a sincere desire to see ourselves as we are seen by our Judge. The sight is crushing, even to those persons who are the most outspoken against concealment. It takes all our virtues from us, and even all our good qualities and the self-esteem they had acquired for us. We feel that we have lived until then in illusions and falsehood; that we have nourished ourselves on painted flesh, have judged virtue by its garments and its jewels, neglecting the foundation because that foundation is the ascription of all to God and to his salvation; it is to despise self in all things, not from a wiser vanity, not from pride more enlightened and of better taste, but from a feeling of its wrongfulness and its misery."

The rest of the letter is equally admirable and in the same suitable and pressing tone: "Therefore, you who have dreamed, cease your dreams. You who esteem yourself *true* among others, and whom the world flatters that you are so, you are *not* so; you are only half so and falsely so; your virtue without God was only good taste." And farther on I find a sentence on those years "for which you have not yet sincerely repented because you are still astray enough to excuse your weakness and to love that which caused it."

One year before her death, Mme. de La Fayette

wrote Mme. de Sévigné a little note which describes
her illness without repose night or day and her resignation to God, ending with these words: "Believe,
my very dear one, that you are the person I have
most truly loved." The other affection that she did
not name and counted no longer, was it buried, consumed at last in sacrifice?

Her life harmonises to the end and is then consummated. Mme. de Sévigné writes to Mme. de Gui-
tand, June 3, 1693, two or three days after the fatal
day, deploring the loss of a friend of forty years:

"Her infirmities for the last two years had become extreme; I de-
fended her always, for people said she was crazy in not being willing
to go out She was deathly sad. 'Another folly!' they said, for
was she not the luckiest woman in the world? But I said to those
people so hasty in their judgments: 'Madame de La Fayette is not
crazy'; and I kept to that. Alas! madame, the poor woman is more
than justified now. . . . She had two polypuses in her heart, and
the point of her heart was withered. Was not this enough to cause
the desolations of which she complained? She was reasonable in her
life, she was reasonable in her death, never was she without that divine reason which was her principal quality. . . . She was uncon-
scious during the four days of her last illness. . . . God did her,
for our consolation, a special grace which shows a true predestination:
it is that she confessed on the day at the little Fête-Dieu, with scrupulous exactitude, and with a sentiment that could come only from
him, and received our Lord in the same manner. Therefore, my dear
madame, we regard this communion, which she was accustomed to
make on Whit-Sunday as a mercy of God, who desired to console us
for her not being in a state to receive the viaticum."

Thus lived and died, in a mingling of sad sweetness
and sharp suffering, of wisdom according to the
world and of repentance before God, the woman

whose ideal production still enchants us. What more can be added as matter for reflection and instruction? The letter to Mme. de Sablé, the *Princesse de Clèves*, and the letter of Du Guet, are they not the whole record of a life?

XII.

Madame, Duchesse d'Orléans.

XII.

Ibenrietta Anne of England.

Madame, Ducbesse d'Orléans.

TWO volumes written by Daniel de Cosnac, a man of Louis XIV's century and of whom Mme. de Sévigné said, "He has much intelligence," cannot be read with too much attention. At first, these Memoirs please but slightly, and seem to respond imperfectly to the reputation of the author: it is only little by little, as we advance, and after we have finished them, that we perceive how much they have increased our knowledge and enriched our judgment on many points. To-day, I take pleasure in detaching their most beautiful and most interesting figure, that of MADAME, to whom Cosnac had the honour of devoting himself of his own free choice, and for whom he had the glory to suffer. The portrait he makes of her does not pale beside even the greatest and the most affecting that we possess; it can be read with pleasure after Bossuet's Funeral Oration, and it adds much to what Mme. de La Fayette, Choisy, and La Fare have said of her.

Mme. de La Fayette has given a most charming history of Madame Henriette such as every woman of delicacy, a born princess in heart, must desire. It is a narrative written down from a confidence, and intended for her who gave it, who smiled at seeing herself so justly, so airily painted, and took, at moments, pen in hand to retouch the sketch. Madame, after her dinner, liked to lie upon the floor, near to Mme. de La Fayette, so that her head was almost upon the latter's knees; and in that familiar and charming position, she related the details of her heart, or listened to those already written, looking at herself in the mirror that her friend offered her. Reading to-day this history so delicate, so flowing, so lightly touched, so timely stopped, we have need of some gift of imagination to catch all its grace and recreate its enchantment. Something is there, like the light down on fruits in their first freshness, which melts if you touch it.

The young Princess of England, daughter of Charles I and granddaughter of Henri IV, brought up in France during the troubles of her family, was destined to marry MONSIEUR, the king's brother, as soon as the young king, Louis XIV, had married the Infanta of Spain, which took place about the time that Charles II was restored to the throne of his fathers. Going with her mother to London on a visit to her brother during the first days of his Restoration she inflamed all hearts and made essay of her charms,

HENRIETTA ANNE OF ENGLAND.
MADAME, DUCHESSE D'ORLÉANS

being then, at most, seventeen years old. "She had," says Choisy, "black eyes, lively and full of contagious fire, that men could not fixedly look at without feeling the effect; her eyes seemed themselves affected with the desire of those who looked into them. Never was there so touching a princess." On her return to France, she became the object of all imaginable assiduities, including those of Monsieur, "who paid her, until their marriage, attentions in which only love was lacking; but the miracle of inflaming the heart of that prince was granted to no woman in the world."

Near to Monsieur, was a young seigneur who, in those days, was his favourite. This was the Comte de Guiche, the handsomest young man at Court, the best-made, bold, proud, with a certain air of assumption that is not displeasing to young women, and perfects to their eyes a hero of romance. The Comte de Guiche, in all respects, was perfect. Monsieur, without being in love, was jealous, which is not rare. But he was not so at first of the Comte de Guiche, whom he introduced into the privacy of the young princess, making him admire charms that of themselves were sufficiently felt and irresistible. Those years (1661–1662) were unique seasons of freshness and youth which may properly be called the spring-tide of Louis XIV's reign. All things opened themselves to joy, to gallantry, to thoughts of glory and of love; and intellect also bore its part; for, no sooner was Madame married and separated from the queen, her mother, who had kept her until then at her side, than "a new discovery was made of her mind which was as lovable as all the rest."

Sometime after her marriage, Madame came to live with Monsieur in the Tuileries, which she did not quit until she went some years later to the Palais-Royal; so that she became in reality a Parisian princess. Monsieur himself, indolent as he was, piqued himself on being liked in Paris. When the Court was elsewhere, he was fond of making little trips and sojourns in the capital; he even put a sort of malice to the king, whom he thought these trips displeased, into making them:

"But the truth is," says Cosnac, "they gave him the joy of having a Court of his own; he was enchanted when he saw a great influx of fine people at the Palais-Royal, coming there for love of him, he said, though it was wholly for Madame. He neglected nothing to cajole each one, and it was visibly remarked that he was more or less gay according as a small or a large Court appeared at his house. Nevertheless, as I could not see that these trips produced the effect he desired, on the contrary, I judged from what he himself told me, that though in the beginning they might have vexed the King, His Majesty ended by laughing at them. I did not have the compliance to applaud such conduct. I told Monsieur I did not think it was prudent to give small displeasures to those who could so easily give him great ones. But Monsieur was so pleased at being able, every time he went to Paris, to ask ten or a dozen persons privately, ' Well, did you see what a large company I had to-day ? ' that it was only opposing one's self to his pleasures to tell him these truths; and his pleasures always carried the day in his mind over the most important matters."

Thus Monsieur, that father of the Orléans branch, a father so feeble and so little worthy, had this in

common with his successors, that he liked to hold his
Court in the Palais-Royal, to be well thought of in
Paris, and to make a sort of rivalry to the king;
nullity that he was, vanity in him forestalled and divined policy.

But I leave this forward glance and presage, which
would be an anachronism in all that concerns Madame
and the wholly ideal charm of her beginnings (1661).
She installed herself in the Tuileries and made choice
of her ladies and her friends, whom Mme. de La Fayette
enumerates:

"All these persons," says the pleasant historian, "passed their afternoons with Madame.   They had the honour to follow her on her
drives; returning, the party supped with Monsieur; after supper, all
the men of the Court arrived, and the evening was passed in the
pleasures of cards, comedies, violins ; in short, they amused themselves with every imaginable diversion, and without the slightest
mixture of grievances."

On a trip to Fontainebleau that was made soon after,
Madame carried joy and pleasure with her.   The
king who, previously, had not smiled upon the idea
of marrying her, "found when he came to know her
better how unjust he had been in not thinking her the
most beautiful person in the world."   Here begins
the romance, or rather many romances in one.   Madame became the queen of the moment, and that moment lasted till her death; she gave the tone to the
young Court, was the cause of all parties of pleasure,

"which were made for her, and it seemed as if the King had no
pleasure in them except through that which they gave to her.   It was

then the middle of summer. Madame went to bathe every day; she
started in a coach on account of the heat and returned on horseback,
followed by all her ladies gracefully dressed, with many feathers on
their heads, and accompanied by the King and all the young nobles
of the Court. After supper, they entered calèches, and to the music
of violins, drove, for a part of the night, around the canal."

Mme. de La Fayette, who gives us thus the framework of the novel, puts also into our hands some of
the threads that entangled and agitated these young
hearts: the king, more touched than a brother-in-law
should be; Madame, more affected, perhaps, than a
sister-in-law should be; La Vallière dawning, and
coming at the right instant to break the spell; the
Compte de Guiche, at the same moment, making as
much way with Madame as La Vallière was making
with the king. Jealousies, suspicions, rivalries, con-
cealments, confidants thrusting themselves forward
and playing the traitor — in short, the eternal history of all groups young and amorous when left to
themselves at leisure beneath the leafage. But here it
was royal youth, glittering in the morning of a splendid reign; history has crystallised them; literature, in
default of poesy, has consecrated them; a woman's
pen has told their tale in polished language full of permissible negligences; posterity glances back upon
them with envy.

To explain to ourselves how, in the midst of the
pitfalls and perils among which she played, Madame
did not succumb and could say sincerely to Monsieur
on her death-bed: "*Monsieur, je ne vous ai jamais*

manqué'' [I have never wronged you], we must remember her situation, always so watched, also her youth with the sort of innocence that accompanies the imprudence of early years. To me, all these great and these semi-passions, such as Mme. de La Fayette shows them to us in her History, and such as I believe them to have been, can be explained by first youth only. When the Comte de Guiche was exiled in 1664, Madame, just twenty, had become more prudent: "Madame," says Mme. de La Fayette, "did not choose that he should bid her farewell, because she knew she should be observed, and she was no longer at the age when that which is dangerous seemed to her so agreeable." Therefore, all her amiable pledges, adventures, entanglements of fancy and intrigues of heart belong to those early years before she was twenty

These amours and the exile of the Comte de Guiche gave rise to scandal, and the result was one of those libels printed in Holland to which Bussy-Rabutin has the sad honour of having set the example by his *Histoires Amoureuses*. Madame, informed in time, and dreading the effect on Monsieur, requested Cosnac to inform the prince and forestall his displeasure. What particularly distressed her was the printing of the libel; Cosnac undertook to stop it. He sent an intelligent man to Holland, M. Patin, son of Gui Patin, with orders to go to all the publishers who might have the book in hand.

"So well did he accomplish his errand," says Cosnac, "that he obtained from the State's government a prohibition to print it, and withdrew eighteen hundred copies already printed, which he brought to me in Paris, and I gave them, by Monsieur's order, to Merille, head valet-de-chambre.   This affair cost me much trouble and money, but far from regretting either I considered myself too well paid by the gratitude Madame showed to me."

This affair bound Cosnac more closely than before to Madame, and from that moment we see him on all occasions espousing her interests and serving them. This was the period when he acted zealously on the mind of Monsieur to induce him to become a prince worthy of esteem and of his lofty birth.   He failed. The influence of the Chevalier de Lorraine at the close of the campaign of 1667 ruined all his efforts; and that unworthy favourite, who saw in Cosnac a natural enemy, neglected nothing to destroy and send him into exile.

I shall say nothing of the miserable domestic intrigues through which, at this epoch, the soul of Madame, so delicate, so elevated, was forced to struggle.   Cosnac fills up here a gap left unfilled in Mme. de La Fayette's History, and he takes us into all the wretchedness, while the latter gives us only the romance.   This attachment to Madame is certainly the finest and most honourable part of Cosnac's life. When he was exiled to his diocese (he was Archbishop of Aix) Madame never ceased to write to him and wish for him; she asked for his recall, and her insistence even went contrary to the king's will:

"The king," says Cosnac, "thought Madame could not preserve so violent and constant a desire for my return unless we had some great bond together which made me necessary to her; and this bond, from ideas that were given to him, seemed to him some fixed cabal, which could not be too carefully destroyed."

There was no cabal, but Madame, had discovered among the persons attached to her husband one capable man, a generously ambitious man of merit, and she acquired him for herself; she wished to make him serve in the accomplishment of her own views, which were becoming more serious with age. In the wicked libel that Cosnac recovered in Holland, there was one phrase, among others, that was not ill-turned: "She has," it was said of Madame, "a certain languishing air, and when she speaks to any one, as she is very amiable, she seems to be asking for their heart no matter what indifferent thing she may be saying." This tenderness in Madame's look had operated on the rather insensible soul of Cosnac, and, without mingling therewith the slightest tinge of gallant sentiment, he had let his heart be captured by her who asked for it so sweetly and so sovereignly.

While Cosnac was in exile at Valence, Madame found herself chosen by Louis XIV, who appreciated her more and more, as mediatrix with her brother, King Charles II, whom it was desirable to detach from the alliance with Holland, and also to induce him to declare himself a Catholic. Louis XIV, however, held much less to the second point than to the first. The

affair was so advanced, and even on the most delicate
point, the declaration of catholicity, Madame supposed
it so near conclusion, that she thought she could inform Cosnac of a great present and surprise she was
preparing for him.   He received a letter from her
dated at Saint Cloud, June 10, 1669, which said:

"In the sorrow you surely feel at the injustice done you, there
must be some comfort in thinking that your friends are devising consolations which might aid you in bearing your misfortunes.   Mme.
de Saint-Chaumont " (governess to the Orléans children), "and I have
resolved, in order to do this, that you shall have a cardinal's hat.
That thought, I am certain, will seem to you visionary at first, seeing
that those on whom such favours depend are so far from giving them
to you; but, to clear up the enigma, you must know that, among
the multiplicity of matters that are treated of between France and
England, this last one will, in a short time, be made of such consequence in Rome, where they will be so glad to oblige the king my
brother, that I am quite certain they will refuse him nothing; and I
have made advances to him so that he would ask for a cardinal's hat
without naming for whom; the which he has promised me; and it
will be for you; therefore you can count upon it."

This cardinal's hat, which she shows thus unexpect-
edly as about to fall upon the head of a man in disgrace, has an odd effect, and we remain convinced,
even after reading her letter, that there was something
a little visionary and fanciful about it, such as women
of the best minds are apt to mingle with their politics.
We must do Cosnac the justice to say that he did not
allow himself to be dazzled by it; and that he chiefly
saw in the idea, what we see to-day, a noble testimony to Madame's esteem for him: "However ambitious the world may have thought me," he says, "I

can say with sincerity that what flattered me the most
in this letter, was to see the increase of Madame's
friendship. This was, speaking with truth, the one
honour that I felt the most." He was on these terms
of friendship and close correspondence with the noble
princess in the spring of 1670, and was receiving from
her all sorts of new proofs of affection and of sympathy for his unfortunate misadventure in Paris.
During a journey to Dover, whither she went to see
the king, her brother, and bring him to sign the treaty
with Louis XIV (June 1st) she thought of "that poor
M. de Valence." On her return from that journey,
four days before her death on the 26th of June, she
wrote to him:

" I am not surprised at the joy you tell me you feel at my journey
to England; it has been very agreeable; and however much I was convinced of the friendship of the king my brother, I found it greater than I
could have hoped. Also, I found in all the things that depended on
him as much willingness as I could wish. The king also, on my
return, showed me a great deal of kindness; but as for Monsieur, nothing can equal his implacable determination to complain of me. He
did me the honour to tell me that I was all-powerful and that I could
do what I choose; and, consequently, if I did not bring back the
Chevalier" (the Chevalier de Lorraine, then exiled by order of the
king) "I did not care to please him, and to that he added threats for
the time to come. I represented to him how little that return depended on me; and how little I could do what I wished inasmuch as
you were where you are. Instead of seeing the truth of what I said
and being softened by it, he took this occasion to do you harm with
the king, and to do me an ill turn also."

This letter also gives expression to a sorrow that to
a mother was very keen. Cosnac had written a little
letter to Madame's daughter, then about eight years

old, for whom he had taken a fancy when seeing
her with Mme. de Saint-Chaumont, her governess.
This letter, which was delivered with a sort of
mystery, had produced a bad effect, and Madame adds
to the above letter :

"I have several times blamed the tenderness you have for my
daughter; in God's name give it up. She is a child who is incapable
of feeling about it as she ought; and she is being brought up to hate
me. Content yourself with loving those who are as grateful as I am,
and who feel as keenly as I do the grief of not being in a position to
draw you from that in which you are."

Three days after the writing of this letter, on the
29th of June, about five in the afternoon, Madame,
being at Saint-Cloud, asked for a glass of iced chicory
water; she drank it, and nine or ten hours later, at
half-past two in the morning of June 30th, she died
in all the agony of a violent colic. We have the details of her slightest actions and words during that
interval. Throughout this sudden attack, when death
took her, as it were, by the throat, she kept her
presence of mind, thought of essential things, of God,
of her soul, of Monsieur, of the king, her family, her
friends; addressing to all simple and true words,
charming in restraint and, if I may say so, supreme
in their decorum.

In the first moments they sent for the learned
Feuillet, canon of Saint-Cloud, a stern rigorist; he
did not spare the princess; he spoke to her harshly;
let us listen to his own account of it: " At eleven o'clock

at night she sent to call me in a great hurry.   Having arrived at her bedside, she made all present retire and said to me: 'You see, Monsieur Feuillet, the state in which I am.' 'In a very good state Madame,' I replied, 'for now you will confess that there is a God, whom you have known very little during your life.'" He goes on to tell her that all her past confessions counted for nothing, that her whole life had been nought but sin; he helped her, as much as time permitted, to make a general confession.   She made it with feelings of great piety.   A Capuchin, her usual confessor, being with M. Feuillet beside her bed, the good man wished to speak to her, and wandered into long discourse.   She looked at Mme. de La Fayette, who stood by, with a mixture of pity and distress; then, turning to the Capuchin: "Let M. Feuillet speak, my father," she said with wonderful gentleness (as if she feared to hurt him), "you shall speak in your turn."   Nevertheless, M. Feuillet said to her, in a loud voice, the harshest words: "Humble yourself, Madame; behold all your deceitful grandeur annihilated beneath the heavy hand of God.   You are nought but a miserable sinner, an earthen vessel, about to fall and be broken to pieces; of all this grandeur not a trace will remain."   "It is true, O my God!" she exclaimed, accepting all with submission from the lips of a deserving but rough priest, giving in exchange, what was unalterable in her, something kind and gentle.

They had sent to Paris in all haste for M. de Condom, Bossuet. The first messenger could not find
him: they sent a second, then a third. She was
dying, and had just taken a last potion when he arrived. Here the account of the stern Feuillet changes
in tone and is sensibly affected: "She was as glad to
see him," he says, "as he was afflicted at finding her
at the last gasp. He prostrated himself upon the
ground and made a prayer which charmed me; he
mingled in it acts of faith, of confidence, and of love."

Prayer of Bossuet prostrate by the death-bed of Madame, natural and instant effusion of that great, tender
heart ! you were the inward treasury whence he drew
the touching grandeurs of his Funeral Oration; that
which the world admires is but the echo of the accents
that gushed forth then and were lost in the bosom of
God with groans from the plenitude of the spirit.

As Bossuet ceased speaking, the head waiting-
woman came forward to give the princess something
that she needed; taking advantage of the occasion,
Madame said to her in English, so that Bossuet could not
understand, keeping until death all the delicacy of her
actions and the courtesy of her spirit: "Give M. de
Condom, when I am dead, the emerald I have had
made for him." This was what Bossuet remembered
in his Funeral Oration when he said: "That art of
giving agreeably, which she had practised throughout her life, followed her, as I know, into the arms of
death."

Was Madame poisoned? It is agreed to-day to deny it; and it seems to be a settled thing to say that she died of cholera-morbus. The official autopsy, required, in part, by policy, appears to declare it; much stress was also laid on constitutional lesions which were covered by that graceful exterior. The feeling, or rather the inward sensation of Madame, was that she had been poisoned. She said so before Monsieur, requesting that the water she had drunk should be examined. Mme. de La Fayette says:

"I was in the alcove, near to Monsieur, and, though I thought him very incapable of such a crime, a bewilderment as to human malignity made me observe him with attention. He was neither moved, nor embarrassed by Madame's opinion; he said the water must be given to a dog; and he agreed with Madame that oil and counter-poison should be sent for, to take from Madame's mind so painful a thought."

It is in such temperate and circumspect words that Mme. de La Fayette justifies Monsieur. The letter written to Cosnac in June showed us Monsieur more "implacable" than ever against Madame, and "threatening her in the future." In another letter, written on the eve of her journey to England, April 28, 1670, Madame expressed her fears and her sad forebodings in very energetic and very precise language: "Monsieur is still too bitter about me, and I must expect many troubles when I return from this journey. . . . Monsieur insists that I shall have the Chevalier brought back, or he will treat me as the lowest of creatures." Observe that as soon as she was dead the Chevalier reappeared at Court. But it does not appear that Cosnac drew any precise induction from the letters addressed to him, or that he gave them any evil meaning. He expresses no suspicion of his own. He simply let his sorrow find vent, and here I ask permission to quote at length a page that does honour to him who wrote it, and which nobly completes the circle of funeral orations of which Madame was the subject.

"I shall not attempt," he says, "to express the state in which I was on hearing of her death. Inasmuch as there have been persons who died of grief, it is shameful in me to have survived mine. All that respect, esteem, gratitude, ambition, self-interest could inspire of dreadful reflections passed a thousand times through my mind. My constitution resisted it, I was not even ill; but my mind became so grieved, so languid, that I was hardly better than if I had been dead. As for the loss of my fortunes, I was not very conscious of that; I had never been able to persuade myself that the hopes held out to me were solid, though, to judge by all appearances, success was indubitable; but to lose so great, so perfect, so good a princess, a princess who could repair the harm my fall had done me — no, if I had had a truly delicate and feeling heart it must have cost me my life. To justify my devotion to this princess, and for my own consolation, I trace here a slender idea of her virtues. . . ."

Here follows a formal Portrait in the style of the day:

"Madame's mind was solid and delicate; she had good sense, knowledge of choice things, a soul lofty and just, enlightened on all she ought to do, but sometimes not doing it, either from natural indolence, or from a certain haughtiness of soul, which came of her origin and made her look upon duty as a degradation. She mingled with all her conversation a gentleness that is never found in other royal personages; it was not that she had less majesty, but that she knew how to use it in an easy and touching manner;

so that with qualities that were wholly divine she never ceased
to be the most human of beings. One might say that she appropriated hearts instead of leaving them in common; and it was
that that gave rise to the belief that she liked to please everybody and to win the liking of all sorts of persons.

" As for the features of her face, we seldom see any so complete;
her eyes were keen without being rude, the mouth admirable,
the nose perfect,— a rare thing ! for nature, to the contrary of art,
makes nearly all eyes well and nearly all noses badly. Her skin
was white and smooth beyond expression, her figure mediocre, but
refined. One might say that her mind as well as her soul animated
her body; she had it even in her feet and danced better than any
woman in the world.

" As for that *je ne sais quoi* so talked about, and given in pure
wantonness to so many unworthy persons, that ' I know not what '
which goes at once to the bottom of all hearts, persons of delicacy
agreed that while in others it was copy, in Madame it was original.
Whoso approached her remained convinced that no one more perfect
could be seen.

" I have nothing more to say of this princess, except that she
would have been the glory and the honour of her century, and that
her century would have ad red her, had it been worthy of her.

" With this princess I lost the desire and the hope of my return, and,
utterly disgusted with the world, I turned all my aims to my ministry."

The event of Madame's death brought a crisis to
many lives. La Fare relates that on that day he
brought back from Saint-Cloud M. de Tréville, a particular friend of Madame, one of those she most appreciated for his elegant mind, somewhat subtile and
extremely accomplished: " Tréville, whom I brought
back that day from Saint-Cloud and kept to sleep at
my house, so as not to leave him a prey to his sorrow,
left the world and gave himself up to devotion, which
he has always continued ever since." Mme. de La
Fayette herself, after losing Madame, retired from the

Court, and lived with M. de La Rochefoucauld that
more private life which she never afterwards quitted.

Dying at twenty-six years of age, having been for
nine years the centre of charm and of pleasures,
Madame marks the finest, or at least the most graceful period of the Court of Louis XIV. After her, at
that Court, there was, perhaps, more splendour, more
imposing grandeur, but less of distinction and refinement. Madame loved intellect, distinguished it for
itself, went in search of it, awakened it in the older
poets, Corneille, for instance, favoured it and embold-
ened it in the younger, such as Racine; she wept at
Andromaque, when the young author first read it to
her: "Pardon me, Madame," wrote Racine in the
preface to his tragedy, "if I dare to boast of that fortunate beginning of its destiny." In all the Courts
which had but recently preceded that of Madame, at
Chantilly, at the hôtel Rambouillet and its surround-
ings, there was a mingling of taste already past and
about to become superannuated: with Madame begins, properly speaking, the modern taste of Louis
XIV's reign; she contributed to fix it in its purity.

Madame naturally calls for comparison with that
other interesting princess of the last years of Louis
XIV, the Duchesse de Bourgogne. Without pretending to sacrifice the one to the other, let us merely
note some differences. The Duchesse de Bourgogne,
cherished pupil of Mme. de Maintenon, whom she
sometimes distressed by disobedience, belonged to

the generation of young women who loved pleasure, cards, and at times the table, immoderately; in short, she was well fitted to be the mother of Louis XV. Madame who, had she come in the days of the Duchesse de Bourgogne, might, perhaps, have loved all those things, did, in point of fact, love the things of the mind; solidity and good sense mingled insensibly with her graces; decency and good manners never deserted her. Louis XIV, in allying himself to her with a true friendship that conquered love, seems to have desired to regulate that happy nature and to give it some of his own good qualities; "he made her in a short time one of the most finished persons in the world." In the few days she spent at Saint-Cloud, on her return from England, and just before her death, La Fare pictures her to us enjoying the beauty of the weather and the conversation of her friends, "such as M. de Turenne, M. de La Rochefoucauld, Mme. de La Fayette, Tréville, and several others." That is not, I imagine, the circle that the Duchesse de Bourgogne, more giddy and frolicsome, would have chosen and grouped around her.

The letters of Madame, written to Cosnac, are short, friendly, sufficiently well-turned, but with nothing remarkable; evidently she had not the imagination that can reach to a distance; hers was one of those light and blessed spirits that we must catch and adore at their source. Literature has nothing here to do except to record the testimony of contemporaries and, in a way, to cut them out from the pages of other days. That is what I have tried to do with as much simplicity and as little effort as possible, asking indulgence of my readers, for we too, servants of the public, are sometimes tired out ourselves.

XIII.

Louis XIV.

XIII.

Louis XIV.

his Memoirs by himself.

UNDER the improper title of "Works," there exist six most interesting and most authentic volumes which it would have been more correct to entitle the "Memoirs of Louis XIV." They are in reality true memoirs of his reign and of his principal actions, which he undertook to write for the instruction of his son. The narrative is often interrupted by moral and royal reflections that are very judicious. The six or seven years after the death of Cardinal Mazarin, which constitute the first epoch of Louis XIV's reign (1661–1668) are exhibited and related consecutively in almost uninterrupted detail. The following years, till 1694, are represented in a series of letters which concern, more especially, the campaigns and military operations. A number of private letters, relating to all the epochs of his reign are added thereto; the whole forming a body of documents, notes, and instructions emanating directly from Louis XIV himself, and casting the strongest light both on his actions and on the spirit that presided over them.

One day, in 1714, the old king, near his end, sent the Duc de Noailles to his desk to bring him the papers that were written by his own hand: " At first he burned several that concerned the reputations of various persons; he was then about to burn the rest, notes, memoirs, fragments of his own composition on war or policy. The Duc de Noailles begged him earnestly to give them to him, and obtained that favour." The originals, deposited by the Duc de Noailles in the Bibliothèque du Roi, are preserved there. From those manuscripts the publication was made, in 1806, of the six volumes of which I speak; to which, I know not why, the public has never done justice or given them the attention they deserve. The volumes have long been for sale at a very cheap price. It is but a few years since the same could be said of the nine volumes of Napoleon's authentic Memoirs. As for those of the great Frederick, there is such mixture in them that it is not surprising the fine historical parts that form their basis should long have been hidden under the literary rubbish that at first sight covers and compromises them. Nothing of the kind appears in the Memoirs of Louis XIV, nor in those of Napoleon; they are pure history, the reflections of men who speak of their art, and the greatest of arts, that of reigning. Our levity shows here: the worst frivolous political pamphlets were read by everybody, yet many distinguished and serious minds never troubled themselves even to know

LOUIS XIV
From a portrait by Van der Meulen

whether it would be well to read those writings,
attached to great names, where, on every page, they
could have verified the stamp of their genius or their
good sense.

Louis XIV had nothing more than good sense, but
he had a great deal of it. The impression made by
the reading of his writings, especially those that date
from his youth, is well fitted to double our respect
for him. The smile that we cannot restrain in certain
places, where he superabounds with the idea of his
glory, soon dies upon our lips and gives place to a
higher feeling when we remember that an inward
spring is necessary to all souls, and that a prince who
doubted himself, a king sceptical of his greatness
would be the worst of kings. The wheel of history,
ever turning, has brought us back to the point of view
that is necessary to comprehend better what a royal
and sovereign nature is, and of what use it is in a society. Let us give ourselves the pleasure of considering it in Louis XIV, in its purity and its hereditary
exaltation, and before the days of Mirabeau.

From childhood Louis XIV was remarkable for
peculiar traits and serious graces that distinguished
him from others of his age. The virtuous and sensible Mme. de Motteville has drawn some charming
portraits of him in his early years; of a ball that took
place in Cardinal Mazarin's apartments while he was
still a child, she says:

"The king wore a coat of black satin with gold and silver

embroidery of which the black showed only enough to set off to advantage the embroidery. Carnation-coloured plumes and ribbons completed his adornment; but the beautiful features of his face, the gentleness of his eyes joined to their gravity, the whiteness and brilliancy of his skin, together with his hair, then very blond, adorned him much more than his clothes. He danced perfectly; and though he was then only eight years old, one could say of him that he was the one of the company who had the best air, and assuredly the most beauty."

Speaking elsewhere of his intimacy with the young Prince of Wales (afterwards Charles II) who was then in France, she says: "The king, whose beauty had charm, though young, was very tall. He was grave; in his eyes we saw a serious look that marked his dignity. He was even prudent enough to say nothing for fear of not speaking well."

About this time (1647) the king fell ill of the smallpox; his mother felt the keenest anxiety, for which he showed her a tender and touching gratitude:

"In this illness he showed himself to all who approached him a prince full of gentleness and kindness. He spoke humanely to all who served him, saying witty and obliging things to them, and was docile to all that the doctors desired. The queen received from him marks of affection that touched her keenly."

These first traits are essential to remark. One of the severest contemporaries of Louis XIV, Saint-Simon, who never saw or knew him till the last twenty-two years of his life, says, in the midst of the penetrating analyses he made of him on all sides:

"He was born virtuous, moderate, discreet, master

of his motions and of his tongue. Will it be believed? he was born good and just; God had given him enough to be a good king, perhaps, even a fairly great king."

That there was in Louis XIV an early foundation of kindness, gentleness, and humanity, which disappeared too often in the idolatry of supreme rank, Saint-Simon recognises and, surprised though he was, bears witness to it. Mme. de Motteville makes us see it as the natural character of the child-king, and more than one saying of Louis XIV in the sincere pages of his youth will confirm it to us.

Gravity and gentleness, all contemporaries agree to note those two manifest traits, though the gentleness gave place more and more to gravity. "I often noticed with astonishment," says Madame de Motteville "that in his games and in his amusements the king never laughed." We have a letter of his in which he asks the Duke of Parma (July, 1661) to send him a Harlequin for his Italian troop; he asks it in terms of the utmost seriousness, without the least little word of gaiety. If he was at a ball, if he danced, Mme. de Sévigné, who watched him with anxiety during Fouquet's trial, applied to him Tasso's words, showing that even in a ballet he had, like Godefroy de Bouillon "a countenance that induced more fear than hope." "He was," she says, "amiable in his person, civil and easy of access to every one, but with a grand and serious air that impressed respect and fear on the public, and prevented those whom he most esteemed from feeling free with him even in private; although he was familiar and lively with ladies." The gentleness that mingled in his speech is singularly certified and depicted to us in this fine passage of Bossuet:

" Whoso would like to know how far reason presides in the councils of this prince has only to lend an ear when it pleases him to explain his motives. I could here call to witness the wise ministers from foreign Courts, who found him as convincing in his discourse as he was formidable in arms. The nobleness of his expressions came from the nobleness of his sentiments, and his precise words are the image of the accuracy that reigns in his thoughts. While he speaks with so much force, a surprising gentleness opens to him all hearts and gives, I know not how, a new splendour to the majesty it tempers."

That passage would be the best epigraph to put at the head of the writings of Louis XIV; it would be found, in part at least, justified as we read them.

In choosing, at twenty-three years of age, to reign wholly by himself, Louis XIV placed in the number of his necessary occupations and duties that of noting down in writing his principal actions, rendering an account of them to himself, and, later, making them the ground of instruction to his son in order to train him in the art of reigning. The idea of glory, inseparable from Louis XIV, mingled in this work, and as history would some day concern itself with his actions, as the passion and genius of many writers would be exercised upon them, he wishes that his son should find in his work that which would correct history wherever it might be mistaken.

Louis XIV, with little knowledge of Letters, and whose early education was much neglected, had, nevertheless, received that far superior instruction which a just and upright mind and a lofty heart derive from events the play of which they have known from childhood. Mazarin, who during his last years understood the king, gave him in conversing the counsels of a statesman, which the young man grasped and comprehended better than minds reputed more cultivated and more acute might have done. Mazarin declared to some who seemed to doubt the future of the young king, that "they did not know him; for he had the stuff in him to make four kings and one honest man."

In these Papers or Memoirs, Louis XIV has exhibited the first idea that he himself had of things, and the first interior education that gradually worked through his mind, his first doubts in view of difficulties, and his reasons for waiting and deferring, "because," he says, "preferring, as I do, to all things and to life itself a lofty reputation, if I can acquire it," he comprehended at the same time that his first proceedings would lay its foundations or else make him lose for ever even the hope of it; so that the sole and same desire for glory which urged him forward restrained him almost equally:

"Nevertheless," he says, "I did not cease to practice and test myself, in secret and without a confidant, reasoning alone and within myself on all the events that happened ; full of hope and joy when

I discovered sometimes that my first thoughts were the same as those arrived at in the end by able and accomplished persons; and convinced in my heart that I had not been put and preserved upon the throne with so great a passion for doing right without being able to find the means of doing it."

Mazarin dead, there was no longer any motive for Louis XIV to delay:

"I began, therefore, to cast my eyes upon the different parties in the State; and not with indifferent eyes, but with the eyes of a master, keenly touched by not seeing one that did not invite me and urge me to lay my hand upon it; but observing carefully what time and the arrangement of things might permit me."

Louis XIV, religious as he is, believes that there are lights proportioned to situations, and particularly to that of kings: "God who will make you king," he tells his son, "will give you the lights that are necessary to you, so long as you have good intentions." He believes that a sovereign sees, by nature, the objects that present themselves in a more perfect manner than the common run of men. Such a conviction we feel is dangerous; it will soon mislead him. Nevertheless, reduced and understood in a certain sense, that idea is a just one: "I do not fear to tell you," he writes, "that the higher the position the more it has objects that cannot be seen or known until we occupy it."

Saint-Simon, whom I shall venture to contradict and refute on this point, says:

"Born with a mind below mediocrity, but a mind capable of forming itself, correcting and refining itself, of borrowing from others without imitation, and without awkwardness, he profited immensely by having, all his life, lived with persons who, of all the world, had the best minds, and the most varied sorts of minds, both men and women, of all ages, all styles, all characters."

He returns quite frequently to this idea, that Louis XIV's mind was "below mediocrity," but that he was very capable of acquiring, and of forming himself and appropriating what he saw in others. There was one thing, however, that Louis XIV did not need to borrow from any one, and which is very original to himself, I mean *state;* that true function of sovereignty, which no one at that time about him had any idea of, which the troubles of the Fronde had allowed to perish in the minds of all, and which Mazarin, even after the restoration of power, had very poorly restored to public reverence. Louis XIV had the instinct within him, and revealed, perceptibly to all, its character. Nature had made him for it physically by giving him a unique mixture of decorum and majesty. Wherever he might be, he would at once have been distinguished and recognised as we recognise "the queen among the bees." His solid qualities, the laborious application of his mind, the feelings of his heart, responded to this intention of Nature and to the rôle of his destiny. Later, and soon, he overpassed it; but in the beginning he simply fulfilled it to perfection and with majestic propriety.

Saint-Simon, who came toward the close of the

reign and at an epoch when the spirit of opposition was reappearing, has not sufficiently recognised this first period of pure and integral royal originality in Louis XIV. His long reign was beginning to weary the people of France; everywhere they were aspiring to some respite. But the true answer to Saint-Simon is that of Louis XIV himself in terms that are worthy of both of them:

" We scarcely notice," says the sensible king, " the wonderful order of the universe, and the course, so regulated and useful, of the sun until some irregularity of the seasons, or some disorder apparent in the system, obliges us to give it a little more reflection. So long as everything prospers in a State we may forget the infinite blessings produced by royalty, and envy only those that royalty possesses: man, naturally ambitious and proud, never finds in himself why another should rule him until his personal need makes him feel it. But to that need, as soon as it has a constant and regular remedy, custom renders him insensible. It is only extraordinary events that make him consider how much that is useful he daily derives from it, and that without such rule he would be a prey to the strongest, and find in this world neither justice, nor reason, nor security for what he possesses, nor resource for what he may lose; and it is in this way that he comes to love obedience as much as he loves his life and his tranquillity."

That is what Louis XIV wrote. Saint-Simon has related to us at great length two or three audiences that he obtained with him, and has vividly conveyed to us the impression of respect, submission, and grateful joy that he brought away with him. Superior as he himself is as an observer, he felt his master on approaching him, and the detail with which he relates the matter proves it. The page I have just quoted leads me to believe that if (by impossibility) a political conversation had taken place between them, Louis XIV, simple in tone and with easy good sense, would have kept, on all essential points, his sovereign superiority. Let us give to each the name that correctly designates him: Saint-Simon was a great painter and a great moralist; Louis XIV was a king. He wished to show to the whole earth (and it is he himself who says it) that "there was still a king in the world."

In the reforms of all kinds that Louis XIV undertook and carried on, in finances, in law and justice, in military regulations, in affairs with foreign countries, he never shows undue eagerness. He examines, he listens, he consults; then he decides for himself: "Decision," he says, "needs the mind of a master." This last point was always the great concern of Louis XIV: not to let himself be governed; to have no prime minister. It has been remarked that this was more an appearance than a reality; he had head-clerks who, by art and flattery, were able to make him adopt as if by his own impulse what they themselves desired. But at the start, and during the first seven or eight years of his youth, Louis XIV certainly escaped that reproach. The form of his mind was judicial and reasoning; it was a practical mind, liking business, finding pleasure in utility, and taking account of facts in the greatest detail. "Every man who is illinformed," he remarks, "cannot prevent himself from arguing badly"; and he adds shrewdly in a conclusion worthy of a moralist: "I believe that whoso should be well informed and well convinced of things as they are would do only as he ought to do."

He takes true pleasure in diligent application and in gaining information; he enjoys unravelling matters that are obscure. "I have already begun," he writes on the day of Fouquet's arrest, "to taste the pleasure there is in working oneself at the finances; having, in the little application I have given to them this afternoon, observed important things of which I had previously seen nothing; and it cannot be doubted that I shall continue to do so." He makes us feel at every moment the sort of charm there is in the exercise of good sense. He thinks that good sense, put to the test of practice and experience, is the best counsellor and the surest guide; and he is sometimes tempted to regard written counsel as useless, and hold to that only which he gives his son. But he instantly revises that opinion, and considers it profitable for all good minds to be put on their guard in advance and be cautioned against error. Regretting that he came so late to the study of history, he considers that " the knowledge of the great events produced by the world through many centuries, digested by solid and active minds, will serve to fortify the reason in all important deliberations."

Note the words, "solid and active minds," clothe

them with majesty and splendour, and there you have
the best definition that can be given of him in the
days of his youth. His wholly royal soul kept its
equilibrium even when it soared the highest; his
greatest heights have something that is moderate in
their principle. He seeks to elevate the heart of his
son, not to swell it; he says: "If I can explain to
you my thought, it seems to me that we ought to be
humble as to ourselves and, at the same time, proud
for the place we occupy."

Some of these first pages set forth dispositions of
mind more extended, more varied than he was able to
maintain. "He had a soul greater than his mind,"
says Montesquieu. He desires that princes who are
really able should know how to transform and re-
make themselves to fit conjunctures. It does not
suffice a prince, in order to be great, that he be born
àpropos. "There are several in the world," he says,
"who have obtained a reputation for ability through
the sole advantage of having been born at a time
when the general state of public affairs was in exact
proportion to their capacity," but as for him, he
aspires to something better; he desires to be of those
who suffice through their minds for all situations,
even contrary ones: "For it is not an easy thing to
transpose oneself at all times into the right way," and
"the face of the world is subject to such different
revolutions that it is not in our power to keep long
to the same measures." In reading this passage it

seems as though Louis XIV foresaw the rock on which, in after years, his pride was to strike. He was not of those whose minds can grasp the renewals of the age, and his final policy was only an exaggeration of his first policy in the midst of public circumstances that were incessantly being modified.

When we read these notes, written day by day, these reflections drawn from each event, when we join to that a reading of the diplomatic instructions he was, at the same time, addressing to his ambassadors and agents at various Courts, we cannot help admiring, in the midst of his *carrousels* and fêtes, the industrious, solid, prudent, and persevering character of this ambitious young man. How little levity, how little rash enthusiasm he has! How he reasons out a thing! how he disputes the ground foot by foot, and argues each advantage bit by bit! Then, too, how much secretiveness and discretion he possesses—royal qualities as necessary to success as they are to respect and reverence, the mere absence of which casts so many men in politics aside: "for great talkers," he remarks, "often talk great nonsense." He prefers, as he does in everything, the slowest but the safest course. In treaties, above all, he thinks there should be no spurring on:

"He who tries to go too quickly," he says, "is liable to make many false steps. It is no matter in how much time, but with what conditions a negotiation ends. Better conclude an affair much later than ruin it by haste; and it happens often that we retard by our own impatience what we tried to hurry on."

This procedure served him at the peace of Aix-la-Chapelle (1668). The young king has those precepts of safe, deliberate slowness that belonged to Philippe de Commynes, and come naturally to the pupil of Mazarin.

I think I find a wonderful relation between Louis XIV's manner of seeing and doing and that of the distinguished men of his time. Boileau advised doing work over and over a score of times, and he taught Racine to make with difficulty very easy verses. Louis XIV gives to his son precisely the same, or analogous precepts on politics; he advises him to turn a thing over in his mind twenty times before proceeding to execute it; he wishes to teach him to find slowly the easy method in each affair. Also, in many a moral reflection that he mingles with his policy, Louis XIV shows himself a worthy contemporary of Nicole and of Bourdaloue.

Even in affairs of war and in the sieges that he undertook, he yielded to the difficulties put before him, "convinced," he says, "that whatever desire one may have to signalise oneself, the safest road to glory is always that which shows the most reason." I do not say that in his conduct he did not, many a time, derogate from this early resolution; it suffices me, in order to characterise him, that he proposed it to himself amid the first fire of his ambition.

When he feels a leading and ruling passion, however noble it may be, Louis XIV endeavours not to listen to it alone, but to counterbalance it by others which shall be equally for the good of the State: "Variety is needed in glory, as in all things else, and more in the glory of princes than of private persons; for whoso says 'great king,' says nearly all the talents of his most excellent subjects combined." There are talents, however, in which he thinks a king ought not to excel too much; it is good and honourable in him to be surpassed in them by others; but he ought to appreciate them all. Knowledge of men, discernment of minds, the selection of each for the employment for which he is best fitted and can be most useful to the State, that is properly the great art and perhaps the chief talent of a sovereign. Some princes have good reason to fear allowing themselves to be approached too closely, and communicating freely with others; he believes that he is not of them; sure as he is of himself and lending himself to no surprise, he thinks he gains by this easy communication the power to penetrate more deeply into those with whom he speaks, and to learn for himself who are the honest men of his kingdom.

It has been said that Louis XIV made the monarchy despotic and Asiatic: that was never his thought. Having recognised that "liberty, gentleness, and, so to speak, facility of the monarchy had passed all proper limits during his minority, and the troubles of the State, and had become license, confusion and disorder," he believed it his duty to restrain these excesses by endeavouring in the first place to preserve to the monarchy its humane and affectionate character, to gather persons of quality about him in an "honourable familiarity," and to keep in communication with the people by pleasures and spectacles conformed to their minds. In this, Louis XIV only half succeeded; evidently, he forced the character of the French monarchy in his pomps and glories, and, as he grew an old man, he ceased to be in harmony with the public spirit of the nation. Nevertheless, he did not see it thus in his youth.

He thought, and he expressly says it to his son, that "empires are preserved only as they are acquired, that is to say, by vigour, by vigilance, by toil." When a wound is inflicted on the body of the State "it is not enough to repair the evil if we do not add more good than there was before." He wishes that his son, instead of stopping on the road and looking around him and beneath him on those who are worth least, should turn his eyes higher:

"Think rather of those whom we have most reason to esteem and admire in past ages; who from private life or very moderate power, by the sole force of their merit, have founded great empires, passed like lightning flashes from one half of the world to the other, charmed all the earth by their great qualities, and left, through many long ages, an eternal memory of themselves, which seems, instead of being destroyed, only to increase and strengthen with the lapse of time."

The misfortune of Louis XIV's descendants is never to have meditated on that thought. The condition of hereditary kings was about to become more and more like that of founders of empires; they needed, for preservation, the same genius and the same courage which had been needed to create and to acquire. I leave aside Louis XV and the base unworthiness of his reign; but it may be said that the good, honest, moderate, respectable Bourbons who succeeded him were not any more at the height of their circumstances; they did not know how to fulfil the hope and the counsel of their great ancestor. Therefore, the empire went to those " who passed like lightning flashes from one part of the world to the other."

Judicious and sensible as Louis XIV usually was, and desirous as he showed himself to foresee all and apply his reason to all, he felt there were moments when, as king, it was absolutely necessary to risk and devise at a venture, under pain of failing in wisdom itself. The religious thought that was joined to this in his mind adds rather than takes away from what this royal maxim has that is politically remarkable; it is in such parts as these that we recognise in Louis XIV the true man of talent in the difficult art of reigning:

" Wisdom," he says, " requires that in certain junctures we leave much to chance; reason itself then counsels us to follow I know not what blind instincts or impulse, above reason, which seem to come from heaven, known to all men, and more worthy of consideration in those whom heaven itself has placed in the first rank. To say when we ought to deny them and when abandon ourselves to them, no one is able; neither books, nor rules, nor experience will teach it; a certain exactitude, a certain boldness of mind will always find it, and, without comparison, more freely in him who owes account of his action to no one."

"Exactitude and boldness of mind"; do you not admire the excellent choice and happy conjunction of those words and the grand and noble style he carries naturally into simple sayings?

It may be said that the text of these Memoirs was written out by a secretary from the king's notes, but whoever that secretary may have been, Pellisson or some other, I find nothing in these pages that does not show, from beginning to end of them, the presence and dictation of the master. All is simple and worthy of him who said: "We notice almost always a difference between the letters which we give ourselves the trouble to write, and those that our secretaries, even the most skilful, write for us; we discover in the latter a something, I know not what, that is less natural, and the uneasiness of a pen that fears eternally to say too much or too little." I find nothing of that uneasiness, nothing of that rhetoric, or that affected simplicity in the pages that form the historic Memoirs of Louis XIV. All is there unfolded with calmness, continuity, and perfect clearness, which answers completely to what contemporaries (Mme. de Caylus, Mme. de Motteville, Saint-Simon) have told us of the unique appropriateness, the easy nobility of the king's words: "His commonest speech was

never without a natural and obvious majesty." One
day, during Louis XIV's youth, Brienne was reading
to the queen-mother in her chamber a draft of the
Letters-patent for the removal of the relics of Sainte-
Madeleine. He had made M. d'Andilly, well known
for his piety, write them. The king chanced to
enter the room, requested that the reading might
begin again, and then interrupted it by saying: "You
make me talk like a saint and I am not one." Brienne
told him the Letters were written by one of the ablest
men in France for style and eloquence. "Who is that
able fool?" asked the king. Being told it was M.
d'Andilly, "Very well," he said, "but all that does
not suit me at all," and tearing up the Letters he threw
them to Brienne, saying: "Write others, and make
me speak like a king, not a jansenist."

Louis XIV's style has not the quick, brusque brevity
that characterises the original writings of Napoleon,
what Tacitus calls *imperatoria brevitas*. That incisive character of the conqueror and the despot, that
short, hasty, staccato rhythm, beneath which we feel
the genius of action and the demon of battles palpitat-
ing, differs wholly from the more tranquil style, the
fuller and, in a way, hereditary style of Louis XIV.
When this monarch forgets himself and is negligent
his sentences are long, like those that have since become the appanage of the Younger Branch, and of
which we see no end: it is there that Louis XIV
comes when he slumbers. But usually, in his habit-

ual manner, his style has the good proportions, the
accuracy, the golden mean of the sanest of languages.
Henri IV, the first Bourbon king, had in his vivid style
something warlike and Gascon which Louis XIV was
without. The pitiable Louis XIV, who was not without intelligence, a few pregnant sayings of his being
quoted, was, in his habitual conversation, long-winded
and given to eternal repetitions; that was the Bourbon
style in what was already its weakness and enerva-
tion. Louis XIV alone presents to us that style in its
true plenitude and perfection, its veritable and regal
stature.

It was said of Louis XIV that no one related things
better than he: "he could tell a story better than any
man in the world, and also a narrative." He put into
it "infinite grace and a noble or shrewd turn of
phrase that was all his own." We have a specimen
of his manner of describing and painting in his letter
written from Montargis to Mme. de Maintenon on the
arrival in France of the Duchesse de Bourgogne, but
narrative, properly so called, or tale of his we do not
possess.

Pellisson, who was a little the Fontanes of those
days, and whom Louis XIV took out of the Bastille
[he had been Fouquet's secretary] to attach him to
his service and make him his rhetorician in ordinary,
transmits to us a conversation, or rather a discourse,
which he took down from the lips of the king himself
at the siege of Lille, August 23, 1667. It is a discourse

on glory, and on the motives that filled the king's soul at that moment. He had exposed his life in an affair two days earlier, and, being reproached for it, he gives his reasons with naive solemnity. This course lays bare to us the young king in his first magnificence of ambition: "It seems to me," he says, "that they strip me of my glory when they can have any without me." That word "glory" is ever on his lips, and he ends by perceiving this himself: "But it would ill-become me to say more of my glory to those who witness it." In this beginning of exultation and apotheosis we find him better and more worthy than he is later; he has certain words of sympathy for the friends, the servitors, who expose and devote themselves before his eyes: "There is no king," he says, "provided his heart is in the right place, who can see so many brave men throwing away their lives like refuse in his service, and yet remain with his arms crossed." That is why he decided to leave the trenches and expose his life under fire in the open; above all, on an occasion, he says: "When all appearances were that we should have a fine action where my presence should do all, I believed that I ought to make visible in open daylight something more than buried valour."

Louis XIV was little of a soldier; but he had the pretension of being one; and nothing shows his foible better than this discourse, this extraordinary apology which he thinks he ought to make because he went once into the trenches, and another time in front of them.

If we pursue him in the direction of vain-glory it would be only too easy to grow frivolous and irreverent towards him. In his own discourses we find him, from time to time, stopping short to congratulate himself with reason and reflection; he takes himself to be naturally the type and figure of the perfect prince; he sees himself in that attitude and at full length before posterity. But it is more useful to insist on the lofty impulses that underlaid this faith and this royal consciousness and made him say, in the midst of political dangers: "But at least, whatever be the outcome, I shall always have within me all the contentment that a brave soul should have when it has satisfied its own virtue."

Speaking of these six volumes of Memoirs when they appeared, M. de Chateaubriand judged them very rightly in saying:

"The Memoirs of Louis XIV increase his renown: they disclose no meanness, they reveal none of those shameful secrets that the human heart too often hides in its abysses. Seen more closely and in the privacy of life, Louis XIV does not cease to be Louis the Great; one is charmed to find that so fine a bust has not an empty head, and that the soul responds to the exterior nobleness."

This feeling is that which rules the reader and triumphs over all criticisms and all restrictions that a just mind may rightly make.

Since it is here a question of Louis XIV as a writer and one of the models of our speech, I shall, in concluding,

point out a direct benefit affecting the whole order
of literature which we owe to him. I have enumer-
ated elsewhere the men of letters grouped around
Fouquet and flourishing in rivalry under his auspices.
If we suppose for an instant that Fouquet had remained in power and firmly established, Louis XIV
leaving him to do as he would, we cannot help perceiving the elements and spirit of the literature that
would then have prevailed; it would have been a
literature freer in every sense than it actually was
under Louis XIV; the eighteenth century would have
been in part forestalled. We should have had La
Fontaine without restraint, Saint-Évremond, Bussy,
the Scarrons, the Bachaumonts, the Hesnaults; many
libertines and epicureans would have glided into the
front rank. This first literature of the morrow of the
Fronde and before Boileau and Racine, not being
restrained by the eye of the master, would have developed, and become more and more emancipated
under a less rigid Mæcenas. It was all ready, as we
can now see; licentiousness and wit would have been
the double danger; a foundation of corruption was
already laid. The young king came, and he brought,
he gave rise to his young literature, he put a corrective
to the old and, save for certain shining infractions,
he impressed upon the body of the productions of
his time a character of solidity and finally of morality,
which is also that which reigns in his own writings
and in the habit of his thought.

XIV.

The Duchesse de La Valliere.

Louise de La Baume Le Blanc.

The Duchesse de La Vallière.

M ME. DE LA VALLIÈRE is one of those subjects and those names that are ever youthful, ever fresh; she represents the ideal of the loving woman, with all the qualities that we delight in giv· ing to it — unselfishness, fidelity, unique and delicate tenderness; and no less does she represent in its perfection a touching and sincere repentance. Seen close by and in its actuality her life answers well to the idea we formed of it from a distance and through its halo; the person herself resembles at all points the charming memory she has left to us. Without pretending to discover anything new about her, let us give ourselves the pleasure of considering her for a moment.

Françoise-Louise de la Baume Le Blanc de La Vallière was baptised in the parish church of Saint-Saturnin at Tours August 7, 1644, having probably been born on the preceding evening. She lost her father early; her mother, who married for her second husband a man who had an office at Court, placed her

437

as maid of honour to Madame, daughter of Cnarles II,
when the latter married Monsieur, brother of the king
(1661). The Court of Madame was all youth, wit,
beauty, amusement, and intrigue. Mlle. de La Vallière, then seventeen years old, seemed at first merely
"very pretty, very gentle, and very artless." The
young king was more occupied than he should have
been with Madame, his sister-in-law. The queen-
mother, Anne of Austria, jealous of her son's friendship
which Madame was taking from her, found much to
say, in the name of propriety, against that intimacy.
In order to carry it on and cover it it was agreed between Madame and the king that he should feign to
be in love with some one of Madame's maids of honour, and thus have a pretext for being at all her
parties and for going to see her at all hours. They
chose to take three of these make-believe loves, the
better to hide their own game; and the three selected
were Mlle. de Pons, Mlle. de Chemerault, and Mlle.
de La Vallière. The latter was particularly the one
whom the king chose to seem in love with. But
while in bringing forward the pretty young girl he
thought only of putting society on the wrong scent
and of dazzling the eyes of the public with her, he
dazzled himself and became in love with her seriously.

Mlle. de La Vallière's beauty was of a nature, a
quality, tender and exquisite, about which there is
but one voice among contemporaries. The engraved
portraits and the painted portraits give us no just idea

to-day of the sort of charm that belonged to her. Freshness and brilliancy, a delicate brilliancy with shaded tones and sweet, made an essential part of it. "She was lovable," writes Mme. de Motteville, " and her beauty had great charm from the whiteness and rosiness of her skin, from the blueness of her eyes which were very gentle, and from the beauty of her flaxen hair [*cheveux argentés*] which increased that of her face." These charms were accompanied by a touching tone of voice that went to the heart; all things blended in her harmoniously. Tenderness, which was the soul of her person, was tempered, visibly, by a foundation of virtue. Modesty, grace— a simple, ingenuous grace—an air of chastity that won respect, inspired and controlled all her motions delightfully: "Though she was slightly lame she danced extremely well." A little slow in walking, she could suddenly, when necessary, find wings. Later, in the cloister, one of her greatest annoyances and mortifications concerned her shoes, which were made, in the world, to fit her slight infirmity. Very slender, and even a little thin, a riding-habit became her well. The close-fitting corsage showed to advantage the slimness of her waist, while " cravats made her seem rather fatter." On the whole, it was a touching, rather than a triumphant beauty, one of those beauties that are not complete in themselves, that are not demonstrated to the eye solely by the perfections of the body, but need that the soul be mingled in them (and with her the soul was ever mingled); she was of those of whom no one could keep from saying at once and at a glance: "There is a face and soul to charm."

The king loved her, and during several years solely and very warmly. As for her, she loved nothing in him but himself, the king not the royalty, and the man still more than the king. Born modest and virtuous, she had great distress in her love even while yielding to it; and she resisted as much as she could all the testimonials of distinction and favour that tended to declare it. Louis XIV lent himself to this and conspired in the secrecy as long as the queen-mother lived. We have in a note from Colbert a circumstantial account of the birth of Mme. de La Vallière's first two children. Colbert was charged to provide for everything in the greatest secrecy. These children, two boys, lived only a short time, and were presented for baptism by old servants, poor people, one a parish pauper. But what is more surprising is that in October, 1666, at the time of the birth of Mlle. de Blois (afterwards Princesse de Conti) Mme. de La Vallière, who was then at Vincennes in attendance upon Madame, concealed everything so carefully up to the last moment, that she passed almost from the salon of the princess into the hands of the midwife, who was in hiding close by, and on the very evening of her confinement she reappeared in Madame's apartment before all the company, in ball-dress, as if nothing had happened. We may conjecture from this what she morally suffered, since shame compelled her to put such constraint upon herself. As the queen-mother was dead at that time, nothing subjected her to this degree of suffering but her own shame. The mistresses of the king who succeeded her did not constrain themselves as much.

Referring one day to Mlle. de Fontanges, that rather silly and boastful mistress, Mme. de Sévigné wrote, comparing her to Mme. de La Vallière: "She is always languid, but so affected by grandeur that you must imagine her the very opposite of *that little violet hiding under the leaves,* who was so ashamed of being mistress, mother, and duchess; there will never be another of that mould."

From the very first period of her connection with the king Mme. de La Vallière had thoughts of the cloister; twice she took refuge there before her last retreat which was final. The first time she fled to it was during the early and most beautiful days of her love. The Court of Madame was, as I have said, a labyrinth of intrigues and tangled gallantries. Mme. de La Vallière had learned, through a friend's confidence, something about the manœuvres of Madame with the Comte de Guiche; she said nothing of it to the king. But, being too simple and too naturally straightforward to be able to dissimulate long, the king perceived that she was hiding something from him, and he flew into a passion. La Vallière was frightened, but, having promised secrecy to her friend, she continued to keep silence, on which the king left her, more and more irritated. "They had agreed many times," says Mme. de La Fayette, "that whatever quarrel they might have together they would never sleep without writing to each other and being reconciled." The night passed without news or message; in the morning, Mme. de La Vallière, who thought that all was over, left the Tuileries in despair and went to hide herself in a convent, not at Chaillot this first time, but at Saint-Cloud. The king was beside himself when told that no one knew what had become of her. He instituted a search in person, and, soon learning where she was, he rode at full speed to Saint-Cloud to bring her back instantly; ready to burn the convent down if she was not restored to him.

Such efforts were not needed; he found La Vallière lying on the ground, broken-hearted, in the parlour outside of the convent, to which she had been refused admittance. The king said to her, bursting into tears: "You do not love me; you do not care for those who love you." Louis XIV at this period was madly in love with her, to the point of being jealous of the past and of making himself uneasy lest he was not the first to have a place in her heart, fearing that she might have had in the provinces some early inclination for a M. de Bragelonne.

The second flight of Mme. de La Vallière to a convent took place under very different circumstances. The years of happiness had passed. Mme. de Montespan, witty, haughty, dazzling, had taken her place and was enthroning herself more and more in the heart of the master; the poor La Vallière paled. On the Shrove-Tuesday of 1671, there was a ball at Court, at which she did not appear. It was learned that she had gone for refuge to the convent of Sainte-Marie at Chaillot. This time the king did not fly to bring her back himself; he sent Lauzan and Colbert to do so. It is said that he wept, but his tears were few, and the last. Mme. de La Vallière returned, no longer in triumph, but as a victim. The three years longer that she stayed at Court were to her mind only a long trial and punishment.

She often said to Mme. de Maintenon, during this interval when she was nerving herself and arranging all for her last retreat: "When I have painful things to bear at the Carmelites I shall remember what those people" (the king and Mme. de Montespan) "have made me suffer here."

She suffered, from a rival, what she herself, gentle and kind as she was, had made another suffer. The queen, Marie Thérèse, wife of Louis XIV, had felt very keenly the favour shown to Mme. de La Vallière, which began so little time after her marriage; and she shed more tears than persons thought possible from her apparent coldness. "Do you see that girl with the diamond earrings?" she said one day to

Mme. de Motteville, pointing to Mlle. de La Vallière,
who was just then crossing the room. "It is she
whom the king loves." The queen's heart, at that
moment, was only suspicious of the king's infidelity;
but when she was informed of it later beyond a doubt
the certainty made her shed many bitter tears. In
May, 1667, the king, before departing for the army,
had sent an Edict to parliament, with a preamble
(said to have been written by the fine pen of Pellisson) by which he acknowledged a daughter he had
had by Mme. de La Vallière and conferred upon the
mother the title and honours of a duchess. The
queen and the ladies of the Court went to pay a visit
to the king, then in camp with the army in Flanders.
Mme. de La Vallière, though confused and distressed
by her new grandeur, was carried away by her love;
she arrived at the same time as the queen, almost in
spite of herself and without being summoned by her
Majesty. When the party came in sight of the camp,
Mme. de La Vallière, in spite of the queen's express
command that no one should precede her, could
restrain herself no longer, but ordered her carriage
to be driven at full speed across the fields. "The
queen saw it, was tempted to have her arrested, and
flew into a frightful passion." That the modest La
Vallière allowed herself to do such an act in view
of the whole Court, shows how true it is that the
shyest and most timid are so no longer when their
passions, once unchained, get the better of them.

Did she not have good reason to say in after years, accusing herself in her "Reflections on the Mercy of God," that her glory and her ambition (we must understand here her ambition and joy in being loved and preferred) had been "like furious horses dragging her soul to the precipice." That sentence has been thought too strong for the gentle La Vallière. I think I see its justification in the above circumstance.

Among the ladies who proclaimed themselves scandalised by this unusual audacity of Mme. de La Vallière one, especially, was remarked, who said: "God preserve me from ever being mistress of the king! but if I were so unfortunate I should never have the effrontery to present myself before the queen." That scrupulous lady who talked so loudly was Mme. de Montespan, she, who from that moment, sought in every way, by all the charms of coquetry and the sallies of her brilliant wit to supplant the poor La Vallière in the master's favour.

It is time to come to the feelings of sorrow and repentance which have purified the passion of Mme. de La Vallière and given to the thirty-six last years of her life a consecration, without which she would have been no more than a mistress of a king, rather touching, but ordinary.

When she returned to Court in 1671, after her flight to the convent of Chaillot, there was much jeering. All the women in society, all the women of wit and intelligence, even Mme. de Sévigné herself, thought she lacked dignity. The fact is, dignity and love will not go together; and so long as we love, so long as we hope, small as that hope may be, all the rest counts for nothing. So society laughed at Mme. de La Vallière and her religious fancies that came to nought: "With regard to Mme. de La Vallière," writes Mme. de Sévigné to her daughter, February 27, 1671, "we are in despair at not being able to get her back to Chaillot; but she stands better at Court now than she has for a long time; so we must bring ourselves to leave her there." We read in the Memoirs of Canon Maucroix, on the occasion of a journey he made to Fontainebleau in August, 1671:

"Having seen the carriages of His Majesty in the Oval Court, I waited nearly an hour; and at last I saw the king get into his calèche; Mme. de La Vallière was placed first, then the king, and then Mme. de Montespan; all three sat on the same seat, for the calèche was very wide. The king was very well dressed in a brown stuff with much gold trimming; his hat was edged with the same; he was rather red in the face. La Vallière seemed to me very pretty, and fatter than I had been told she was. I thought Mme. de Montespan very handsome, especially her complexion which was wonderful. They all disappeared in a moment."

Again Mme. de Sévigné writes (December 15, 1673): "Mme. de La Vallière no longer talks of retreat; it was enough to have talked about it." We see the poor immolated woman figuring not only at Court but in the train of her rival: "Mme. de Montespan, abusing her advantages," says Mme. de Caylus, af-

fected being served by her, gave her many praises,
declaring that she could not be satisfied with her
toilet unless she put the last touches to it. This
Mme. de La Vallière did with all the zeal of a waiting-
maid whose fortune depends on the charms she can
give to her mistress."

Such was the talk of society which loves to humble and disparage all that once was brilliant, ready to
pity later the very object of its rigour, and thus play
all the chords of emotion for the benefit of conversation. Must we believe what Madame, mother of the
Regent says, when she tells us with her Germanic
frankness:

" The Montespan, who had more wit, ridiculed her publicly, treated
her very badly, and obliged the king to do the same. It was necessary to go through La Vallière's room to reach that of the Montespan.
The king had a pretty spaniel named Malice. At the instigation of
the Montespan he took the little dog and tossed it to the Duchesse de
La Vallière, saying: ' There, Madame, there is your company, and it
is enough ' This was all the harder, because, instead of remaining
with her, he only passed through to go to the Montespan. However,
she bore it patiently." [1]

What was passing, during that time, in the sincere
and tender soul, the repentant soul, which drank thus
willingly the bitterness of the cup that she might let
herself be punished in the way that she had sinned?

[1] No; for it is to be remembered that Madame, in her delightfully
amusing daily letters to her German relatives, wrote down all the
malicious Court gossip and news that was brought to her. The
present incident is not characteristic of Louis XIV, one of whose
strongest personal points was decorum and a sense of what was out-
wardly due to others.—TR.

She herself has recorded the secret feelings of her
heart in a series of "Reflections on the Mercy of
God," which she wrote during these years, after her
recovery from a serious illness.

That little writing, which appeared for the first time
in 1686, during Mme. de La Vallière's lifetime, has often
been reprinted; but I warn all readers who think they
know it from any of the later editions, that the style
has been continually altered and weakened, so that
they have not in their hands the true and pure con-
confession of Mme. de La Vallière.

She compares herself, in the beginning, to three
great sinners, the Canaanitish woman, the woman of
Samaria, and the Magdalen.   Speaking of the first, she
cries out: "Lord help me, look upon me sometimes
as I approach thee like that poor stranger, that poor
dog, who thinks herself too fortunate to gather of the
crumbs that fall from the table where thou dost feed
thine elect." The expression is frank to crudity, but
it is sincere, and in reproducing the text of Mme. de La
Vallière, nothing should be suppressed.

Side by side with this we find sweet thoughts more
in keeping with the idea that we form of this delicate
and shrinking soul: "For, alas! I am so weak, so
changeable, that my best desires are like the flowers
of the field of which thy Prophet-king has said that
they blossom in the morning and are withered before
night." To save herself from these relapsings, these
weaknesses, "from the sweet poison of pleasing this

world and loving it," she invokes the bestowal of
one of those " blows of mercy" that afflict, humiliate,
and, at the same time, turn back the soul to God.
That word "mercy," which is on the title-page, recurs at every instant; it overflows her lips, it is her
cry; it is also the name under which she entered the
religious life: Sœur Louise de la Miséricorde — Sister
Louise of God's mercy.   Lately, there has been some
attempt to doubt if the little paper was really written
by Mme. de La Vallière, but that one word Mercy,
thus placed with manifest intention does it not become, as it were, her signature ?

We find, and we divine allusions more or less covered to her sufferings, her humiliations:

" If to impose upon me," she says, " a penance in some way suited
to my offences thou willest, O my God ! that, for indispensable duty,
I remain in the world to suffer on the scaffold where I have so much
offended thee, if thou wilt draw from my sin itself my punishment, in
making those I had made idols my torturers: *Paratum cor meum,
Deus*—My heart is ready, Lord."

While awaiting the great stroke she hopes for, she
makes a resolution to profit by the slightest internal
succour to advance in the path of return:

" I will not wait, O my God, till I come out or my dangerous
slothfulness, till the full sun of thy righteousness be risen.   So
soon as the dawn of thy grace begins to break I will begin to
act, to labour at the work of my salvation. . .   Contenting
myself to advance and grow in thy love, like the dawn, softly and
imperceptibly."

It is natural to compare these words with those of

Bossuet writing on the subject of Mme. de La Vallière on the eve of her complete conversion: "It seems to me," he says, "that she advances a little in her own manner, quietly and slowly." Thus her habitual bearing and progression, even in the path of salvation, was gently slow, and as if with an air of soft indifference until the moment came when love, the divine love, gave her wings to rise.

"Whoso loves, runs, flies, and rejoices; he is free, nothing can stop him." The "Imitation of Jesus Christ" says that. Mme. de La Vallière, who had so deeply felt it in the order of human feelings, was now to say them to herself in the path of her heavenward progress.

We perceive, toward the end of the "Reflections," eager soarings of a tender love about to transform itself into a divine passion, and into charity. The "semi-repentant woman," as she calls herself, is wholly occupied in persuading her soul to transport, to *transpose* her love; that soul must turn and render to God alone that which it had wasted on a god of earth: "It loves thee, O Lord, with a keen and loving sorrow for its past unfaithfulness, and with all the respect and religious trembling that is due to thy sovereign Majesty."

In estimating a writing of this simplicity, talent and imagination, properly so-called, cannot fairly be brought into the question. Two or three passages alone give a rather figurative and vivid impression:

" If it is true, Lord, that the prayer of a Carmelite who has retired into solitude and no longer does ought but fill herself with thee, is like a sweet perfume-box which needs only to be held to the fire to give forth its fragrant odour, that of a poor creature who is still attached to earth, and who can only creep in the path of virtue is like those muddy waters that must be distilled little by little to make a useful liquor of them."

The letters of Mme. de La Vallière to the Maréchal de Bellefonds, and those of Bossuet to the same maréchal on the subject of Mme. de La Vallière, complete the interior picture of her conversion. The Maréchal de Bellefonds, a man of worth and piety, had a sister who was a nun in the Carmelite convent of the Fauboug Saint-Jacques, where Mme. de La Vallière had a project of retiring. He exhorted and strengthened, as best he could, that poor distressed soul, as Bossuet sustained and incited it on his side:

" I have seen M. de Condom [Bossuet] and I have opened to him my heart," writes Mme. de La Vallière to the maréchal, November 21, 1673; " he admires the great mercy of God to me, and urges me to execute at once his holy will; he is even convinced that I shall do it sooner than I think. For the last two days the report of my retreat has been so spread about that my friends and relatives now speak of it to me. They are very pitying, in advance, upon my fate. I know not why they speak of it, for I have not done anything to show it. I believe it is God who permits this talk to draw me to him more quickly."

We do not find in her letters one word that is not natural, humble, and kind; with lively gratitude to those who wish her well, and perfect indulgence for all others. "My affairs do not advance," she writes (January 11, 1674), "and I find no help in persons from whom I might expect it: I must have the mortification of importuning *the master;* and you know what that is for me. . . ." And elsewhere she says: "To quit the Court for the cloister does not cost me anything; but to speak to the king, oh! that is my torture." The sight of her daughter, Mlle. de Blois, moved her, but did not shake her: "I own to you that I felt joy in seeing how pretty she is; but at the same time I had a scruple; I love her, but she cannot hold me back a moment; I see her with pleasure and I shall leave her without pain; make that accord as you please; but I feel it just as I tell it to you." These struggles, these last difficulties dragged on, and were prolonged for some time, until persevering resolution prevailed and one morning the tone of deliverance breaks forth:

" At last I quit the world," she cries, March 19, 1674, "without regret, but not without pain; my weakness has kept me here long without pleasure, or, to speak more truly, with a thousand griefs. You know the greater part of them; you know how sensitive I am; that feeling has not diminished; I am conscious of it daily; I see that the future will not give me any more satisfaction than the past and the present. You judge rightly that according to the world I ought to be content, and according to God I ought to feel transported. I do feel myself warmly urged to respond to the grace that He has done me, and to abandon myself wholly to Him.

" Everyone leaves here the last of April; I leave too, but it is to take the surest way to heaven. God grant that I may advance in it, as I must, if I would obtain the pardon of my sins. I feel within me inclinations so sweet and so cruel and, at the same time, so decided (accord that opposition that is within me as you can) that the persons to whom I open my heart admire more and more the extreme mercy that God is showing to me."

Speaking of Bossuet she says: "As for M. de Condom, he is an admirable man for his mind, his goodness, and his love of God." And, in truth, when we read at the same time Bossuet's letters relating to Mme. de La Vallière, we are struck with the qualities of kindness, perfect charity, and even humility in the great director and the sublime orator. He had begun by thinking that she advanced rather slowly: "A nature a little stronger than hers would have made more way," he writes, "but we must not bind her to more than she is able to carry on." Her final resolution, when declared, did not lack opposition and, above all, ridicule. Mme. de Montespan, particularly, scoffed at the project of the Carmelites, and it was feared that the king would forbid it: it was necessary to conduct the matter cautiously. Bossuet followed the alternations of delay and progress with fatherly solicitude. "It seems to me," he said of the humble convert, "that without her making any movement her affair is advancing. God never quits her, and, without violence he is breaking her bonds." Then, suddenly, when the last tie is worn through and breaks, when the dove takes her flight, he is full of the joy of triumph, of wonderment in his turn:

"I send you," he writes to the Maréchal de Bellefonds, "a letter from Mme la Duchesse de la Vallière, which will make you see that by the grace of God, she is about to execute the intention that the Holy Spirit put into her heart. The whole Court is edified and astonished at her tranquillity and her joy, which increase as the time approaches. In truth, her feelings have in them something so divine that I cannot think of them without being in a state of continual thanksgiving. The mark of the finger of God is in the strength and the humility which accompany all her thoughts; that is the work of the Holy Spirit . . . that transports me, and confounds me; I speak, she acts; I discourse, she does the work. When I consider these things I feel a desire to be silent and hide myself . . . poor channel through which the waters of heaven pass, and which can hardly retain a few drops."

Thus spoke and thought about himself with touching simplicity the great bishop, the oracle of his times, the greatest of mankind through his talent.

The evening before the day on which she quitted the Court Mme. de La Vallière supped with Mme. de Montespan; she chose to drink the cup to its last dregs and to "taste the rejection of the world," as Bossuet said, to the last remains of its bitterness. The next day, April 20, 1674, she heard the mass of the king who was starting for the army; leaving the mass she went to ask pardon on her knees of the queen for her offences; then she got into her carriage and went to the convent of the Carmelites in the Faubourg Saint-Jacques, where a great crowd of people lining the way awaited her. Entering, she threw herself on her knees before the superior and said: "My mother, I have always made so bad a use of my will that I come to place it in your hands." Without waiting for the end of her novitiate, on the very day of her entrance into the Cloister, she made them cut off her hair, "the admiration of all those who have spoken of her person," making haste to despoil herself of her last earthly crown. Mme. de La Vallière, when she entered the Cloister, was thirty years old.

Bossuet could not preach the sermon for the *vêture,* or taking of the habit, which took place in June, 1674; but he did for that of the *profession,* that is to say, the irrevocable vow, which was taken in June of the following year. Mme. de La Vallière, then become Sister Louise de la Miséricorde, solemnly received the black veil from the hands of the queen. We can judge of the strain of such an occasion: "That beautiful and courageous person," writes Mme. de Sévigné, "did this action, like all the others of her life, in a noble and winning manner; her beauty surprised every one ; but what will astonish you is that the sermon of M. de Condom [Bossuet] was not as divine as was hoped for." When we read that sermon to-day we comprehend and, I must own, share a little in the impression of Mme. de Sévigné; we say to ourselves that we expected something else. So much the worse for those who had that expectation, and for us! Bossuet, before being an orator was a religious man, a true bishop, and, on the present occasion, he felt to what a point it behoved him to be grave and not lend himself in any way to a smile, nor to an illusion, nor to the secret malice of hearts that would have taken pleasure in certain memories, certain descriptions. He transported his audience at once into higher and purer regions. He took for his text the words of Him who is seated on the throne in the Apocalypse: "Behold, I make all things new," and he applied it to the present case. The more he had

seen of Mme. de la Vallière during the time of her
novitiate the more he had been struck with her
strength, with the soaring of her spirit, and her entire
renewal of heart. What he desired above all in
preaching before her was to bear to that soul a *good
word,* and not to shine in the eyes of worldlings by
one of those miracles of eloquence which were to
him so easy and so familiar:

" Take notice, Messieurs, that we must here observe more carefully
than ever the precept given us by the Preacher: ' The wise man
listens to the wise word, lauds it, and applies it to himself.' He looks
neither to the right nor to the left to see whom it may fit; he applies
it to himself, and finds his profit in it. ' My sister,' " he added, turning toward the new nun, " ' from among the things I have to say to
you, you will know how to distinguish those that apply to you.
Do you likewise, Christians. . . ."

It was in these simple terms, cutting short all vain
and alien curiosity, that Bossuet approached his subject and applied himself to describe the two loves,
profane and divine; " the love of self pushed to contempt of God," and " the love of God pushed to
contempt of self."

Having entered the path of prayer and penitence,
Mme. de La Valliére never looked back for a single
instant. She was visited sometimes by the queen,
and by Mme. de Montespan herself; but she withdrew
as much as possible from communication with the
outside. When Mme. de Montespan asked her one
day, whether, really and truly, she was as glad as
people said she was, she replied, with a tact that the

mind borrowed from the heart, "No, I am not glad,
I am content." *Content* is, in truth, the Christian
word, the one that expresses tranquillity, peace, submission, joy without effusion, something *contained*
withal.

Mme. de La Vallière on entering the convent had
two children living. Her son, the Comte de Verman-
dois, died in the flower of his age (1633), tainted
already by the vices of the young Court. Bossuet
was charged with announcing to the mother her
painful loss. At first she could answer only with
tears, but as soon as she was in a fit state to reply,
the penitent within her rose above all, and she said .
"I have wept enough for a son whose birth I have
not mourned enough." Her daughter, Mlle. de Blois,
who married the Prince de Conti, was a model of
grace; it was of her that La Fontaine said, describing
her light and as it were aërial step : "A blade of grass
could bear her; a flower would scarce have bent
beneath the imprint of her feet." When she married
the Prince de Conti people hastened from all parts to
congratulate the mother, who bore this last homage
of the world, which to her was humiliation, with a
modesty, a good grace, and a perfect decorum, which
have been much celebrated. Mme. de Sévigné began
by jesting about it, as even the best persons in society
did not refrain from doing: "They say that she
[Mme. de La Vallière] has adapted her style to her
black veil perfectly, and seasons her tenderness as a

mother with that of the spouse of Jesus Christ." But
when she went herself to the convent grating and saw
with her own eyes Mme. de La Vallière, she has only
a cry of admiration for a simplicity so truly humble
and yet so noble:

"What an angel appeared to me at last! . . . To my eyes,
there were all the charms we used to see in other days; I found her
neither bloated nor yellow; she is less thin and more content; she has
the same eyes, the same glance; austerely bad food, and little sleep
have not hollowed nor dulled them; that strange garb takes nothing
from her grace, nor from her elegance; as for modesty, it is no greater
than when she gave birth to a Princesse de Conti, but that is enough
for a nun. She said many kindly things to me, and spoke to me of
you [Mme. de Grignan] so well, so appropriately, all that she said was
so in keeping with herself that, as I think, nothing could be better."

And she ends this strain of eulogy by the following
very mundane reflection: "In truth, that garb and
that retreat give her great dignity."

Mme. de La Vallière was certainly not thinking of
making them into a dignity. Completely given up
to the calmness and the consolations of her hidden
life, she thought she could not sufficiently purchase
them by austerities and mortifications which she imposed upon herself with ardour and a species of
subtlety. Those who have written the narrative of
her penitent life have taken pleasure in producing
some singular examples of it, which would move us
very little to-day; but the principle that inspired them,
the end that she approached by such means, are for-
ever worthy of respect in all ages and from whatever
point of view we look at them: "I hope, I believe, I

love," she said; "it is for God to perfect his gifts."
"Faith and hope are two great virtues; but those
who have not charity have nothing; they are like
sterile plants that the sun never shines upon."

This beautiful soul, realising henceforth in her own
being the qualities of divine love, considered herself to
the end one of the lowest in God's eyes. "I do not
ask him," she said, "for those great gifts which are
only put into the great souls he sends into the world
to enlighten it; I could not contain them: but I do
ask him to incline my heart, according to his promise,
to seek his law and meditate upon it night and day."
Such desires of the soul, no matter in what form they
wrap themselves, are for ever precious; they lead in
all ages to the great moral heights.

Mme. de La Vallière died on the 6th of June, 1710,
after thirty-six years of cloistered life. Louis XIV
had seen her enter the convent with a dry eye. He
retained for her, Saint-Simon says, "esteem and a
dry consideration." Here is dryness enough, but,
even so, it tells too little. He had long ceased to
love her; but when she proved to him that she could
tear herself from him and prefer another to him, even
though that other were God himself, she entirely detached and alienated him from her, and he never forgave it. "She has often said to me," relates Madame,
mother of the Regent, "that if the king came to the
convent she should refuse to see him and would hide
herself where he could not find her. She has been

excused from that trial, for the king has never gone
there. He has forgotten her as much as if he had
never known her."

Of the three women who veritably occupied the
mind of Louis XIV and divided his heart and his
reign among them, Mme. de La Valliére, Mme. de
Montespan, and Mme. de Maintenon, the first remains
by far the most interesting; the only one truly interesting in herself. Much inferior to the two others in
mind she is incomparably their superior in heart: one
may say that in this respect she inhabits another
sphere which those two women of intellect (the
latter, moreover, a woman of judgment) could never
reach. Whenever we try to make for ourselves the
image of a perfectly loving woman, we think of La
Vallière. To love for the sake of loving, without
pride, without coquetry, without arrogance, without
one secret thought of ambition, of self-interest, of
narrow calculation, without a shadow of vanity—and
then to suffer, to make herself of no account, to sacrifice even her dignity so long as there was hope, to
allow herself, when hope was gone, to be humiliated
as an expiation; and, when the hour came, to immo-
late herself courageously in a higher hope, to find in
prayer and in the presence of God treasures of energy,
of a new tenderness; to persevere, to ripen and
strengthen at every step, to arrive at the plenitude of
her soul by her heart — *such was her life*, the last
part of which developed resources of vigour and

Christian heroism which were not to have been expected from her early fragility. As a loving woman she recalls Heloise, or even the Portuguese Nun, but with less violence and flame; for they had not only the genius of passion but also its transports and its madness; La Vallière had its tenderness only. Soul and beauty delicate and sweet, she had more of Berenice than the other two. As a nun, a Carmelite, daughter of Saint Teresa, it is not for us to seek comparisons for her here. Let us only say, in our least profane tone, that when we read that wonderful fifth chapter of the Third Book of the "Imitation" in which are shown the effects of divine love, which in that chapter is the ideal of the other love, Mme. de La Vallière is one of the living figures that explain it to us in their person, and are its best commentary.

PORTRAITS OF THE SEVENTEENTH CENTURY

Collation of Texts

For the benefit of those readers who may want to compare these translations to the original, the following table indicates the sources and dates of each essay. A detailed collation has not been included in the collection as being specialized in interest and too cumbersome to tabulate. It has, however, seemed vital to an understanding of Sainte-Beuve's original articles to give the date and reference to the ones which appear here. The references are to the standard current editions of his works.

P.L.	*Portraits littéraires*	
C.L.	*Causeries du lundi*	(third edition)
P.F.	*Portraits des femmes*	
P.C.	*Portraits contemporains*	(ed. in 5 vols.)

Volume I

1. RICHELIEU

    Dec. 20 & 27, 1852   C.L. VII, 224-265
    (2 articles in one) part. II begins p. 27

2. DUC DE ROHAN

    July 7, 14, & 21,   C.L. XII, 298-355
    1856

    art. II p. 60
    art. III p. 83

3. MAZARIN

    July 1, 1850   C.L. II, 247-265
    p. 114-122 inserted from 1856   C.L. XIII, 379-389

4. LA ROCHEFOUCAULD

    Jan. 15, 1840   P.F. 288-331

5. MADAME DE LONGUEVILLE

    Aug. 1, 1840   P.F. 322-357

6. CARDINAL DE RETZ

    Oct. 20, 1851   C.L. V, 40-61
    Dec. 22, 1851   C.L. V, 238-254

    art. II p. 223

ERRATA

Vol. I P. 11 note 1. (Tr. note)

    113 1. 26   Séquier should read: Séguier
    173 1. 23   1662 should read 1652
    214 1. 1   Ile-Saint-Louis should read: Ile-Notre-Dame
    431 1. 4   Louis XIV should read: Louis XV